THE INCONVENIENT INDIAN

Other Books by Thomas King
Published by the University of Minnesota Press

One Good Story, That One: Stories
A Short History of Indians in Canada: Stories
The Truth About Stories: A Native Narrative

The
INCONVENIENT
INDIAN
A Curious Account of Native
People in North America

Thomas King

University of Minnesota Press

Minneapolis

Originally published in 2012 by Doubleday Canada
First published in 2013 in the United States by the University of Minnesota Press

Published by the University of Minnesota Press
111 Third Avenue South, Suite 290
Minneapolis, MN 55401-2520
http://www.upress.umn.edu

Library of Congress Cataloging-in-Publication Data
King, Thomas,
    The inconvenient Indian : a curious account of native people in North America / Thomas King.
    Includes index.
    ISBN 978-0-8166-8976-7 (hc)
    ISBN 978-1-5179-0446-3 (pb)
1. Indians of North America—History. 2. Indians of North America—Social life and customs. 3. Indians, Treatment of—North America. 4. North America—Ethnic relations. I. Title.
E77.K566 2013
970.004'97—dc23

2013027013

Printed in the United States of America on acid-free paper

The University of Minnesota is an equal-opportunity educator and employer.

23   4

For the grandchildren I will not see

CONTENTS

PROLOGUE

WARM TOAST AND PORCUPINES

I am the Indian
And the burden
Lies yet with me.

—Rita Joe, *Poems of Rita Joe*

About fifteen years back, a bunch of us got together to form
a drum group. John Samosi, one of our lead singers, suggested we
call ourselves "The Pesky Redskins." Since we couldn't sing all that
well, John argued, we needed a name that would make people smile
and encourage them to overlook our musical deficiencies.

We eventually settled on the Waa-Chi-Waasa Singers, which
was a more stately name. Sandy Benson came up with it, and as
I remember, *waa-chi-waasa* is Ojibway for "far away." Appropriate
enough, since most of the boys who sit around the drum here in
Guelph, Ontario, come from somewhere other than here. John's

from Saskatoon. Sandy calls Rama home. Harold Rice was raised on the coast of British Columbia. Mike Duke's home community is near London, Ontario. James Gordon is originally from Toronto. I hail from California's central valley, while my son Benjamin was born in Lethbridge, Alberta, and was dragged around North America with his older brother and younger sister. I don't know where he considers home to be.

Anishinaabe, Métis, Coastal Salish, Cree, Cherokee. We have nothing much in common. We're all Aboriginal and we have the drum. That's about it.

I had forgotten about "Pesky Redskins" but it must have been kicking around in my brain because, when I went looking for a title for this book, something with a bit of irony to it, there it was. *Pesky Redskins: A Curious History of Indians in North America.*

Problem was, no one else liked the title. Several people I trust told me that *Pesky Redskins* sounded too flip and, in the end, I had to agree. Native people haven't been so much pesky as we've been . . . inconvenient.

So I changed the title to *The Inconvenient Indian: A Curious History of Native People in North America*, at which point my partner, Helen Hoy, who teaches English at the University of Guelph, weighed in, cautioning that "history" might be too grand a word for what I was attempting. Benjamin, who is finishing a Ph.D. in History at Stanford, agreed with his mother and pointed out that if I was going to call the book a history, I would be obliged to pay attention to the demands of scholarship and work within an organized and clearly delineated chronology.

Now, it's not that I think such things as chronologies are a bad idea, but I'm somewhat attached to the Ezra Pound School of

History. While not subscribing to his political beliefs, I do agree with Pound that "We do NOT know the past in chronological sequence. It may be convenient to lay it out anesthetized on the table with dates pasted on here and there, but what we know we know by ripples and spirals eddying out from us and from our own time."

There's nothing like a good quotation to help a body escape an onerous task.

So I tweaked the title one more time, swapped the word "history" for "account," and settled on *The Inconvenient Indian: A Curious Account of Native People in North America*. Mind you, there is a great deal in *The Inconvenient Indian* that *is* history. I'm just not the historian you had in mind. While it might not show immediately, I have a great deal of respect for the discipline of history. I studied history as part of my doctoral work in English and American Studies at the University of Utah. I even worked at the American West Center on that campus when Floyd O'Neil and S. Lyman Tyler ran the show, and, over the years, I've met and talked with other historians such as Brian Dippie, Richard White, Patricia Limerick, Jean O'Brien, Vine Deloria Jr., Francis Paul Prucha, David Edmunds, Olive Dickason, Jace Weaver, Donald Smith, Alvin Josephy, Ken Coates, and Arrel Morgan Gibson, and we've had some very stimulating conversations about . . . history. And in consideration of those conversations and the respect that I have for history, I've salted my narrative with those things we call facts, even though we should know by now that facts will not save us.

Truth be known, I prefer fiction. I dislike the way facts try to thrust themselves upon me. I'd rather make up my own world. Fictions are less unruly than histories. The beginnings are more engaging, the characters more cooperative, the endings more in line with expectations of morality and justice. This is not to imply that fiction is exciting and that history is boring. Historical narratives can be as enchanting as a Stephen Leacock satire or as terrifying as a Stephen King thriller.

Still, for me at least, writing a novel is buttering warm toast, while writing a history is herding porcupines with your elbows.

As a result, although *The Inconvenient Indian* is fraught with history, the underlying narrative is a series of conversations and arguments that I've been having with myself and others for most of my adult life, and if there is any methodology in my approach to the subject, it draws more on storytelling techniques than historiography. A good historian would have tried to keep biases under control. A good historian would have tried to keep personal anecdotes in check. A good historian would have provided footnotes.

I have not.

And, while I'm making excuses, I suppose I should also apologize if my views cause anyone undue distress. But I hope we can agree that any discussion of Indians in North America is likely to conjure up a certain amount of rage. And sorrow. Along with moments of irony and humor.

When I was a kid, Indians were Indians. Sometimes Indians were Mohawks or Cherokees or Crees or Blackfoot or Tlingits or Seminoles. But mostly they were Indians. Columbus gets blamed for the term, but he wasn't being malicious. He was looking for India and thought he had found it. He was mistaken, of course, and as time went on, various folks and institutions tried to make the matter right. Indians became Amerindians and Aboriginals and Indigenous People and American Indians. Lately, Indians have become First Nations in Canada and Native Americans in the United States, but the fact of the matter is that there has never been a good collective noun because there never was a collective to begin with.

I'm not going to try to argue for a single word. I don't see that one term is much better or worse than another. "First Nations" is the current term of choice in Canada, while "Native Americans" is the fashionable preference in the United States. I'm fond of both of these terms, but, for all its faults and problems—especially in Canada—"Indian," as a general designation, remains for me, at least, the North American default.

Since I'm on the subject of terminology and names, I should mention the Métis. The Métis are one of Canada's three official Aboriginal groups, Indians (First Nations) and the Inuit being the other two. The Métis are mixed-bloods, Indian and English, Indian and French, for the most part. They don't have Status under the Indian Act, but they do have designated settlements and homelands in Ontario, Manitoba, Saskatchewan, and Alberta. Many of these communities maintain a separate culture from their White and First Nations neighbors, as well as a separate language—Michif—which features components of French and Aboriginal languages.

Terminology is always a rascal. I've tried to use "reservations" for Native communities in the United States and "reserves" for Native communities in Canada, and "tribes" for Native groups in the United States and "bands" for Native groups in Canada. But in a number of instances, when I'm talking about both sides of the border, I might use "reservation" or "reserve" and "band" or "tribe" or "Nation," depending on rhythm and syntax. I actually prefer "Nation" or a specific band or tribal name, and I try to use this whenever possible.

And Whites. Well, I struggled with this one. A Japanese friend of mine likes to call Anglos "crazy Caucasoids," while another friend told me that if I was going to use the term "Indians" I should call everyone else "cowboys." Both of these possibilities are fun, but there are limits to satire. Besides, "Whites" is a perfectly serviceable term. Native people have been using it for years, sometimes as a description and sometimes as something else. Let's agree that within the confines of this book the term is neutral and refers to a general group of people as diverse and indefinable as "Indians."

There is an error in the text of the book that I have not corrected. "The Bureau of Indian Affairs" is the correct designation for the U.S. agency that is charged with looking after matters pertaining to Indians in that country, but for Canada, I have continued to use the "Department of Indian Affairs" even though the ministry is now called "Aboriginal Affairs and Northern Development Canada." I simply like the older name and find it less disingenuous.

In the end, I'm not so much concerned with designing a strict vocabulary as I am with crafting a coherent and readable narrative.

One of the difficulties with trying to contain any account of Indians in North America in a volume as modest as this is that it can't be done. Perhaps I should have called the book *The Inconvenient Indian: An Incomplete Account of Indians in North America*. For whatever I've included in this book, I've left a great deal more out. I don't talk about European explorers and their early relationships with

Native people. I haven't written much about the Métis in Canada and, with the exception of the Nunavut Land Claims Agreement, I don't deal with the Inuit at all. I touch on early settlement and conflicts, but only in passing. I spend a great deal of time on Native people and film, because film, in all its forms, has been the only place where most North Americans have seen Indians. I talk about some of the resistance organizations and the moments that marked them, but I don't spend any time on Anna Mae Aquash's murder or on the travesty of Leonard Peltier's trial and imprisonment.

Nor do I talk about Native women such as Brenda Wolfe, Georgina Papin, and Mona Wilson, women whom Robert "Willie" Pickton murdered at his pig farm in British Columbia, or the Native women who have gone missing in Vancouver and along the highway between Prince Rupert and Prince George. Nor do I bring up the murder of Ditidaht First Nation carver John T. Williams, who, in 2010, was gunned down in Seattle by a trigger-happy cop.

While I spend time in the distant and the immediate past, I've also pushed the narrative into the present in order to consider contemporary people and events. This probably isn't the best idea. The present tends to be too fresh and fluid to hold with any surety. Still, as I argue in the book, when we look at Native–non-Native relations, there is no great difference between the past and the present. While we have dispensed with guns and bugles, and while North America's sense of its own superiority is better hidden, its disdain muted, twenty-first-century attitudes toward Native people are remarkably similar to those of the previous centuries.

Finally, no doubt, someone will wonder why I decided to take on both Canada and the United States at the same time, when choosing one or the other would have made for a less involved and more focused conversation. The answer to this is somewhat complicated by perspective. While the line that divides the two countries is a political reality, and while the border affects bands and tribes in a variety of ways, I would have found it impossible to talk about the one without talking about the other.

For most Aboriginal people, that line doesn't exist. It's a figment of someone else's imagination. Historical figures such as Chief Joseph and Sitting Bull and Louis Riel moved back and forth between the two countries, and while they understood the importance of that border to Whites, there is nothing to indicate that they believed in its legitimacy.

I get stopped every time I try to cross that border, but stories go wherever they please.

1

FORGET COLUMBUS

Out of the belly of Christopher's ship
a mob bursts
Running in all directions
Pulling furs off animals
Shooting buffalo
Shooting each other
        . . .
Pioneers and traders
bring gifts
Smallpox, Seagrams
and rice krispies
Civilization has reached
the promised land.

　　　　　—Jeannette Armstrong, "History Lesson"

When I announced to my family that I was going to write a book about Indians in North America, Helen said, "Just don't start with Columbus." She always gives me good advice. And I always give it my full consideration.

In October of 1492, Christopher Columbus came ashore somewhere in the Caribbean, a part of world geography with which Europeans were unfamiliar, and as a consequence, he was given credit for discovering all of the Americas. If you're the cranky sort, you might argue that Columbus didn't discover anything, that he simply ran aground on an unexpected land mass, stumbled across a babel of nations. But he gets the credit. And why not? It is, after all, one of history's jobs to allocate credit. If Columbus hadn't picked up the award, it would have been given to someone else.

The award *could* have gone to the Norse. They arrived on the east coast of North America long before Columbus. There is even evidence to suggest that Asians found their way to the west coast as well.

But let's face it, Columbus sailing the ocean blue is the better story. Three little ships, none of them in showroom condition, bobbing their way across the Atlantic, the good captain keeping two journals so that his crew wouldn't realize just how far they had drifted away from the known world, the great man himself wading ashore, wet and sweaty, flag in hand, a letter of introduction to the Emperor of the Indies from the King and Queen of Spain tucked in his tunic.

A Kodak moment.

And let's not forget all the sunny weather, the sandy beaches, the azure lagoons, and the friendly Natives.

Most of us think that history is the past. It's not. History is the

stories we tell about the past. That's all it is. Stories. Such a definition might make the enterprise of history seem neutral. Benign.

Which, of course, it isn't.

History may well be a series of stories we tell about the past,
but the stories are not just any stories. They're not chosen by
chance. By and large, the stories are about famous men and celebrated events. We throw in a couple of exceptional women every
now and then, not out of any need to recognize female eminence,
but out of embarrassment.

And we're not easily embarrassed.

When we imagine history, we imagine a grand structure, a
national chronicle, a closely organized and guarded record of
agreed-upon events and interpretations, a bundle of "authenti-
cities" and "truths" welded into a flexible yet conservative
narrative that explains how we got from there to here. It is a
relationship we have with ourselves, a love affair we celebrate
with flags and anthems, festivals and guns.

Well, the "guns" remark was probably uncalled for and might
suggest an animus toward history. But that's not true. I simply
have difficulty with how we choose which stories become the
pulse of history and which do not.

In 1492, Columbus sailed the ocean blue.

On second thought, let's not start with Columbus. Helen was
right. Let's forget Columbus. You know, now that I say it out
loud, I even like the sound of it. Forget Columbus.

Give it a try. Forget Columbus.

Instead, let's start our history, our account, in Almo, Idaho.
I've never been there, and I suspect that most of you haven't
either. I can tell you with certainty that Christopher Columbus

didn't discover the town. Nor did Jacques Cartier or Samuel de Champlain or David Thompson or Hernando Cortés. Sacajawea, with Lewis and Clark in tow, might have passed through the general area, but since Almo didn't exist in the early 1800s, they couldn't have stopped there. Even if they had wanted to.

Almo is a small, unincorporated town of about 200 tucked into south central Cassia County in southern Idaho. So far as I know, it isn't famous for much of anything except an Indian massacre.

A plaque in town reads, "Dedicated to the memory of those who lost their lives in a most horrible Indian massacre, 1861. Three hundred immigrants west bound. Only five escaped. Erected by the S&D of Idaho Pioneers, 1938."

Two hundred and ninety-five killed. Now that's a massacre. Indians generally didn't kill that many Whites at one time. Sure, during the 1813 Fort Mims massacre, in what is now Alabama, Creek Red Sticks killed about four hundred Whites, but that's the largest massacre committed by Indians that I can find. The Lachine massacre on Montreal Island in Quebec in 1689 killed around ninety, while the death toll in nearby La Chesnaye was forty-two. In 1832, eighteen were killed at Indian Creek near Ottawa, Illinois, while the 1854 Ward massacre along the Oregon Trail in western Idaho had a death toll of nineteen. The 1860 Utter massacre at Henderson Flat near the Snake River in Idaho killed twenty-five. The 1879 Meeker massacre in western Colorado killed eleven. The Fort Parker massacre in Texas in 1836 killed six.

It's true that in 1835, just south of present-day Bushnell, Florida, Indians killed 108, but since all of the casualties were armed soldiers who were looking for trouble and not unarmed civilians who were trying to avoid it, I don't count this one as a massacre.

By the way, these aren't my figures. I borrowed them from William M. Osborn, who wrote a book, *The Wild Frontier*, in which he attempted to document every massacre that occurred in North America. The figures are not *dead* accurate, of course. They're approximations based on the historical information that was available to Osborn. Still, it's nice that someone spent the time and effort to compile such a list, so I can use it without doing any of the work.

I should point out that Indians didn't do all the massacring. To give credit where credit is due, Whites massacred Indians at a pretty good clip. In 1598, in what is now New Mexico, Juan de Onate and his troops killed over eight hundred Acoma and cut off the left foot of every man over the age of twenty-five. In 1637, John Underhill led a force that killed six to seven hundred Pequot near the Mystic River in Connecticut. In 1871, around one hundred and forty Pinal and Aravaipa Apaches were killed in the Camp Grant massacre in Arizona Territory. Two hundred and fifty Northwestern Shoshoni were killed in the 1863 Bear River massacre in what is now Idaho, while General Henry Atkinson killed some one hundred and fifty Sauk and Fox at the mouth of the Bad Axe River in Wisconsin in 1832. And, of course, there's always the famous 1864 Sand Creek massacre in Colorado, where two hundred peaceful Cheyenne were slaughtered by vigilantes looking to shoot anything that moved, and the even more infamous Wounded Knee in 1890, where over two hundred Lakota lost their lives.

Of course, body counts alone don't even begin to tell the stories of these slaughters, but what the figures do suggest—if you take them at face value—is that Whites were considerably more successful at massacres than Indians. So, the 1861 Almo massacre by the Shoshone-Bannock should stand out in the annals of Indian bad behavior. After the massacre at Fort Mims, Almo would rank as the second-largest massacre of Whites by Indians.

Three hundred people in the wagon train. Two hundred and ninety-five killed. Only five survivors. It's a great story. The only problem is, it never happened.

You might assume that something must have happened in Almo, maybe a smaller massacre or a fatal altercation of some sort that was exaggerated and blown out of proportion.

Nope.

The story is simply a tale someone made up and told to someone else, and, before you knew it, the Almo massacre was historical fact.

The best summary and critical analysis of the Almo massacre is Brigham Madsen's 1993 article in *Idaho Yesterdays*, "The Almo Massacre Revisited." Madsen was a historian at the University of Utah when I was a graduate student there. He was a smart, witty, gracious man, who once told me that historians are not often appreciated because their research tends to destroy myths. I knew the man, and I liked him. So, in the spirit of full disclosure, I should say that I have a bias toward his work.

Bias or no, Madsen's research into Almo settles the question. No massacre. As Madsen points out in his article, attacks by Indians did not go unmarked. The newspapers of the time—the *Deseret News* in Salt Lake City, the *Sacramento Daily Union*, the *San Francisco Examiner*—paid close attention to Indian activity along the Oregon and California trails, yet none of these papers had any mention of Almo. Such an event would certainly have come to the attention of Indian Service agents and the military, but again Madsen was unable to find any reference to the massacre either in the National Archives or in the records that the Bureau of Indian Affairs kept for the various states and territories. Nor does the Almo massacre appear in any of the early histories of Idaho.

You would expect that the rescue party from Brigham who supposedly came upon the carnage and buried the bodies of the slain settlers—or the alleged five survivors who escaped death— would have brought the massacre to the attention of the authorities. Okay, one of the survivors was a baby, but that still left a chorus of voices to sound the alarm.

And yet there is nothing.

In fact there is no mention of the matter at all until sixty-six years after the fact, when the story first appeared in Charles S. Walgamott's 1926 book *Reminiscences of Early Days: A Series of Historical Sketches and Happenings in the Early Days of Snake River Valley*. Walgamott claims to have gotten the story from a W.M.E. Johnston, and it's a gruesome story to be sure, a Jacobean melodrama complete with "bloodthirsty Indians" and a brave White woman who crawls to safety carrying her nursing child by its clothing in her teeth.

A right proper Western.

That the plaque in Almo was erected in 1938 as part of "Exploration Day," an event that was designed to celebrate Idaho history and promote tourism to the area, is probably just a coincidence. In any case, the fact that the story is a fraud didn't bother the Sons and Daughters of Idaho Pioneers who paid for the plaque, and it doesn't bother them now. Even after the massacre was discredited, the town was reluctant to remove the marker, defending the lie as part of the culture and history of the area. Which, of course, it now is.

But let's not blame Almo for spinning fancy into fact. There are much larger fictions loose upon the land. My favorite old chestnut features Pocahontas and Captain John Smith. The original story, the one Smith told, is that he was captured by the Powhatan in 1607, shortly after arriving in what is now Virginia. He was taken to one of the main villages, and just as the Indians made ready to kill him, he was saved by the daughter of the head man, a young woman whom all of us know as Pocahontas.

It's a pretty good tale. And 1607 wasn't the first time Smith had used it. Before he came to America, he had been a soldier of fortune, had found himself in a number of tight spots, and, according to the good Captain, had been befriended and/or saved by comely women. Smith makes mention of three such women in his writings, the Lady Tragabigzanda in Turkey, the Lady Callamata in Russia, and Madam Chanoyes in France, all of whom "assisted" him during his trials and tribulations as a young mercenary.

Lucky guy.

Of course, the story of heroes being saved by beautiful maidens is a classic and had been around for centuries. Personally, I don't believe that Smith knew Pocahontas. I certainly don't believe that she saved him or that they had any sort of relationship. His first mention of her doesn't come until Pocahontas arrived in England in 1616. By then, as an authentic American Indian princess, she had acquired a certain fame and notoriety, and Smith, I suspect, eager to bathe once again in the warmth of public glory, took the stock story out of storage, dusted it off, and inserted Pocahontas's name in the proper place.

Helen likes details, and she is inordinately fond of footnotes.

I'm not. But because I love her, I try to accommodate her needs. So, here are the facts, as we know them. Smith does come to Virginia in 1607. He is most likely captured by the Powhatan people. Whether they want to kill him or not is a moot point. The reality is they don't. He gets back to the colony in one piece, is injured in a gunpowder explosion, and returns to England in 1609. Did he know Pocahontas? There's nothing to indicate that he did. Did he have a relationship with her as the Disney folks suggest in their saccharine *jeu d'esprit*? Well, at the time of the supposed meeting, Smith would have been twenty-seven and Pocahontas would have been about ten, maybe twelve years old. Possible, but not probable.

Still, the story, false though I believe it to be, has been too appealing for North America to ignore. And we have dragged the damn thing—with its eroticism and exoticism, its White hero and its dusky maiden—across the continent and the centuries.

There's an 1885 musical called *Po-ca-hon-tas, or the Gentle Savage* by John Brougham, a 1924 film directed by Bryan Foy called *Pocahontas and John Smith*, a racehorse named Pocahontas, a Pocahontas train that ran between Norfolk, Virginia, and Cincinnati, Ohio, for the Norfolk and Western Railway in the 1950s and '60s, a Pocahontas coal field in Tazewell, West Virginia, a Pocahontas video game, as well as the towns of Pocahontas in Arkansas, Illinois, Iowa, Missouri, and Virginia.

There's a town in Alberta just a little north of Jasper called Pocahontas, where you can rent your very own cabin (with kitchenette) in the heart of the heart of nature, relax in the curative waters of Miette Hot Springs, and enjoy a meal at the Poco Café.

I don't know about you, but it's on my bucket list.

The irony is that there are a great many stories that are as appealing as the story of Pocahontas and that have more substance than the fiction of the Almo massacre.

The Rebellion of 1885, with Louis Riel playing the lead, is one such story, as is the 1876 Battle of the Little Bighorn, starring George Armstrong Custer. Each is a moment in the national identities of Canada and the United States, though in terms of prominence and fame, they are not historical equals. While the 1885 Rebellion as a historical moment and Louis Riel as a name are well known throughout Canada, the event and the man hardly register in America. I would say that they don't register at all, but I ran into someone in San Francisco about twelve years back who knew something about Batoche and was able to use "Duck Lake" and "Gabriel Dumont" in the same sentence. On the other hand, Custer's name and the legend of the Little Bighorn are well known in both countries, even though the battle in Montana was not nearly as important or as long as the Métis fight for independence. In part, that's not history's fault. You can blame the extra brightness of Custer's star on nineteenth-century American outrage and twentieth-century Hollywood.

Nevertheless, each of these events gave us a man of historical note. To call them "heroes" might be stretching the noun, for, while Riel and Custer are enduring, larger-than-life figures, they also have mixed reputations. Riel may have negotiated the terms under which Manitoba became a part of Canada, but he is also remembered as a messianic nutcase. Custer may have been a successful Civil War commander and one of the officers on hand at General Robert E. Lee's surrender, but he is also burdened with a reputation as an arrogant officer who made a fatal mistake and died fighting a superior force. One man was Métis, one was White. Custer died on the battlefield from wounds that were, in a manner of speaking, self-inflicted, while Riel was hanged for treason at the insistence of Prime Minister John A. Macdonald.

In *Prairie Fire*, their 1984 book on the North-West Rebellion, Bob Beal and Rod Macleod argue that "when most Canadians think of the North-West Rebellion of 1885, they picture a righteous and determined Louis Riel leading, for the last time, a band of dissatisfied Métis in a desperate reaction against the Government's treatment of their people." I don't disagree with that general image, but most Canadians, like most Americans, have a shockingly poor grasp of their own history. Dates, people, the large and small nuances of events have all been reduced to the form and content of Classic Comics. This isn't a complaint. It's an acknowledgment that people are busy with other things and generally glance at the past only on holidays. Given our hectic schedules, the least I can do is to provide a little historical background so no one will feel left out when our story gets complicated.

The Battle of the Little Bighorn. Or the Battle of Greasy Grass, as it is also known. The 7th Cavalry, under the command of George Armstrong Custer, versus the Lakota and Northern Cheyenne, led by Crazy Horse, Sitting Bull, Gall, et al. Five companies under Custer's command—258 soldiers—were wiped out, along with 7 civilians and 3 Arikara scouts.

There were never any figures on Northern Cheyenne and Lakota casualties.

Mind you, this was not the worst defeat that Native forces had inflicted on the U.S. military. In 1791, at the Battle of the Wabash, Little Turtle of the Miami, Blue Jacket of the Shawnee, and Buckongahelas of the Delaware sent their warriors against an army of about one thousand, led by General Arthur St. Clair. Over half of St. Clair's forces were killed, the other half wounded. Only forty-eight men escaped unharmed.

But the Battle of the Wabash did not make it into the public's limited consciousness in the same way that the Battle of the Little Bighorn did. While both were utter defeats, the Little Bighorn was framed as a romantic tragedy. We're fonder of that kind of story. Arthur St. Clair was a plodding but efficient military man, who was simply outmaneuvered by Little Turtle, whereas the legend that is Custer was, in large part, a convergence of political interests and national pride. His defeat occurred as America was celebrating its hundredth birthday and news of the rout ruined the party.

And we've told the story of Custer's defeat so many times, in so many ways, that his moment on the plains of Montana has become a metaphor for heroic but ill-advised and failed endeavors.

Custer's Last Stand.

Of course, we don't have much call for this particular metaphor any more. In our gated, modern world, fault now gets deflected. Ruinous incursions such as Cuba, Vietnam, Iraq, and Afghanistan are no longer assigned to one individual. Rather, we have, through a well-developed, propagandistic sleight-of-hand, made the people and places we attack responsible for our aggression.

If you can read only one book on the Little Bighorn, read Evan Connell's *Son of the Morning Star*. Connell takes no prisoners, White or Red. He understands that the fight was not about the national pride of an emerging nation or the pursuit of one man's glory. It was about killing. He understands that, when the killing starts, whether it's on the plains of Montana or in the deserts of Iraq, everyone ends up covered with blood.

But if you have time for a second book, Brian Dippie's *Custer's Last Stand: The Anatomy of an American Myth* offers a detailed look at how the Custer myth was created and, more important, how it has been maintained.

Almost immediately after word reached the world that Custer had got his ass kicked in Montana, America's artistic class went to work. Henry Wadsworth Longfellow, Walt Whitman, Frederick Whittaker, and the like lifted Custer out of the Montana dirt, hoisted him high on their metered shoulders, and rhymed him around the country in free verse and heroic couplets. At the same time, artists began recreating and reimagining the story with paint and canvas. My three favorites are John Mulvany's *Custer's Last Rally*, painted in 1881, Cassilly Adams's 1884 *Custer's Last Fight*, which was the basis for the better known 1896 Otto Becker lithograph commissioned by the Anheuser-Busch company, and E. S. Paxson's 1899 painting *Custer's Last Stand*, which contains so many figures that the canvas looks like a cowboy and Indian version of *Where's Waldo?*

Okay, I exaggerate. Paxson painted a yellow flag just above Custer, which makes him easier to find.

In all three paintings and the lithograph, Custer stands tall in a murdering crowd of soldiers and Indians, his pistol going bang-bang, his vorpal blade going snicker-snack, as he fights his way into history. And story.

Of course, none of the paintings is an accurate depiction of what did happen. There's just no way they *could* be accurate. There was no one on the battlefield with a camera or a cellphone.

The scenes that the paintings show are all guesswork in the service of heroism and bravery. Yet the story that they tell is that Custer stood fast to the last and that he went down boots on, guns blazing, when in fact he might have cut and run, might have gone scampering off across the coulees while his company tried to hold the high ground. Or he might have been killed in the first skirmish and been just another body rotting on the prairies when the fighting reached its zenith.

Nor has time changed the allure of the myth to any great degree. Contemporary artists such as Mark Churms, Alton Tobey, Thom Ross, and William Reusswig have continued to recreate a defiant, heroic Custer. Evanston, Illinois, hosts an annual Custer's Last Stand Festival of the Arts. And, each year, there is a reenactment of the battle at Hardin, Montana, during Little Bighorn Days, where you can watch the whole drama sweep across the landscape and, later, meet some of the cast and crew.

In other words, we don't need the truth. We have the legend. And even if we were somehow able to know what transpired on that day in June of 1876, that knowledge would not set us free. As with John Smith and Pocahontas, we like the story of Custer's Last Stand too much ever to give it up.

I've discussed these stories at public lectures and in the classes I teach, and the communal desire to believe that John Smith and Pocahontas really were lovers, and that Custer most certainly fought well and died valiantly, is palpable.

Okay, perhaps they were. Perhaps he did.

Louis Riel's is a somewhat longer story. It officially begins in 1869 with what has come to be called the Red River Rebellion or the Red River Resistance, and it ends with the 1885 North-West

Rebellion. In 1869, Canada bought Rupert's Land from the Hudson's Bay Company. It was a huge chunk of real estate, some 3.9 million square kilometers that had York Factory at its center, took in all of Hudson Bay, and ran out to include all of Manitoba and large parts of Saskatchewan, Alberta, Quebec, and Ontario, along with small pieces of Minnesota, Montana, and North and South Dakota. It was the same sort of purchase that the Americans had made in 1803, when they bought the 828,000 square miles known as the Louisiana Purchase—land that would later be carved up into fourteen states and parts of two Canadian provinces—from Napoleon and the French for $15 million. Rupert's Land, a larger, albeit more desolate chunk of real estate, cost the government of Canada some 300,000 pounds, which makes it, square kilometer for square mile, the better deal.

The problem was that the Hudson's Bay Company didn't own the land it sold to the Canadian government, any more than the French owned the land they sold to the Americans. They didn't even control it. The purchases were no more than paper promises and wishful thinking.

Not that this bothered either government. As soon as Canada bought Rupert's Land, Ottawa appointed William McDougall—a man not fond of the French—as governor. In August of 1869, McDougall sent surveyors into the territory to cut up the land into nice, square township blocks, which ignored the seigneurial system that the Métis had established of long narrow lots that ran back from the river. Push came to shove, and, in November, the Métis forced the surveyors to retreat.

Out of this confrontation, and the continuing irritant of competing French and English interests, arose Louis Riel. Riel led the fight for a Métis homeland. He helped to form a provisional government for the territory and tried, along with others, to negotiate peacefully the matter of who controlled what. All in all, things were going along nicely until February of 1870, when Charles Boulton, John Schultz, Charles Mair, and Thomas Scott tried to overthrow the Manitoba provisional government by force. The coup failed, and Boulton and Scott were captured, while Mair and Schultz scurried back to Toronto. Riel pardoned Boulton and, in an ill-advised move, executed Scott. Predictably, the execution set off an explosion of anti-Métis, anti-Catholic, anti-French sentiments, and Riel was forced to flee Canada for the safety of the United States.

By 1885, Canada had been a nominal confederation for eighteen years and was still trying to sort out the nasty bits of nationhood, particularly English–French and Indian–White relations, issues that continue to vex and annoy the country's current Chief Factors. Many of the Métis had moved from Manitoba to Saskatchewan and formed a large settlement at Batoche on the South Saskatchewan River. By now it was clear that the Dominion of Canada, as the fledgling country called itself, was not at all interested in negotiating Métis rights or listening to Métis concerns.

And in that year, Riel returned to lead the North-West Rebellion.

Between April and June of 1885, the Métis fought a series of engagements with government forces, the pivotal battle being fought at Batoche. It was there that Riel, Dumont, and the Métis made their stand. For three days they held out against superior forces until their ammunition ran out. Riel surrendered, and Dumont, along with many of his troops, escaped across the border into Montana.

At Prime Minister John A. Macdonald's insistence—"though every dog in Quebec bark in his favour"—Riel was hanged for treason, and English Canada patted itself on the back, confident that it had settled the Métis question once and for all. This nineteenth-century instance of national smugness might call to mind a singular moment during the U.S. invasion of Iraq that featured President George W. Bush standing on the deck of the aircraft carrier USS *Abraham Lincoln* in May of 2003 under a banner that blithely announced to the world: "Mission Accomplished."

Louis Riel. George Custer. All that history. And the names of these two men are what we have to show for it. Oh, sure, we have other names as well—Gabriel Dumont, Crazy Horse, Sitting Bull—all of which may well trigger a synaptic flash within the general populace. Dumont, who was an excellent strategist and a more effective leader than Riel, continued to be a pain in English Canada's Protestant *derrière* for the rest of his life, but since he didn't die heroically or tragically, his value as a cultural icon is limited.

Crazy Horse was stabbed and killed by soldiers at Camp Robinson, while Sitting Bull was shot and killed by police at the Standing Rock Agency in North Dakota. Which should have given each some measure of sparkle. But their deaths occurred at several removes from that pivotal moment on the rolling prairie above Greasy Grass Creek, and since they didn't die with Custer—with their boots on, as it were—their value has slipped, though both men continue to be part of the imagination of the West and the subject of contemporary biographies.

Perhaps I'm too harsh. Still, apart from Custer and Riel scholars, I don't know of anyone, including me, who knows the names of

the Indians or the soldiers who died with Custer that June day in
Montana, or the names of the Métis who fought with Dumont, or
the names of the Whites who marched with Middleton at Batoche.
No surprise, I suppose. I've visited the Vietnam Veterans Memorial
in Washington, D.C., looked at the names on that cold piece of
black granite, and can't remember one of them. All I do know is
that my brother's name is not there.

Still, I object, in an ineffective and somewhat churlish way, to
the manner in which Crazy Horse and Sitting Bull and Dumont
have been allocated minor roles in the "public history" of North
America, while George Armstrong Custer is read into the books
because he made a sophomoric military mistake and got himself
killed. Though perhaps that's not the reason. Perhaps it's simply
because he's White, and the rest are not.

So, am I suggesting that race is a criterion in the creation of
North American history? No, it wasn't a suggestion at all.

But then what about Riel? He's not White. If race were the issue,
you might expect that General Middleton would get the glory, that
his name would be the one that hangs over Batoche. After all, he
defeated Riel and Dumont, and scattered the Métis. So I guess I'm
wrong about the role of race in the construction of history and I
will try not to mention it again.

I have to stop here for a moment, because I'm struck by an
amusing thought, albeit not an original one. One of our problems
in understanding Indian history is that we think we don't have all
the pieces. We believe our understanding of, say, the nineteenth
century is like buying a thousand-piece puzzle from the Salvation
Army, taking it home, and discovering that one-third of the card-
board squiggles are missing. Whereas, today, with our ability to

record any detail, hardly anything of note goes unmarked. If the twenty-first century were a puzzle, we could well have more pieces than we might reasonably manage.

Too little information or too much, what history encourages us to do is to remember the hindrances that Native people posed to the forward momentum of European westward migration, even though Native people were more often an assistance, showing Europeans river systems and trade routes, taking them around the neighborhood and introducing them to family and friends. I don't mention this because I think such encouragements were a particularly good idea. I bring it up because popular history for the period tends to ignore this aid and focuses instead on the trouble Indians caused. Worse, when the names of Native people who *did* help Europeans or who *did* try to bridge the gap between the two groups come up, we don't applaud their efforts. In many cases, such as that of Sacajawea, we tend to look sideways at the alliance and wonder about their intent and morals.

As Sylvia Van Kirk points out in her book on women in the fur trade, *Mary Tender Ties,* these intermediaries were often Native women, which answers the implicit question of intent and morality. Helen, who is attuned to the ways in which women have been used throughout history, has reminded me that most, if not all, of the European explorers, soldiers, trappers, map makers, and traders were men, and that dealing with a Native woman they could sleep with held more appeal than dealing with a Native man whom they might have to shoot. Sure, there might have been gay explorers, but if there were, history has buried them right alongside equally forgotten Native figures such as Washakie, Standing Bear, Ely Parker, Carlos Montezuma, Osceola, and Jane Schoolcraft.

Just not in the same grave.

The sad truth is that, within the public sphere, within the collective consciousness of the general populace, most of the history of Indians in North America has been forgotten, and what we are left with is a series of historical artifacts and, more important, a series of entertainments. As a series of artifacts, Native history is somewhat akin to a fossil hunt in which we find a skull in Almo, Idaho, a thigh bone on the Montana plains, a tooth near the site of Powhatan's village in Virginia, and then, assuming that all the parts are from the same animal, we guess at the size and shape of the beast. As a series of entertainments, Native history is an imaginative cobbling together of fears and loathings, romances and reverences, facts and fantasies into a cycle of creative performances, in Technicolor and 3-D, with accompanying soft drinks, candy, and popcorn.

In the end, who really needs the whole of Native history when we can watch the movie?

2

THE END OF THE TRAIL

The *indian* is a daemon, a modernist simulation of the other
in the wicked cause of savagism and civilization.

—Gerald Vizenor, *Fugitive Poses*

When my brother and I were kids, we would dress up and
play cowboys and Indians with the rest of the kids. I have a
photograph of Chris and me in our leather vests, leather chaps,
and cowboy hats, looking laconic and tough as cowboys looked.
For a nine-year-old, I cut a fine figure in my Western garb. I'm
carrying a rifle, with two six-guns strapped to my waist, so
there's no mistaking who I'm supposed to be. Now that I think
about it, I don't remember anyone who wanted to be an Indian.
Not my brother. Not my cousins. Not even the girls in the
neighborhood, who were generally good sports about such things.

Having said that, I should acknowledge that a friend of mine, the Canadian historian Brian Dippie, did like to dress up like an Indian. He sent me pictures of himself as a bare-chested young lad in a headdress, complete with drum and tomahawk, emulating his hero, Straight Arrow, the popular character from the radio show of the same name that ran from about 1949 to 1952.

Straight Arrow, as some of you might remember, was a Comanche who was orphaned and raised by a White family. As an adult, he posed as a White man named Steve Adams, but whenever "danger threatened innocent people . . . and when evil-doers plotted against justice," Adams would rush off to his secret gold cave, get dressed up in "traditional" Comanche garb, grab his golden bow and golden arrows, leap onto the back of his golden Palomino stallion, Fury, and ride off to right wrongs.

At the time, it was the only show that I knew that featured an Indian as the hero, a hero who pretended to be a White in order to mask his secret Indian identity. So maybe that was it. Maybe I wore my cowboy outfit to hide my secret identity. Although, if that was my intention, it wasn't particularly effective.

My six-guns have long since vanished, but I still have my vest and chaps. One Hallowe'en, when Benjamin was eighteen, he asked if he could wear my old outfit to a Halloween party. The chaps were much too tight, the vest much too small, but there was a certain nostalgia in watching my son walk down the street in the snow. An Indian disguised as a cowboy. Maybe when my grandkids are old enough, they'll want to continue this family tradition.

I should ask Dippie if he kept his Straight Arrow outfit.

I don't expect that kids in seventeenth- and eighteenth-century North America lined up to play Indians any more than we did, though their parents found Indians interesting enough. Almost as soon as colonies were established at Plymouth, Jamestown, Acadia, and Quebec, and folks found time for more contempla-tive and artistic activities, Indians began appearing in literature, art, and popular culture.

Native people in this early period were a critical part of every-day life. Even though diseases had greatly reduced populations along the eastern seaboard, Indians were still a potent military force, and they were also players in colonial economies. Native people had not been pushed west just yet, had not been reduced and relegated to reserves and reservations just yet. That would come later. In the beginning, Indians were more difficult to ignore.

Explorers who treated with Indians in the early years tended to report on Indian–White relationships in generally positive terms. Colonists, who had to live with Indians, were more dis-posed to dwell on what they saw as the darker side of Native character. Armed with the divine imperative to subdue the earth, they were, no doubt, annoyed that the virgin lands they had imagined, the empty wildernesses they had been promised, were occupied, and, gazing through the lens that seventeenth-century Christianity provided, most were only able to see the basic dichotomy that framed their world, a world that was either light or dark, good or evil, civilized or savage.

A world in which you were either a cowboy or an Indian.

Strangers in a strange land, European squatters quickly crafted an easy narrative that ignored Native humanity and reduced Indians to instruments of divine punishment. In an elegant amalgam of desire and doctrine, colonizers framed Indian attacks not as a con-sequence of colonial arrogance or mutual misunderstandings, but as God's way of making sure that his chosen people were paying attention. Indian depredations were a test to measure the force and depth of faith. Pass/fail. No extra credit available. Don't even ask.

English Puritans were the designated apologists for God's bad behavior, but the concept of therapeutic suffering was not the exclusive domain of Puritanism. All the different flavors of seventeenth-century Christianity featured a deity who might hurt you as a way of demonstrating his love. While the hardware of civilization—iron pots, blankets, guns—was welcomed by Native people, the software of Protestantism and Catholicism— original sin, universal damnation, atonement, and subligation— was not, and Europeans were perplexed, offended, and incensed that Native peoples had the temerity to take their goods and return their gods. As though there was a money-back guarantee on God's love.

Still, colonists, whose feelings had been hurt, could always console themselves with the knowledge that Whites, who had found their way to North America, were part of God's master plan. And Indians, who had been here all along, were not.

A more practical answer as to why explorers tended to be more generous with Indians than colonists can be found in the frictions of propinquity and competition. Explorers, their curiosity salted with excitement, came and went, never staying long enough to rub relations raw, whereas the colonists, who stepped off the ships and found themselves up to their pious prejudices in a "howling wilderness" inhabited by "murderous wretches" and "hell-hounds," were not nearly as enthusiastic. In the early days, there were certainly concerted attempts to put differences aside, and there is no doubt that colonists knew how to share. They simply did not want to share with Indians.

From the early part of the seventeenth century until the close of the nineteenth, Indians and Europeans were continuously "not sharing" somewhere in North America. From 1622 to 1644, the Powhatan Confederacy fought with Virginia colonists. Connecticut and Rhode Island were the sites of the 1637 Pequot War, while Massachusetts and Rhode Island found themselves embroiled in the 1675–78 King Philip War. The French and Indian War, which officially began in 1754 and ended in 1763, involved most of the landscape between Virginia and Nova Scotia, with the Algonquian nations fighting as allies of the French and the Iroquois nations fighting as allies of the British. The Tuscarora War broke out in North Carolina in 1711, while the Yamassee War erupted in South Carolina in 1715 and ran for three years. Pontiac led an alliance to drive the British out of the Ohio River Valley in 1763, a conflict that continued in one form or another until 1774. This is generally referred to as Lord Dunmore's War. Conflict broke out again in Ohio and Indiana in 1790 and continued until 1794.

From there we have the Battle of Tippecanoe at the Wabash and Tippecanoe rivers (1811), the Creek War in Georgia and Alabama (1814), the First Seminole War in Florida (1817–18), the Black Hawk War in northern Illinois and southwestern Wisconsin (1832), the Second Seminole War in the Florida Everglades (1835–42), the running conflicts with the Navajo in Arizona and New Mexico (1849–63), the Sioux Wars in Wyoming, Minnesota, and South Dakota (1854–56).

And then there's the Rogue River War in Oregon (1855–56), the Third Seminole War in the Everglades once again (1855–58), the skirmishes with the Apache in New Mexico, Arizona, Texas, and Mexico (1861–1900), the Ute Wars in Utah (1865–68 and later in 1879), the Modoc War in northern California and southern Oregon (1872–73), the Red River War in northwestern Texas (1874–75), the Battle of Rosebud in southern Montana (1876), the Nez Perce War in Oregon, Idaho, and Montana (1877), and the Wounded Knee Massacre in South Dakota (1890).

Nor should one assume that the intervening periods of time were islands of peace. From the beginning of the European colonization of North America, Indian–White relations were an itch that both parties scratched until someone broke the skin. Agreements for peace were made. Treaties were signed. But the constant temptation to pick at the scabs was, in the end, just too much to resist.

In December of 1895, almost five years after the 1890 massacre at Wounded Knee, an article appeared in the *New York Times* (reprinted from the *Westminster Review* in England) that tried to draw a line between the treatment afforded Indians by Canadian, in contrast to American, authorities. "The great fact stands boldly forth that Canada has never fought the Indians," said the article, "and she will not begin to do so now. Never has Canada had an Indian war."

This is correct if you don't count Red River, Duck Lake, Frog Lake, Batoche, Frenchman's Bluff, Cut Knife, and Loon Lake as proper "Indian" conflicts, since they had more to do with the Métis. And while drawing a line in this fashion is technically accurate, it also serves as a way to disguise aggression and make it appear that conciliation and forbearance were cornerstones of Canadian Aboriginal policy.

Of course I could mention the 1858 Fraser Canyon War in British Columbia. During the Fraser Canyon gold rush a group of miners raped a Nlaka'pamux woman, and the Nlaka'pamux retaliated, killing the miners and dumping them into the river, where their headless bodies floated around in an eddy near the town of Yale. Panic set in and six ragtag regiments formed up. They were of two minds. One group, the New York Pike Guards under the command of a Captain Snyder, called for a war of pacification, while a second group, the Whatcom Company, commanded by a Captain Graham, argued for a war of extermination.

An interesting distinction. I'd always thought that war was war.

The regiments roamed up and down the canyon, engaging in minor skirmishes here and there, but there were no major battles. The worst casualties were inflicted on the Whatcom Company, which was wiped out in an overnight battle with itself. The story is that a rifle fell over and went off, and the soldiers, unable to see in the dark, began shooting at each other until there was almost no one left alive.

In the end, the Nlaka'pamux and the miners signed a series of six treaties known as the Snyder Treaties, none of which has survived. But all this fighting happened before British Columbia was a legal part of Canada, so I suppose we shouldn't count it.

The author of the *Westminster Review* article goes on to explain why Canada hasn't had any Indian uprisings or massacres. "She [Canada] is too poor to seek glory by slaughtering the natives born of her soil, and too proud to defame her character or stain her escutcheon." "Contrast this," the writer continues, "with the policy of the United States that is nearly always fighting its redmen. Indian wars are very expensive matters to deal with. The small episode of last year, beginning with the Messiah craze and ending with the tragedy at Pine Ridge Agency, covering but a few weeks, cost the United States Government $2 million, besides the lives lost, and in addition unsettled the natives throughout the country."

"Born of *her* soil?" "*Its* redmen?" A rather possessive attitude. As though both countries had stopped off at the mall and bought us on clearance.

This is probably as good a place as any to bring up the matter of race. The concept has been with us at least since the ancient Egyptians, whose *Book of Gates* set up categories for "Egyptians," "Asiatics," "Libyans," and "Nubians," and the Bible, in which Noah's three sons, Shem, Ham, and Japheth, are credited with fathering the Semites, the Hamites, and the Japhethites, the three races from which Asiatic, African, and Indo-European peoples are supposed to have descended. Johann Friedrich Blumenbach, the German physician and anthropologist, in his 1775 *The Natural Varieties of Mankind*, offered up five classifications of race: Caucasoid, Mongoloid, Ethiopian, American Indian, and Malayan. Charles Darwin, in *The Descent of Man* (1871), a book that everyone likes but few have read, makes the argument for the superiority of Europeans over other races, an idea that was central to the Atlantic–African slave trade. Eugenics, a natural byproduct of the discussion of race, was a very popular idea in the early part of the twentieth century, until Hitler and the Nazi regime went and wrecked it for everyone.

Certainly, race is what James Fenimore Cooper was invoking in his 1841 novel *The Deerslayer* when he brought up the idea of "gifts." "God," Cooper argued, "gave each race its gifts. A white man's gifts are Christianized, while a red-skin's are more for the wilderness."

But this wasn't simply the old city/country, cultivated/wilderness dichotomy. What Cooper was talking about was the division of *Homo sapiens* into categories that had clear and concise boundaries and attributes. Cooper allowed that both Whites and Indians had souls and that both would be judged by God according to how well each race had adhered to its "gifts." And this "generosity" made Cooper sound almost modern and progressive, until you discovered that what Cooper was implying when he said "gifts" was that Whites had a pre-frontal cortex and Indians did not.

Sure, Cooper admitted that Indians were better in the wilderness than Whites, and that Whites were better with a rifle than Indians, since this technology was European, but what he made clear in description after description was that Whites were human, while Indians were still working their way up the evolutionary ladder.

"White is the highest color," says one of the characters in the novel, "and therefore the best man; black comes next, and is put to live in the neighborhood of the white man, as tolerable, and fit to be made use of; and the red comes last, which shows that those that made 'em never expected an Indian to be accounted as more than half human."

My quarrel is not with the Coopers of the period. He didn't come up with these ideas on his own. They were part of the air he breathed, the water he drank. As with other writers before and after him, Cooper simply reminded his readers that race was a divine sanction, a scientific certainty, and an economic imperative.

Of course, the need for race precedes race. But let's ignore that for the moment.

While much of the early literature tended to cast Indians as surly scoundrels and unrepentant pagans, nineteenth-century literary offerings, such as John Augustus Stone's play *Metamora* (1829), John Richardson's poem *Tecumseh* (1828), and Lydia Marie Child's novel *Hobomek* (1824), spun those representations on their axis and reimagined Indians as romantic figures, heroes who were noble, honest, and trustworthy. But only one at a time. One Indian per play. One Indian per poem. One Indian per novel. Male, almost without exception. And all of them doomed, dying, or dead. In the end, though, neither the Indian as savage nor the Indian as hero changed the dynamics of racism.

Then there were the painters such as George Catlin, Charles Bird King, and Paul Kane. In 1830, Catlin began travelling the West and painting the Indians he encountered along the Mississippi and Missouri rivers. Charles Bird King was, for the most part, a studio painter and did not go West. Instead he spent his time painting the portraits of the members of Native delegations that came to Washington, D.C. Paul Kane, the Irish-born Canadian painter, worked out of Toronto and, like Catlin, went into the field, touring the Canadian Northwest and the Rocky Mountains, painting the Indians he saw on his travels.

And if you look at Catlin's painting of Mah-to-toh-pe (1833), King's portrait of the Pawnee Petalesharo (1822), and Kane's dramatic *Assiniboine Hunting Buffalo* (circa 1851–56), you will see in the work of these early artists some of the ideas and images that would later serve as prototypes for the D. W. Griffiths, the Bruce Beresfords, the John Fords, the Kevin Costners, and the James Camerons of the world.

Equally visual and of far greater influence on North American culture were the Wild West shows. Buffalo Bill Cody started up his famous Wild West Show in 1883 with Whites playing Indians in redface. But by the late 1880s, American Horse, Jack Red Cloud, and Red Shirt were performing with Cody's Congress of Rough Riders. Sitting Bull joined Buffalo Bill in 1885. The Métis leader Gabriel Dumont, who had fled to the United States after the Battle of Batoche and the execution of his friend Louis Riel, signed on with Cody in 1886. Indian leaders such as Red Cloud appeared in Colonel Frederick T. Cummins's 1901 Pan-American Exposition in Buffalo, New York, while Chief Joseph and Geronimo were in Cummins's Indian Congress and Life on the Plains exposition when it opened at Madison Square Garden in 1903.

Did people such as Sitting Bull and Dumont and Geronimo enjoy these shows? Perhaps. Sitting Bull and Dumont stayed with Buffalo Bill for only a few months. Geronimo, on the other hand, was more active, working with Buffalo Bill, Colonel Cummins, and Pawnee Bill, as well as doing a stint with the Miller Brothers at their 101 Ranch in Oklahoma Territory. Whatever else the shows were, they were an intriguing alternative to being locked down on a reservation or sitting alone in a prison cell. Keep in mind, many of these individuals were considered dangerous by North America. After all, the Battle of the Little Bighorn and Wounded Knee were still in the rear-view mirror, and, at the turn of the century, no one was quite sure what might appear up ahead through the windshield.

On the one hand, using Indians in Wild West shows had a certain crass, commercial quality to it. Indians were the scary, unknown element that brought in the crowds, and the men who managed these extravaganzas knew it. On the other hand, Native performers were generally well treated. They were paid and fed. And they had the opportunity to travel with the show to Europe to see the sights (if you're an optimist) or (if you're a satirist) to see whence came their oppression.

While Cody's was the biggest, the best known, and the longest running of the Wild West shows, there were many others. Dr. W. F. Carver, Luella-Forepaugh Fish, the McLoughlin brothers, Tiger Bill, the Kemp sisters, Buckskin Joe, Montana Frank, Texas Jack, California Frank, the Irwin Brothers, and Tim McCoy all put together exhibitions that used Indians as a major part of their entertainment package. Indians were more than a staple in Wild West shows and expositions. They were an essential part of the Western spectacle, the Western myth. It would not be an exaggeration to say, "No Indians, no show."

The pageantry of the Wild West shows, along with four centuries of visual and written renderings of Native people, came together in the twentieth century's most famous Indian image, James Earle Fraser's 1915 sculpture *The End of the Trail*. Fraser was also responsible for the Indian Head nickel that the United States minted from 1913 until 1938, but in terms of Indian iconography, *The End of the Trail* was his masterwork.

I don't know how many people know the sculpture itself or its story, but most everyone recognizes the image of a dejected Indian holding a spear while he slumps over his equally dejected horse. The idea seems to be that both rider and horse have run out of time and space and are poised on the edge of oblivion. Now, it's probably my vivid imagination, but the horse looks as though it's being pushed from behind, that something or someone is trying to shove horse and rider over a precipice.

Most likely the gentle hands of civilization.

But if you look at the sculpture a second time, you can easily reason that the horse is resisting. Its front legs are braced and its back legs are dug in. American expansion be damned. This pony is not about to go gentle into that good night. Such a reading might be expanded to reimagine our doleful Indian as a tired Indian, who, at any moment, will wake up refreshed, lift up his spear, and ride off into the twenty-first century and beyond.

The original sculpture was done in plaster and scheduled to be cast in bronze for the 1915 Panama–Pacific International Exposition in San Francisco, but the war had first call on bronze, and the plaster sculpture remained plaster. If you're keen on seeing the original, it has been restored and is currently housed at the National Cowboy and Western Heritage Museum in Oklahoma City.

The point I want to make is that *The End of the Trail* was the single most powerful icon of Indians in North America. Versions of *The End of the Trail* still appear everywhere. The image and its variations have been slapped on motels, riding stables, restaurants, used-car lots, and rest homes. When I took two of my three children west to see where the Lakota and the Cheyenne had defeated Custer, I stopped at a Wyoming rest stop and there on the back of the shelter was a stencil of *The End of the Trail*.

Hollywood has had a long-standing love affair with Indians, and I've always felt that *The End of the Trail*, both in subject and in rendering, could have been a fine logo for the film industry. In 1890, when Thomas Edison began making images to showcase his Kinetoscope—the first motion-picture viewer—the images he chose to make were of Pueblo villages. Between 1894 and 1930, Hollywood made well over 100 films that featured Hollywood's notion of "real" Indian people and "authentic" Native culture. This was the period of the silent film and the short featurette. After

1930, when you could *hear* the crack of the rifles, the thundering hoofs of the ponies, and the blood-curdling screams of the painted warriors, Hollywood knocked out another 300 films, which means that in the 116 years between 1894 and 2010, Tinseltown conjured up an average of 3.5 films a year. Films with Indian people somewhere in the frames. Which more or less confirms Native filmmaker Chris Eyre's suspicion that "Indian people have been the longest running subject of films out of anyone."

Indians were made for film. Indians were exotic and erotic. All those feathers, all that face paint, the breast plates, the bone chokers, the skimpy loincloths, not to mention the bows and arrows and spears, the war cries, the galloping horses, the stern stares, and the threatening grunts. We hunted buffalo, fought the cavalry, circled wagon trains, fought the cavalry, captured White women, fought the cavalry, scalped homesteaders, fought the cavalry. And don't forget the drums and the wild dances where we got all sweaty and lathered up, before we rode off to fight the cavalry.

The only thing film had to do was to collect such materials and cobble them into a series of functioning clichés. Film dispensed with any errant subtleties and colorings, and crafted three basic Indian types. There was the bloodthirsty savage, the noble savage, and the dying savage. The bloodthirsty savage was the most common. This was the familiar character who rode around wagon trains, burned settlers' cabins to the ground, bashed babies against trees, and trapped cowboys and soldiers in box canyons. The second type was the noble savage, an Indian who assisted Whites in their struggles with bloodthirsty Indians, spoke fluent English, and understood the basic precepts of supply-side capitalism. The dying Indian, on the other hand, was just that. Dying. Not from a wound. Not from any disease. This was the Indian who was simply worn out, who was well past his "best before" date, who had been pulled under by the rip tide of western expansion, drowned, and thrown up on the beach to rot.

You could mix and match these Indians. The bloodthirsty Indian might also be a dying Indian. The dying Indian generally had an element of nobility in him. You normally didn't find all three elements in the same Indian, but you would have no trouble finding all three Indians in the same film.

The good news is that none of these Indians was a threat. To the White heroes in particular and to North America in general. None of them ever prevailed. What we watched on the screen over and over was the implicit and inevitable acquiescence of Native people to Christianity and Commerce. No matter what happened, the question that was asked and answered again and again on the silver screen was: Can Indians survive in a modern world? And the answer, even in sympathetic films such as *Broken Arrow, Little Big Man*, and *Dances with Wolves*, was always: No.

Early film directors such as D. W. Griffith, Thomas Ince, Raoul Walsh, and Jay Hunt used White actors to play Indian roles in their melodramas, but they also used a surprising number of Native actors as well. William Eagle Shirt, a Lakota, was a regular in films made during this period. Elijah Tahamont, an Abenaki from Okanak, Quebec, whose stage name was Dark Cloud, played one of the leads (White Eagle) in D. W. Griffith's *The Squaw's Love* (1911). James Young Deer and his wife Lillian St. Cyr (Princess Red Wing), Nebraska Ho-Chunks who worked with Griffith on a number of projects, also had their own film company, which turned out over thirty films. The majority of their movies were made in a five-year period between 1909 and 1914, but now Deer and St. Cyr have been forgotten except by die-hard movie buffs and scholars, whose job it is to keep such esoterica alive in print and available on video.

The use of "real" Indians in film was not without its difficulties. Chauncey Yellow Robe, a Lakota from the Rosebud reservation, played an Indian in a number of movies, including the 1930 silent film *Silent Enemy*. A bright guy, he understood the issue of image and cultural degradation. Speaking to the third annual conference of the Society of American Indians in Denver in 1913, Yellow Robe argued that Wild West shows and films distorted Indians and Indian culture.

"We see the Indian," Yellow Robe said. "He is pictured in the lowest degree of humanity. He is exhibited as a savage in every motion picture theater in the country. We see the Indian, in his full native costume, stamped on the five-dollar bills as a reminder of his savagery. We see a monument of the Indian in New York harbor as a memorial of his vanishing race. The Indian wants no such memorial monument, for he is not yet dead. The name of the North American Indian will not be forgotten as long as the rivers flow and the hills and the mountains shall stand, and though we have progressed, we have not vanished."

I didn't know that any Indian had been "stamped" on North American currency, so I went looking, and there he was. Running Antelope. The bill in question is the U.S. five-dollar silver certificate, which was released in 1899 and remained in circulation until 1914, when Running Antelope was replaced by Abraham Lincoln. While there are several examples of American coins that feature

Indian iconography—the 1907–33 ten-dollar gold coin (which is really Lady Liberty in a headdress); the 1913–38 five-cent Buffalo nickel; and the 1859–1909 Indian Head penny—the five-dollar silver certificate is, to my knowledge, the only piece of North American paper money that has an Indian as the central design.

Canada produced a Voyager Canoe dollar that featured a fur trader and an Indian in a birch-bark canoe. It was produced from 1935 to 1939, discontinued for World War II, and then returned to circulation from 1946 until 1967. In 1958, the country minted the Totem Pole dollar, which created a stir because the central figure on the pole was that of a raven, and for some Indian groups the raven is a symbol of death. The coin was issued to commemorate the founding of British Columbia and the hundredth anniversary of the British Columbia gold rush, neither of which was a high point in Canadian Native history, so the nickname that the dollar wound up with—the Death Dollar—wasn't completely unwarranted.

And then there are the iconic Indian postage stamps, which include a 1898 four-cent "Indian Hunting Buffalo" stamp, a 1907 five-cent "Pocahontas" stamp, a 1968 six-cent "Chief Joseph" stamp, and a 1989 twenty-eight-cent "Sitting Bull" stamp, all courtesy of the United States. North of the border, Canada was slower off the mark, issuing a "Plains Indians" eight-cent stamp set in 1972, an "Iroquoian Indians" ten-cent stamp set in 1976, a "Native Indians" seventeen-cent stamp in 1981, and a "Great Peace" forty-seven-cent stamp in 2001. A "Chief Tecumseh" stamp was issued in 2012, just in time for the bicentennial of the War of 1812.

Circling back for a moment, there are several delightful stories connected with the Running Antelope five-dollar silver certificate.

The first says that, during the sitting for the image, Running Antelope was asked to wear his full feathered headdress, but that he thought it was inappropriate and refused. The second story has it that Running Antelope wore the headdress, but that it was too tall to use on the bill. The third describes Running Antelope coming to the sitting without a headdress and being given a Pawnee headdress, which he refused to wear, the Pawnee and the Lakota not being on the best of terms. Whichever story is true—supposing that one of them is—the engraver, perhaps fed up with a recalcitrant Indian or knowing what an Indian should look like better than an Indian did, "photoshopped" Running Antelope and the Pawnee headdress, hit "merge," and stuck the image on the certificate.

Fact, fiction. Fiction, fact. I'm reasonably sure that the image on the certificate is that of Running Antelope, but admit that I can't tell whether the feathered headdress is Lakota or Pawnee. All I know is that it looks exactly like the headdress Anthony Quinn wore when he played Crazy Horse in the film *They Died with Their Boots On*.

And that's what is important, isn't it?

The engraved certificate itself is a thing of beauty. I really wanted one for the wall of my office until I found out that, in good condition, the bill can cost thousands of dollars.

Running Antelope was a major figure among the Lakota. He was a chief of the Hunkpapa, an advisor to Sitting Bull, and, from all reports, a gifted orator. But I'm curious to know why Sitting Bull himself, or Crazy Horse or Geronimo or Chief Joseph or Osceola, weren't immortalized as well. Perhaps one Indian was more than enough.

No one has yet asked me which famous Indian I'd like to see on a piece of currency. It would be a tough choice, but since we're talking about entertainment and film, I'd probably go with Will Rogers.

Rogers was a Cherokee who worked as a cowboy, as a vaudeville player, and as an actor. He performed in the famous Ziegfeld Follies and Texas Jack's Circus, did a stint with Buffalo Bill in Cody's Wild West show, and hosted the 1934 Academy Awards. He began acting in 1918 with a picture called *Laughing Bill Hyde* and went on to make well over fifty films. By the mid-1930s, he was the highest-grossing, highest-paid actor in Hollywood.

An Indian.

But Rogers's real reputation was as a social commentator. He was, for his time, the unofficial voice and conscience of America. The man had a fine sense of humor. "An onion can make people cry," he joked, "but there has never been a vegetable invented to make them laugh." On the matter of humor and politics, Rogers said, "There's no trick to being a humorist when you have the whole government working for you," while on the subject of diplomacy, he reminded us that "Diplomacy is the art of saying 'nice doggie' until you can find a rock."

He also said, "We will never have true civilization until we have learned to recognize the rights of others." This last adage isn't particularly funny, but then Rogers wasn't always funny. Sometimes he was hilarious.

Rogers wrote more than four thousand columns that were syndicated in over six hundred newspapers. He had his own radio show, wrote six books, and was declared "Ambassador at Large of the United States" by the National Press Club. In 1928, seven years before his death in a plane crash, *Life* magazine started an editorial campaign to put him on the ballot as the Anti Bunk Party candidate for president.

The cover of the May 31, 1928, issue of *Life* shows an artist's rendering of Rogers with the caption, "Will Rogers Accepts the Nomination." Rogers wrote a byline story for the issue, in which he promised to resign if elected, a promise that, unlike most politicians, he most certainly would have kept.

Rogers didn't want to be president, would probably have been appalled by the prospect, but I would have voted for him. I've always liked Rogers a great deal. We're both Cherokee, so there's probably a bit of tribalism at work here, but what I most admire about the man is his honesty and intelligence, along with a wit that was so sharp and gentle he could cut and heal you with the same stroke.

In the 1930s, he was the most famous man in America, Indian or White, and today he's hardly known outside his home state of Oklahoma. But all is not lost. I figure that if we made a film about his life and revealed that he was the brains behind the victory at the Little Bighorn, he'd be back on top again.

Maybe get Johnny Depp to play Rogers.

Of course, Rogers was not at the Little Bighorn. He was born three years after that battle took place, but if the geniuses at Disney can fling Pocahontas into the arms of John Smith, they'll have little difficulty green-screening Rogers onto a Pinto pony and racing him across the Montana prairies, with Crazy Horse and Sitting Bull at his side.

There's only one problem with this plan. In the fifty-odd films that Rogers made, I don't think he ever played an Indian. I don't recall that he ever put on a headdress or tossed a tomahawk, ever led a charge against a column of cavalry, ran down a herd of buffalo, or rode off with a White woman slung across his horse. The irony is that, to Hollywood's eye, he didn't look Indian enough to play an Indian on the big screen.

Still, Rogers is one of only two Indians to get a star on Hollywood's Walk of Fame. And he got two, one for motion pictures and one for radio. There's a Helen Twelvetrees on the Walk of Fame with a star. I thought, because of her last name, that she might be Native. But she wasn't. And Iron Eyes Cody has a star. Cody, who claimed to be Cherokee or Cree but was really Sicilian, made a good living playing Indian roles because he looked more Native than Rogers. Since I delight in absurd bits of information, I have to point out that there are more cartoon characters (Mickey Mouse, Bugs Bunny, Winnie the Pooh, Snow White, Big Bird) and more dogs (Strongheart, Lassie, Rin Tin Tin) who have stars on Hollywood's Walk of Fame than Indians.

At the same time, there are other celebrities with stars, such as Clint Walker and Cher, who are purported to be part Indian, so perhaps I'm wrong about my figures.

Canada is somewhat more sedate. On its Walk of Fame in downtown Toronto, while there are only two Natives who have stars—the Inuit artist Kenojuak Ashevak and singer-songwriter Buffy Sainte-Marie—there are no dogs or cartoon characters.

And while I'm at it, I should mention Santa Clarita's Western Walk of Western Stars in downtown Newhall, California, which has one Indian with a star, the Canadian actor Graham Greene (Oneida), who is surrounded on the sidewalks of the town by a wagon train of cowboys.

The only Indian besides Rogers who has a star on Hollywood's Walk of Fame is Jay Silverheels. Unlike Rogers, Silverheels did get to play Indians. A Canadian Mohawk from the Six Nations of the Grand River reserve near Brantford, Ontario, Silverheels's real name was Harold J. Smith, and he began his film career as a stuntman and an extra. He played in films with Tyrone Power, Humphrey Bogart, James Stewart, Maureen O'Hara, Anne Bancroft, and Bob Hope. He had a substantial role as John Crow in the 1973 film *Santee*, starring Glenn Ford, and made a momentary appearance in *True Grit* (1969), as a condemned man about to be executed.

But Silverheels's most famous role was as Tonto in the long-running television series *The Lone Ranger*. The show started off on the radio in 1933 and moved to television in 1949. For the radio show, Tonto was originally played by the Irish Shakespearean actor John Todd, who first uttered the famous phrase "Kemo Sabe," which was supposed to mean "faithful friend." Over the years I've wondered if Todd was really trying to say "que no sabe," which in Spanish—with apologies for syntax—translates as "he knows what?" Or, in a less literal translation, "he knows nothing." I could be wrong, of course. My Spanish is lousy.

When the series was brought to television, Todd, who was bald and didn't much look like an Indian, with or without makeup, was dropped, and Silverheels got the job. But Tonto was not about the actor who played him. Tonto was North America's Indian. Trustworthy, loyal, helpful, friendly, courteous, kind, obedient, cheerful, thrifty, brave, clean, and reverent. Some of you might recognize these terms of reference as parts of the Boy Scout Law, but they are just as relevant for Indian sidekicks.

Tonto was the Indian that North America had been waiting for, the Indian that North America deserved. After all, Europeans *had* brought civilization to North America. They *had* shared it with Native people, who hadn't been as gracious about the gift as they might have been, and one could argue that Tonto was North America's way of thanking itself.

For 221 episodes, viewers got to watch Tonto stand shoulder to shoulder with the Lone Ranger, the two *compañeros* fighting crime and/or evil. And sometimes Indians, for that matter. Call me sentimental, but the relationship shared by the masked man and his faithful Indian friend has always struck me as a close bond, friend–friend, brother–brother, United States–Canada.

Silverheels has been criticized for playing a Stepin Fetchit role in the *Lone Ranger* series, but this is a small and mean complaint. Silverheels was an actor and Tonto was a job, and a very good job at that. And it was the first time that you had a White and an Indian on almost equal footing. Sure, the Ranger called the shots, but Tonto rode as well, fought as well, shot as well as the Ranger, and he had skills that the Ranger did not. Yes, it's easy to get grumpy about the pidgin English that Tonto was forced to speak, and, as far as I'm concerned, the producers could have dropped his leather headband in the nearest Goodwill donation bin. I'll even admit that there were those of us who fantasized that Tonto would, one day, shoot the Ranger for cause and ride off into the sunset by himself.

Or, as Lyle Lovett imagines in his song "If I Had a Boat," Tonto might tell the Ranger to kiss his ass as Tonto leaves the Wild West behind, buys a boat, and goes off on his own adventure.

Still, even with an Indian as the co-lead in a television series, *The Lone Ranger* was not about rewriting history. Tonto's character simply affirmed North American history and celebrated the forward thrust of progress. It was proof positive that as Indians were gently pressed through the sieve of civilization, they would come out looking and sounding like Tonto. Well, maybe not sounding like Tonto, but at least possessed of that pleasant, helpful, and obsequious demeanor so prized in ethnic folk.

Two Indians on Hollywood's Walk of Fame. Will Rogers, an Indian who didn't get to play Indians, and Jay Silverheels, an Indian who played only Indians. Curious. And it raises the nasty question, does it matter? In the world of entertainment, does it matter that Branscombe Richmond (Aleut) played an Indian (Bobby Sixkiller) in the television series *Renegade* (1992–97) while Oliver Reed (English) played an Indian (Joe Knox) in *The Great Scout and Cathouse Thursday* (1976)? Does it matter that Graham Greene (Oneida) played an Indian (Joseph) in the film *Maverick* (1994) while Nick Mancuso (Italian) played an Indian (Horses Ghost) in *The Legend of Walks Far Woman* (1982)?

How about a remake of *Beau Geste*, but this time with Adam Beach (Saulteaux) playing Beau, Raoul Trujillo (Apache/Ute) playing John, Nathaniel Arcand (Plains Cree) playing Digby, and Wes Studi (Cherokee) or Gary Farmer (Cayuga) as Sergeant Markoff?

The Cree playwright Tomson Highway, in a 2001 article "Should Only Native Actors Have the Right to Play Native Roles?" in the Canadian magazine *Prairie Fire*, argued that to insist that Native parts go only to Native actors was a good way to silence Native drama and starve Native playwrights, since there were not enough Native actors to mount plays in various cities around North America at the same time. Highway found that if he didn't use non-Native actors to play some of the parts, his plays couldn't be produced.

And what should we make of those truly Hollywood moments, such as the minor controversy over the casting for the movie *New Moon* (2009), in which Taylor Lautner played a Quileute Indian, Jacob Black? At the beginning of the project, Lautner was just another White actor who got to play an Indian. But after he got the part, Lautner discovered that he was part Ottawa and Potawatomi.

New Tribe magazine had no problem with this. One article, "The Twilight Craze: The Rise of Native American Actors in Hollywood," suggested that if White actors didn't get roles as Indians, "these young actors may have never even discovered their family lineages." Which offers up an intriguing scenario. Get a role as an Indian in a major Hollywood production, do some genealogical research, and, presto, you're an Indian.

The article goes on to suggest that, "despite the controversy that Hollywood has caused with its practices of casting, Native Americans are finally beginning to develop in their roles and story lines in Hollywood films," and that this movie franchise is "a gateway for nonindigenous people to view more accurate indigenous characters than those of the past, forever changing how the world sees Native Americans through film."

Right. We used to be portrayed as bloodthirsty savages. Now we're vampire-killing werewolves.

So, does who gets cast as what matter? Nope. With regular type-casting, reasonable makeup, and a good voice coach, almost anyone can be a Hollywood Indian. Does it hurt the veracity of the film? Nope. Film has little veracity to begin with. The only "truth" you see on the screen is the fancy that you see on the screen. We expect too much and too little from Hollywood, and we never get what we desire.

When I was at the University of Utah, I had a chance to be in a Christmas commercial for a local appliance store. They needed an Indian couple, a Latino couple, and a Black couple. Off we went to the studio, and when we arrived we were given our "authentic" ethnic outfits. Yes, mine was a faux-leather vest with a headband and a single red feather. The Latino outfit was a skirt and huipil, along with a serape and an enormous sombrero. Black traditional dress on this occasion consisted of an agbada for him and a dashiki for her.

I had a moustache at the time and probably looked more Mexican than Indian, while the guy who was supposed to play the part of the Latino looked more Indian than Mexican. He was tired of wearing sombreros, he told me, and suggested that we trade places. I've never been one to say no to a complication, so I put on the sombrero, and he put on the headband with the feather. The producers didn't notice or didn't care. "Just stand among the appliances," they told us, "and wish everyone a merry Christmas. In your own language." Fortunately for me, I knew how to say "*Feliz Navidad*," but I had no idea how to say "Merry Christmas" in Cherokee. "Make something up," I told the guy with the feather. And he did. We all did.

Since then, I've found out that *danistayohihv* is more or less "Merry Christmas" in Cherokee. The next time such a situation arises, I'll be ready.

Tony Hillerman, the author of the Jim Chee and Joe Leaphorn mysteries that are set on a Navajo reservation, once told me a story about a producer who couldn't find enough extras for a jungle movie he was making, so he hired a group of Navajo, did them all up in blackface and bad wigs, put them in a dugout, and set them

loose on a river. When the Navajo asked what they were supposed to do, the director told them to paddle and sing something that sounded African, something that sounded fierce. The
Navajo obliged, singing parts of the Night Chant, a Navajo heal-
ing ceremony, as they paddled along. Tony told me that whenever that movie came to drive-ins in the Four Corners area,
Navajo would come from miles around to hear their relatives
singing "African war chants" on the big screen.

So, what's the problem with casting an Indian actor as a doctor
or a lawyer or a baseball player or some rich asshole everyone
hates? Black actors play a wide range of characters. Will Smith
played a fighter pilot in *Independence Day*, a dating coach in *Hitch*,
a superhero in *Hancock*, a man who begins giving away pieces of
his body in *Seven Pounds*, and a lawyer in *Enemy of the State*. Denzel
Washington played an army officer in *The Manchurian Candidate*,
a futuristic warrior in *The Book of Eli*, an angry father in *John Q.*, a
bodyguard in *Man on Fire*, and a corrupt cop in *Training Day*.
Samuel L. Jackson played a cop in *Freedomland*, a gangster in *Pulp
Fiction*, a cop turned private detective in *S.W.A.T.*, a villain in a
wheelchair in *Unbreakable*, and a fight promoter in *Hype*. And
these were all principal or leading roles.

At the same time, Native actors—Eddie Little Sky, Shelia
Tousey, Nathan Lee Chasing His Horse, Irene Bedard, Tantoo
Cardinal, Evan Adams, Byron Chief-Moon, Ben Cardinal, Tina
Louise Bomberry, Shirley Cheechoo, Rodney Grant, Michael
Horse, Billy Marasty, Elaine Miles, Floyd Red Crow Westerman,
Ted Thin Elk, John Trudell, Eric Schweig, Tom Jackson, Alex Rice,
Russell Means—were cast, and for the most part continue to be
cast, with stunning regularity, as Indians. In mostly minor roles.

So, is there a dearth of talent in Indian country? Well, Chief Dan George (Salish) was nominated for an Academy Award for his role as Old Lodgeskins in the 1970 film *Little Big Man*, while Graham Greene was nominated for the same award for his role as Kicking Bird in the 1991 film *Dances with Wolves*. Of course both of these roles were nineteenth-century Indians, and there is a troubling assumption that an Indian playing an Indian is an infinitely easier acting job than, say, an Italian actor playing a mobster or an Irish actor playing a cop. I spent a fair amount of time trying to find Indian actors, apart from Will Rogers, who have been given leading or supporting roles as characters who were not Indian, and I couldn't find many. Gary Farmer (Cayuga) played a Fagin-like character in *Twist* and a police chief in the television series *Forever Knight*. Graham Greene played a cop in *Die Hard: With a Vengeance* and was the narrator on the television crime show *Exhibit A*. Jennifer Podemski (Saulteaux) has played non-Native characters in the television series *Degrassi: The Next Generation* and *Riverdale* and in the 1999 television movie *Mind Prey*. Still, none of these is a major breach in the garrison that is Hollywood.

A good friend of mine, the Choctaw–Cherokee writer Louis Owens, once suggested that Indians were viewed in much the same way as the livestock that had to be requisitioned for a Western film—cattle, a herd of buffalo, a couple of dogs, a dozen horses, maybe a wolf or a bear. You don't cast a cow to play a horse, Louis said, no matter how great an actor the cow is. It was a joke. And we both had a good laugh.

Still, Louis's joke reminds me of the actor Daniel Simmons (Yakama), who went under the name Chief Yowlachie. Originally trained for opera, he switched to acting in the 1920s, and for the next forty years or so you could find him working away in the *Ma and Pa Kettle* films (1949) as Crowbar, in *Yellowstone Kelly* (1959) as a medicine man, in *Oregon Trail Scouts* (1947) as Red Skin, in *Rose Marie* (1954) as Black Eagle, in *The Invaders* (1929) as Chief Yowlache, in *Forlorn River* (1926) as Modoc Joe, in *The Prairie* (1947) as Matoreeh, in *The Lone Ranger* (1949) as Chief Lame Bear, and in *The Yellow Sky* (1949) as Colorado. He had over a hundred film and television credits. And in each and every one, he played an Indian.

"Even if the cow was a great actor . . ." It's a good joke, and it sits at the back of my mind like a benign tumor.

If you wanted to, you could break down the Indian roles that Indians get to play into two categories: historical Indians and contemporary Indians. As you might expect, most Indian actors wind up in historical roles. Provided they look Indian. That's the catch. If you don't look Indian, you don't get historical Indian roles. These are roles in which Italians, Mexicans, Spaniards, Greeks, mixed-blood Asians, and the like will do just as well. One of my favorite examples is that of Mel Brooks in *Blazing Saddles,* where he plays two different parts. Turn him loose with a little paint and a headdress and you have a perfectly respectable Indian chief. Comb his hair and dress him up in a three-piece suit and you have a perfectly sleazy White politician.

For casting the historical Indian, then, race need never be an issue. Things are a little different, however, for the contemporary Indian in film and television.

Now it is true that in the past twenty years Indian actors have found roles that do not involve the nineteenth century, roles that don't require loincloths and full feather headdresses. Canadian broadcasters, in particular, have been good about producing movies—*Medicine River* (1993), *Dance Me Outside* (1994), *Atanarjuat* (2002), *Hank Williams First Nation* (2005), and *Tkaronto* (2007)— and television series—*North of Sixty*, *The Rez*, *Moccasin Flats*, *Moose TV*, and *Mixed Blessings*—that make use of Native actors and that focus on contemporary Native life. As well, the country has the Aboriginal Peoples' Television Network (APTN), the only Aboriginal television network in North America.

While the United States has been slow to shift its focus from the 1800s, it has still managed to put together a reasonable modern movie resumé that includes *Powwow Highway* (1989), *Grand Avenue* (1996), *Smoke Signals* (1998), *Skins* (2002), *The Business of Fancydancing* (2002), and *Dreamkeeper* (2003), but its contributions to series television have been dismal, with *Northern Exposure* being the exception to the rule.

In the end, the history of Indians in Hollywood is more a comedy than a tragedy. The Indians that Hollywood shows on the silver screens of North America bear only a passing resemblance to Native people. Native filmmakers are trying to change this, particularly through documentaries that deal with a contemporary Native world. Phil Lucas (Choctaw) made over one hundred such short films and documentaries in the course of his life. Alanis Obomsawin (Abenaki) has made over thirty. Chris Eyre (Cheyenne–Arapaho), Billy Luther (Navajo, Hopi, and Laguna), Neil Diamond (Cree), Drew Hayden Taylor (Ojibway), Gil Cardinal (Métis), Tracy Deer (Mohawk), Paul M. Rickard (Cree), Sarah Del Seronde (Navajo), Amy Tall Chief (Osage), Lisa Jackson (Ojibway), Ramona Emerson (Navajo), and Jobie Weetaluktuk (Inuit) are just a few of the Native filmmakers currently working in this area, and it is here that some of the best work is being done.

Helen, in her helpful way, suggested that I should cut all the lists in this chapter in half, suggested that no one likes to read lists, suggested that lists are, by and large, pedantic. She's right, of course. I just wanted to see the names, and I wanted to make sure that you saw them too.

The only problem is that most people, Native folks included, don't watch documentaries. Native artists could well be changing the way the world looks at Native people, but because few of these productions ever get to large commercial venues, no one, outside art theaters and the film festival circuit, will ever see them.

Of course, film, even documentary film, isn't "real." As with literature and Hollywood releases, documentaries are just an approximation. If you want real life and real Indians, well, that's another matter altogether.

3

TOO HEAVY TO LIFT

Few looking at photos of mixed-bloods would be likely to say,
"But they don't look like Irishmen."

— Louis Owens, *I Hear the Train*

Indians come in all sorts of social and historical configurations. North American popular culture is littered with savage,
noble, and dying Indians, while in real life we have Dead Indians,
Live Indians, and Legal Indians.

Dead Indians are, sometimes, just that. Dead Indians. But the
Dead Indians I'm talking about are not the deceased sort. Nor are
they all that inconvenient. They are the stereotypes and clichés
that North America has conjured up out of experience and out of
its collective imaginings and fears. North America has had a long
association with Native people, but despite the history that the
two groups have shared, North America no longer *sees* Indians.

What it sees are war bonnets, beaded shirts, fringed deerskin dresses, loincloths, headbands, feathered lances, tomahawks, moccasins, face paint, and bone chokers. These bits of cultural debris—authentic and constructed—are what literary theorists like to call "signifiers," signs that create a "simulacrum," which Jean Baudrillard, the French sociologist and postmodern theorist, succinctly explained as something that "is never that which conceals the truth—it is the truth which conceals that there is none."

God, I love the French theorists. For those of us who are not French theorists but who know the difference between a motor home and a single-wide trailer, a simulacrum is something that represents something that never existed. Or, in other words, the only truth of the thing is the lie itself.

Dead Indians.

You can find Dead Indians everywhere. Rodeos, powwows, movies, television commercials. At the 1973 Academy Awards, when Sacheen Littlefeather (Yaqui–Apache–Pueblo) refused the Best Actor award on behalf of Marlon Brando, she did so dressed as a Dead Indian. When U.S. Senator Benjamin Nighthorse Campbell (Northern Cheyenne) and W. Richard West Jr. (Cheyenne–Arapaho), the director of the American Indian Museum in New York, showed up for the 2004 opening ceremonies of the museum, they took the podium in Dead Indian leathers and feathered headdresses. Phil Fontaine (Ojibway) was attired in the same manner when he stood on the floor of the House of Commons in 2008 to receive the Canadian government's apology for the abuses of residential schools.

I probably sound testy, and I suppose part of me is. But I shouldn't be. After all, Dead Indians are the only antiquity that

North America has. Europe has Greece and Rome. China has the powerful dynasties. Russia has the Cossacks. South and Central America have the Aztecs, the Incas, and the Maya.

North America has Dead Indians.

This is why Littlefeather didn't show up in a Dior gown, and why West and Campbell and Fontaine didn't arrive at their respective events in Brioni suits, Canali dress shirts, Zegni ties, and Salvatore Ferragamo shoes. Whatever cultural significance they may have for Native peoples, full feather headdresses and beaded buckskins are, first and foremost, White North America's signifiers of Indian authenticity. Their visual value at ceremonies in Los Angeles or Ottawa is—as the credit card people say—priceless.

Whites have always been comfortable with Dead Indians. General Phil Sheridan, famous for inventing the scorched-earth tactics used in "Sherman's March to the Sea," is reputed to have said, "The only good Indian I ever saw was a dead one." Sheridan denied saying this, but Theodore Roosevelt filled in for him. In a speech in New York in 1886, some sixteen years before he became president of the United States, Roosevelt said, "I suppose I should be ashamed to say that I take the Western view of the Indian. I don't go so far as to think that the only good Indians are dead Indians, but I believe nine out of every ten are, and I shouldn't like to inquire too closely into the case of the tenth."

Which brings to mind that great scene in the 1994 film *Maverick*, in which Joseph, a Native con man played by the Oneida actor Graham Greene, spends his time pandering to the puerile whims of a rich Russian grand duke, played by Paul L. Smith. Smith is on a grand tour of the West and has become a bit bored with all the back-to-nature stuff. He has shot buffalo, lived with

Indians, communed with nature, and is casting about for something new and exciting to do with his time. Greene, dressed up in standard Dead Indian garb, asks Smith if he would like to try his hand at the greatest Western thrill of all.

"What's the greatest Western thrill of all?" asks Smith.

"Kill Indians," says Greene.

"Kill Indians?" says Smith. "Is that legal?"

Sure, Greene assures him, "White man been doing it for years."

So Greene gets Mel Gibson to dress up like a Dead Indian, and the grand duke gets to shoot him. The greatest Western thrill of all? You bet.

And you don't necessarily have to head west to find Dead Indians. In one of Monty Python's skits, a gas official comes into a British household with a dead Indian slung over his shoulder. The Indian, who isn't quite dead, turns out to be part of the special deal the homeowner got when he bought a new stove. The free dead Indian was "in the very small print," says the gas man, "so as not to affect the sales."

On the other hand, if you like the West and are the outdoors type, you can run out to Wyoming and pedal your bicycle over Dead Indian Pass, spend the evening at Dead Indian campground, and in the morning cycle across Dead Indian Meadows on your way to Dead Indian Peak. If you happen to be in California, you can hike Dead Indian Canyon. And if you're an angler, you can fish Dead Indian Creek in Oregon or Dead Indian Lake in Oklahoma, though the U.S. Board on Geographic Names recently voted to rename it Dead Warrior Lake.

Sometimes you can only watch and marvel at the ways in which the Dead Indian has been turned into products: Red Chief Sugar,

Calumet Baking Powder, the Atlanta Braves, Big Chief Jerky, Grey Owl Wild Rice, Red Man Tobacco, the Chicago Blackhawks, Mutual of Omaha, Winnebago Motor Homes, Big Chief Tablet, Indian motorcycles, the Washington Redskins, American Spirit cigarettes, Jeep Cherokee, the Cleveland Indians, and Tomahawk missiles.

Probably the most egregious example is Crazy Horse Malt Liquor, a drink that one reviewer enthusiastically described as "smooth, slightly fruity with an extremely clean, almost Zinfandel finish that holds together all the way to the dregs of the bottle. Personally we think the chief should be proud." That the Hornell Brewing Company would even think of turning the great Oglala leader into a bottle of booze should come as no surprise. Corporate North America had already spun the Ottawa leader Pontiac into a division of General Motors, the Apache into an attack helicopter, and the Cherokee into a line of clothing and accessories.

I once bought a pair of Cherokee underpants that I was going to send to my brother as a joke, but by the time I got them home and looked at them again, they had become more embarrassing than funny.

One of my favorite Dead Indian products is Land O' Lakes butter, which features an Indian Maiden in a buckskin dress on her knees holding a box of butter at bosom level. The wag who designed the box arranged it so that if you fold the box in a certain way, the Indian woman winds up *au naturel*, sporting naked breasts. Such a clever fellow.

Of course, all of this is simply a new spin on old notions. The medicine shows that toured the West in the eighteenth and early-nineteenth centuries used Aboriginal iconography and invention to sell Dead Indian elixirs and liniments, such as Kickapoo Indian

Sagwa, a "blood, liver, and stomach renovator," Dr. Morse's Indian Root Pills, Dr. Pierce's Golden Medical Discovery, featuring the caption "Used by the First Americans," White Beaver's Cough Cream, Ka-Ton-Ka, and Nez Perce Catarrh Remedy.

All of this pales by comparison with the contemporary entrepreneurs who have made a bull-market business out of Dead Indian culture and spirituality. Gone are the bogus potions and rubs that marked the earlier snake oil period. They have been replaced by books that illuminate an alternative Dead Indian reality, by workshops that promise an authentic Dead Indian experience, by naked therapy sessions in a sweat lodge or a tipi that guarantee to expand your consciousness and connect you to your "inner Dead Indian." Folks such as Lynn Andrews, Mary Summer Rains, Jamie Samms, Don Le Vie Jr., and Mary Elizabeth Marlow, just to mention some of the more prominent New Age spiritual CEOs, have manufactured fictional Dead Indian entities— Agnes Whistling Elk, Ruby Plenty Chiefs, No Eyes, Iron Thunderhorse, Barking Tree, and Max the crystal skull—who supposedly taught them the secrets of Native spirituality. They have created Dead Indian narratives that are an impossible mix of Taoism, Buddhism, Druidism, science fiction, and general nonsense, tied together with Dead Indian ceremony and sinew to give their product provenance and validity, along with a patina of exoticism.

In the late nineteenth century, Kickapoo Indian Sagwa sold for fifty cents a bottle. Today's Indian snake oil is considerably more expensive. In her article "Plastic Shamans and Astroturf Sun Dances: New Age Commercialization of Native American Spirituality," Lisa Aldred makes note of someone called Singing

Pipe Woman, in Springdale, Washington, who advertises a two-week retreat with a Husichol woman priced at $2,450. A quick trip to the Internet will turn up an outfit offering a one-week "Canyon Quest and Spiritual Warrior Training" course for $850 and an eight-night program called "Vision Quest," in the tradition of someone called Stalking Wolf, "a Lipan Apache elder" who has "removed all the differences" of the vision quest, "leaving only the simple, pure format that works for everyone." There is no fee for this workshop, though a $300-350 donation is recommended. Stalking Wolf, by the way, was supposedly born in 1873, wandered the Americas in search of spiritual truths, and finally passed all his knowledge on to Tom Brown Jr., a seven-year-old White boy whom he met in New Jersey. Evidently, Tom Brown Jr., or his protégés, run the workshops, having turned Stalking Wolf's teachings into a Dead Indian franchise.

From the frequency with which Dead Indians appear in advertising, in the names of businesses, as icons for sports teams, as marketing devices for everything from cleaning products to underwear, and as stalking goats for New Age spiritual flimflam, you might think that Native people were a significant target for sales. We're not, of course. We don't buy this crap. At least not enough to support such a bustling market. But there's really no need to ask whom Dead Indians are aimed at, is there?

All of which brings us to Live Indians.

Among the many new things that Europeans had to deal with upon their arrival in the North American wilderness were Live Indians. Live Indians, from an Old World point of view, were an intriguing, perplexing, and annoying part of life in the New World.

My son's girlfriend, Nadine Zabder, a meat science major, once told me: "You can't herd them. They won't follow. And they're too heavy to lift." Nadine was talking about sheep, but she could have been talking about Indians, for the same general sentiment appears in early journals and reports. The good news, the writers agreed, was that they were dying off in large numbers.

Indians. Not sheep.

There is no general agreement on how many Indians were in North America when Europeans first arrived, but most scholars are willing to speculate that the new diseases that fishermen and colonists brought with them killed upward of 80 percent of all Native people along the eastern seaboard. Conflicts and wars did their part as well, and, by the time the nineteenth century rolled around, the death of the Indian was a working part of North American mythology. This dying was not the fault of non-Natives. The demise of Indians was seen as a tenet of natural law, which favored the strong and eliminated the weak.

George Catlin, who travelled around North America in the 1830s painting Live Indians, said of the tribes he visited that "in a few years, perhaps, they will have entirely disappeared from the face of the earth, and all that will be remembered of them will be that they existed and were numbered among the barbarous tribes that once inhabited this vast Continent." General John Benjamin Sanborn, who was part of an Indian Peace Commission formed in 1867, echoed the common sentiments of a nation on the move. "Little can be hoped for them as a distinct people," said Sanborn. "The sun of their day is fast sinking in the western sky. It will soon go down in a night of oblivion that shall know no morning . . . No spring-time shall renew their fading glory, and no future know their fame." The American newspaperman Horace Greeley, on a trip west in 1859, was not quite as kind as Catlin or as eloquent as Sanborn. "The Indians are children," said Greeley. "Their arts, wars, treaties, alliances, habitations, crafts, properties, commerce, comforts, all belong to the very lowest and rudest of human existence . . . I could not help saying, 'These people must die out—there is no help for them.'"

Henry Wadsworth Longfellow's 1855 epic poem *Song of Hiawatha* summed up the sentiments of most North Americans. At the end of the poem, as Hiawatha is getting ready to depart this world for the next, he tells his people to turn everything over to the Europeans. "Listen to their words of wisdom," Hiawatha intones in trochaic meters. "Listen to the truth they tell you." Longfellow's poem was romantic wishful thinking, but, more than that, it confirmed that Indians, understanding their noble but inferior nature, had willingly gifted all of North America to the superior race.

Problem was, Live Indians didn't die out. They were supposed to, but they didn't. Since North America already had the Dead Indian, Live Indians were neither needed nor wanted. They were irrelevant, and as the nineteenth century rolled into the twentieth century, Live Indians were forgotten, safely stored away on reservations and reserves or scattered in the rural backwaters and cityscapes of Canada and the United States. Out of sight, out of mind. Out of mind, out of sight.

All Native people living in North America today are Live Indians. Vine Deloria, the Lakota scholar and writer, didn't use the term "Live Indians" when he wrote his famous 1969 manifesto *Custer Died for Your Sins*. Instead, he talked about Native people being "transparent." "Our foremost plight," said Deloria, "is our transparency. People can tell just by looking at us what we want, what should be done to help us, how we feel, and what a 'real' Indian is really like." Deloria might as well have said that Indians are invisible. North Americans certainly *see* contemporary Native people. They just don't *see* us as Indians.

When I was kicking around San Francisco, there was an Aboriginal photographer, a Mandan from the Fort Berthold reservation in South Dakota named Zig Jackson, who had a wonderful wit. For one of his photographic series, "Entering Zig's Indian Reservation," he took photographs of himself in a feathered headdress wandering the streets of San Francisco, riding cable cars and buses, looking in store windows. What he was after and what he was able to catch were the apprehensive and delighted reactions of non-Natives as they came face to face with their Dead Indian come to life.

Carlisle Indian Industrial School, an early residential school, took photographs of Indians when they first came to that institution and then photographed them after they had been "cleaned up," so that the world could see the civilizing effects of Christianity and education on Indians. Not to be outdone, the Mormon Church, or the Church of Jesus Christ of Latter-Day Saints (LDS), has for years maintained an impressive collection of photographs of Indian children, taken when the children were first brought into the church's Home Placement Program. This was a program in place from 1947 to 1996, through which Native families were encouraged to send their kids off-reservation to live with Mormon families, the expectation being that these children would have a greater chance at success if they were raised and educated in White society. The purpose of the photographs was to track the change in the children's skin color, from dark to light, from savagism to civilization.

Indeed, *The Book of Mormon* specifically teaches that dark-skinned Lamanites (Indians), as they accept Mormon gospel, will turn "white and delightsome." At the 1960 LDS Church conference, the head of the church, Spencer Kimball, rejoiced that Indians were "fast becoming a white and delightsome people," and that Indian children in the church's Home Placement Program were "often lighter than their brothers and sisters in the hogans on the reservation."

When I lived in Salt Lake City, I was privileged to see some of the Church's Polaroids. Frankly, I couldn't see much of a difference between the "before" and "after" shots, but then I wasn't looking at the photographs through the lens of scripture.

In the late 1970s, I went to Acoma Pueblo and took the tour of the old village up on the mesa. One of the adobe houses had a television antenna fixed to the roof, and, as we walked through the narrow streets, we could hear the sounds of Daffy Duck and Bugs Bunny arguing over whether it was rabbit hunting season or duck hunting season. One of the women in the group, a woman in her late thirties from Ohio, was annoyed by the presence of the television set. This was supposed to be an authentic Indian village, she complained to the rest of the group. Real Indians, she told us, didn't have televisions.

In 1997, I was invited to go to France for the St. Malo book fair. I'm not much for travel, but Helen wanted to go, and my friend the late Louis Owens and a number of other Native authors were going to be there, so I went. Now, at that time, I was sporting a moustache. My brother Christopher and I are polar opposites when it comes to body hair. He got it all. I got none. He was able to grow a full beard when he was in his early twenties. I didn't bother shaving more than once a week until I was in my thirties. But I discovered that if I was willing to persevere for a year or so, I could grow a moustache. So I did. I was delighted with the damn thing.

But when I arrived in France, I was promptly told by a photographer, who was taking shots of all the Native authors, that I wasn't Indian. That's not exactly what she said. What she said was, "I know you're Indian, but you're not really Indian, are you?" This wasn't a problem with language. Her English was excellent. What she meant was that I might be Indian by blood and perhaps even by culture, but, with my splendid moustache, I was no longer an authentic Indian. Real Indians, she told me, with no hint of humor or irony, didn't have facial hair.

For us Live Indians, being invisible is annoying enough, but being inauthentic is crushing. If it will help, I'm willing to apologize for the antenna on that house at Acoma. I've already shaved off my moustache, so that should no longer be an issue. If I didn't live in the middle of a city, I'd have a horse. Maybe two. I sing with a drum group. I've been to sweats. I have friends on a number of reservations and reserves around North America. I'm diabetic. If you can think of something else I can do to help myself, let me know.

But I know that nothing will help. In order to maintain the cult and sanctity of the Dead Indian, North America has decided that Live Indians living today cannot be genuine Indians. This sentiment is a curious reworking of one of the cornerstones of Christianity, the idea of innocence and original sin. Dead Indians are Garden of Eden—variety Indians. Pure, Noble, Innocent. Perfectly authentic. Jean-Jacques Rousseau Indians. Not a feather out of place. Live Indians are fallen Indians, modern, contemporary copies, not authentic Indians at all, Indians by biological association only.

Many Native people have tried to counter this authenticity twaddle by insisting on tribal names—Blackfoot, Navajo, Mohawk, Seminole, Hoopa, Chickasaw, Mandan, Tuscarora, Pima, Omaha, Cree, Haida, Salish, Lakota, Mi'kmaq, Ho-Chunk—and while this is an excellent idea, it has been too much for North America to manage. As with the Dead Indian, North America has, for a very long time now, insisted on a collective noun for Live Indians—Indians, Aboriginals, First Nations, Natives, First Peoples—even though there are over 600 recognized nations in Canada and over 550 recognized nations in the United States.

"Recognized." I like that term. Makes me feel almost real.

Dead Indians. Live Indians. You would think that these two Indians would be akin to matter and anti-matter, that it would be impossible for both of them to occupy the same space, but each year Live Indians and Dead Indians come together at powwows and ceremonies and art markets from Alberta to Arizona, Oklahoma to Ontario, the Northwest Territories to New Mexico. At the same time, with remarkable frequency, Live Indians cum Dead Indians show up at major North American social, artistic, and governmental events and galas to pose for the cameras and to gather up any political advantage that might be available.

I never wore a full feather headdress to protests or marches, but I did sport a four-strand bone choker, a beaded belt buckle, a leather headband, and a fringed leather pouch, and when I look at the photographs from those years, the image of myself as a Dead Indian still sends a tremor up my spine.

For Native people, the distinction between Dead Indians and Live Indians is almost impossible to maintain. But North America doesn't have this problem. All it has to do is hold the two Indians up to the light. Dead Indians are dignified, noble, silent, suitably garbed. And dead. Live Indians are invisible, unruly, disappointing. And breathing. One is a romantic reminder of a heroic but fictional past. The other is simply an unpleasant, contemporary surprise.

Tony Hillerman, in his mystery novel *Sacred Clowns*, captures such a moment. In the book, he describes a Tano ceremony in which Jim Chee, a Navajo cop, watches real people, "farmers, truck drivers, loggers, policemen, accountants, fathers, sons, and grandfathers," dancing beneath the masks. Chee can see "the very real sweat glistening on their shoulders, a very ordinary Marine Corps anchor tattoo on the arm of the seventh kachina, the very natural dust stirred by the rhythmic shuffling of their moccasins." And all around, the tourists stand at the edges of the ceremony, looking right at the Live Indians, watching the Dead Indians appear in the plaza. Their cameras at the ready.

Let's be clear, Live Indians dance at powwows. And when we dance, when we sing at the drum, when we perform ceremonies, we are not doing it for North America's entertainment. Where North America sees Dead Indians come to life, we see our families and our relations. We do these things to remind ourselves who we are, to remind ourselves where we come from, and to remind ourselves of our relationship with the earth. Mostly, though, we do these things because we enjoy them. And because they are important.

I know that this sort of rhetoric—"our relationship with the earth"—sounds worn out and corny, but that's not the fault of Native people. Phrases such as "Mother Earth," "in harmony with nature," and "seven generations" have been kidnapped by White North America and stripped of their power. Today, Mother Earth is a Canadian alternative rock band, a Memphis Slim song, an alternative-living magazine, and a short story by Isaac Asimov. "In Harmony with Nature" is an Internet company that sells "nourishing products for home and body." It's also the website for a group of New Age lifestyle educators who offer products and instructions that will "support your transition towards a more holistic lifestyle." "Harmony with Nature" is a hypnosis session that you can download for only $12.95 and which will "gently guide you into a rapturous sense of connection to the whole of natural creation."

"Seven Generations" is a Native institute designed to meet the educational and cultural needs of the ten bands in the Rainy Lake Tribal area. But it is also an Alberta-based company in the business of "unconventional oil and gas resource development," though I'm not sure how you can use "unconventional" and "oil and gas" in the same sentence without creating an oxymoron. There's a "Seven Generations" company out of Burlington, Vermont, that sells "naturally safe and effective household products," while an outfit called "Hellfish Family" will sell you a T-shirt that has a crucifixion scene on the back with "Seven Generations" at the top and "You Are Not My Christ" at the bottom for $12.95.

And then there are the great Indian phrases. I don't know if Crazy Horse ever said, "Today is a good day to die," but I'm told that *"Heghlu'meH QaQ jajvam"* means the same thing in Klingon. You can download Manowar's "Today Is a Good Day to Die" as a ringtone for your phone, and it is the opening line in the movie *Flatliners.*

Dead Indians. Live Indians. In the end, it is an impossible tangle. Thank goodness there are Legal Indians.

Legal Indians are considerably more straightforward. Legal Indians are Live Indians, because only Live Indians can be Legal Indians, but not all Live Indians are Legal Indians.

Is that clear?

Legal Indians are those Indians who are recognized as being Indians by the Canadian and U.S. governments. Government Indians, if you like. In Canada, Legal Indians are officially known as "Status Indians," Indians who are registered with the federal government as Indians under the terms of the Indian Act.

According to the 2006 census, Canada had a population of about 565,000 Status Indians. The census put the total number of Native people in Canada at that time—Indians, Métis, and Inuit—at 1.2 million, but, in that year, at least 22 Indian reserves were not counted, and Statistics Canada admitted that it might have missed even more. Add to that the fact that many First Nations people refuse to participate in a census, seeing it as an affront to sovereignty. Besides, enumeration is not an exact science. So much depends on how it's done and who is doing it. The number 1.2 million is probably too low. But even if there are 1.2 million Indians, Métis, and Inuit, it means that slightly less than 50 percent of all Native people in Canada are Status Indians.

In the United States, federal "recognition," the American version of "Status," is granted to tribes rather than individuals, and in 2009, the government's Federal Register recognized some 564 tribes whose enrolled members were eligible for federal assistance. The total number of individuals who are members of those tribes probably tops out at about 950,000, while the total number of Indians in the United States comes in at around the 2.4 million mark, though again, census figures being what they are, this figure could be lower. Or higher.

As I said, these numbers will never be accurate. But if they are close, it means that only about 40 percent of Live Indians in North America are Legal Indians. A few more than one in three. This is important because the only Indians that the governments of Canada and the United States have any interest in are the Legal ones.

"Interest," though, is probably too positive a term, for while North America loves the Dead Indian and ignores the Live Indian, North America *hates* the Legal Indian. Savagely. The Legal Indian was one of those errors in judgment that North America made and has been trying to correct for the past 150 years.

The Legal Indian is a by-product of the treaties that both countries signed with Native nations. These treaties were, for the most part, peace treaties. Wars were costly, and after a couple of hundred years of beating up on each other, Whites and Indians decided that peace was more profitable. All in all, it was a smart move. For both sides. And because of the treaties, Legal Indians are entitled to certain rights and privileges. They're called treaty rights, and—with the exception of certain First Nations bands in British Columbia and some executive order reservations in the States—Legal Indians are the only Indians who are eligible to receive them.

A great many people in North America believe that Canada and the United States, in a moment of inexplicable generosity, gave treaty rights to Native people as a gift. Of course, anyone familiar with the history of Indians in North America knows that Native people paid for every treaty right, and in some cases paid more than once. The idea that either country gave First Nations something for free is horseshit.

Sorry. I should have been polite and said "anyone familiar with Native history knows that this is in error" or "knows that this is untrue," but, frankly, I'm tired of correcting people. I could have said "bullshit," which is a more standard North American expletive, but, as Sherman Alexie (Spokane–Coeur d'Alene) reminds us in his poem "How to Write the Great American Indian Novel," "real" Indians come from a horse culture.

In Canada, Legal Indians are defined by the Indian Act, a series of pronouncements and regulations, rights and prohibitions, originally struck in 1876, which has wound its snaky way along to the present day. The act itself does more than just define Legal Indians. It has been the main mechanism for controlling the lives and destinies of Legal Indians in Canada, and throughout the life of the act, amendments have been made to the original document to fine-tune this control.

An 1881 amendment prohibited the sale of agricultural produce by Legal Indians in the prairie provinces, to keep them from competing with White farmers. An 1885 amendment prohibited religious ceremonies and dances. A 1905 amendment allowed the removal of Aboriginal people from reserves that were too close to White towns of more than 8,000 residents. A 1911 amendment allowed municipalities and companies to expropriate portions of reserves, without the permission of the band, for roads, railways, and other public works. A 1914 amendment required Legal Indians to get official permission before appearing in Aboriginal costume in any dance, show, exhibition, stampede, or pageant. A 1927 amendment made it a crime to solicit funds for Indian claims without a special license from the government. A 1930 amendment banned Legal Indians from playing pool if they did it too often and wasted their time to the detriment of themselves and their families. And, in 1985, an amendment known in Parliament as Bill C-31 was passed that allowed Native women who had lost their Legal Indian standing through marriage to regain that status.

Until at least 1968, Legal Indians could be "enfranchised," which simply meant that the government could take Status away from a Legal Indian, with or without consent, and replace it with Canadian citizenship. Technically, enfranchisement was proffered as a positive, entailing, among other benefits, the right to vote and drink. All you had to do was give up being a Legal Indian and become . . . well, that was the question, wasn't it. Legal Indian women could be "enfranchised" if they married non-Native or non-Status men. If Legal Indians voted in a federal election, they would be "enfranchised." Get a university degree and you were automatically "enfranchised." If you served in the military, you were "enfranchised." If you were a clergyman or a lawyer, you were "enfranchised."

If you look the word up in the dictionary, you'll find that "enfranchised" means "to be liberated." A Blackfoot friend once told me that "enfranchised" was French for "screwed." It's only funny if you're Indian. Even then, it's not that funny.

In the United States, Legal Indians are enrolled members of tribes that are federally recognized. That's the general rule. However, tribes control how their membership rolls are created and maintained, and eligibility for membership varies from nation to nation. Most base their membership on blood quantum. If you have enough Native blood in you, then you are eligible for enrollment, and, once enrolled, are a Legal Indian.

In Canada, loss of Status has been an individual matter, one Legal Indian at a time. A rather slow process. In the United States, where things reportedly move faster, the government, particularly in the 1950s, set about "enfranchising" entire tribes en masse. They started with the Menominee in Wisconsin and the Klamath in Oregon and, in the space of about ten years, they removed another 107 tribes from the federal registry. At that time, around 1.4 million acres of Legal Indian land were taken from tribes and sold to non-Natives. Over 13,000 Legal Indians lost their federal status and were reduced to being simply Live Indians.

Certainly the sentiment for the extinguishment of the Legal Indian has been around for a while. "I want to get rid of the Indian problem," said Duncan Campbell Scott, head of Canada's Department of Indian Affairs from 1913 to 1932. "Our objective is to continue until there is not a single Indian in Canada that has not been absorbed into the body politic and there is no Indian question, and no Indian Department . . ."

In 1953, the Termination Act and the Relocation Act were concurrently passed by the United States Congress. Termination allowed Congress to terminate all federal relations with tribes unilaterally, while Relocation "encouraged" Native people to leave their reservations and head for the cities. One might say that Termination provided for the death of the Legal Indian, while Relocation provided the mass grave.

In 1969, the Canadian government tried to pull a home-grown Termination Act—the 1969 White Paper—out of its Parliamentary canal. In that year, Prime Minister Pierre Trudeau blithely intimated that there was no such thing as Indian entitlement to land or Native rights and suggested that it was in the best interests of First Nations people to give up their reserves and assimilate into Canadian society. The reaction was immediate and fierce. Almost every Indian organization came out against the plan. Whatever the problems were with the Indian Act and with the Department of Indian Affairs, Native people were sure that giving up their land and their treaty rights was not the answer.

Dead Indians, Live Indians, Legal Indians.

But all North America can see is the Dead Indian. All North America dreams about is the Dead Indian. There's a good reason, of course. The Dead Indian is what North America wants to be. Which probably explains the creation and proliferation of Indian hobbyist clubs, social organizations that have sprung up in North America and around the world as well, where non-Indians can spend their leisure time and weekends pretending to be Dead Indians.

There are Indian clubs in Florida, Texas, California, Washington, Oregon, Idaho, New Mexico, and Arizona. There are Indian clubs in Russia, in Italy, in France, in Poland, in Hungary, and in most of the other eastern European and Scandinavian countries. In a 2003 article for *The Walrus* magazine, Adam Gilders estimates that each weekend over 60,000 Germans dress up like Indians and head out for Indian camps to participate in powwows and sweats. Germany, it should be said, has a long history in the Indian business, a history exemplified by Karl May's adventure novels and the founding of Club Manitou in Dresden in 1910.

But everyone likes to blame the Germans for everything.

I haven't found any clubs in Canada yet, but would guess there must be a couple hidden away here and there. A friend of mine reminded me that, in this regard, Canada can claim Ernest Thompson Seton, who was responsible for the tradition of "summer camp" and the creation of the Boy Scouts. Seton was intrigued with Native people and used Aboriginal crafts and traditions as the centerpiece for his 1902 League of Woodcraft Indians, an organization that combined outdoor activities with Indian culture for the benefit of non-Native children. However, while Woodcraft Indians and the Scouts made use of what they saw as Indian content in their structures and performances, neither was an "Indian club."

Indian clubs are magnets for non-Natives who want to transform themselves, just for a day or two, into Dead Indians. Folks who attend go to dance and sing and participate in pipe ceremonies and sweats. They take on cool Indian names such as Black Eagle and Howling Wolf and Screaming Hawk, and if you ask them what in the hell they're doing, they will tell you with a straight face that they are trying to preserve the culture of North American Indians so it won't be lost.

The one thing that you can say about Indian hobbyists is that they take their fantasies seriously. Still, all of this dress-up, role-playing silliness has as much to do with Indians as an Eskimo Pie has to do with the Inuit.

The irony is that these clubs and the sentiments they espouse would be better served if Live Indians and Legal Indians somehow disappeared, got out of the way. After all, there's nothing worse than having the original available when you're trying to sell the counterfeit.

Live Indians. Legal Indians.

If you listen carefully, you can almost hear North America cry out, in homage to Henry II and his feud with Thomas à Becket, "Who will rid me of these meddlesome Indians?"

And, as luck would have it, Canada and the United States are working on a solution.

4

ONE NAME TO RULE THEM ALL

> growing up in rural Alberta
> in a town with fewer Indians
> than ideas about Indians
> —Marilyn Dumont, *A Really Good Brown Girl*

If North America doesn't like Live Indians and it doesn't like Legal Indians, why doesn't the military-political-corporate complex just kill us off? I know this question sounds melodramatic and absurd, but I've been to rallies, marches, and protests where some clever wit has shouted out from the crowd, "We should have killed all you [expletives deleted] Indians when we had the chance." I'd like to believe that this kind of remark is just the huffing and puffing of bigoted buffoonery. But I've heard it too many times. Such sentiments may not be the rule, but neither are they the exception.

"Why didn't we kill you off when we had the chance?" It's a fair question. Why didn't the United States keep dropping atomic bombs on Japan? If two bombs were good, wouldn't four have been better? Why didn't Turkey keep on killing Armenians after World War I? What stopped the murderous purges of China's Mao Zedong, Russia's Josef Stalin, Cambodia's Pol Pot, and North Korea's Kim Il Sung? A friend of mine suggested that I include George W. Bush for his efforts in Iraq, Afghanistan, and much of the rest of the world, but if I did that, I'd have to throw in AT&T, the World Bank, and the International Monetary Fund, and once you start down that road, there's no end to the list of killers and killings.

Even without the testimony of scholars and social scientists, we know that we don't mind killing as much as we think we should. In particular, contemporary history has demonstrated that we don't mind killing people we don't like, and we don't mind killing if it can be done at a distance and out of sight. And killing is especially acceptable if the slaughter can be attributed to a defect in the victims or to a flaw in their way of life or to an immutable law of nature. Or all of the above. How fortunate it is to have so many excellent ways of destroying a people without getting one's hands damp.

"Why didn't we kill you off when we had the chance?" Maybe the answer isn't all that complicated. Maybe killing is like most everything else. Do it enough times, and it loses its appeal. Maybe it gets boring.

A pervasive myth in North America supposes that Native people and Native culture are trapped in a state of stasis. Those who subscribe to it imagine that, like Vladimir and Estragon in

Samuel Beckett's play *Waiting for Godot*, Natives were unable to move forward along the linear continuum of civilization, that we were waiting for someone to come along and lead us in the right direction. To free us from ourselves.

In Beckett's play, as everyone knows, Godot never arrives. In the Native version, Europeans never leave. In some ways, I envy Vladimir and Estragon. Who knows what unfortunate turns their lives might have taken had Godot managed to land on their shores?

This idea, that Native people were waiting for Europeans to lead us to civilization, is just a variation on the old savagism versus civilization dichotomy, but it is a dichotomy that North America trusts without question. It is so powerful a toxin that it contaminates all of our major institutions. Under its influence, democracy becomes not simply a form of representative government, but an organizing principle that bundles individual freedoms, Christianity, and capitalism into a marketable product carrying with it the unexamined promise of wealth and prosperity. It suggests that anything else is, by default, savage and bankrupt.

Of course, we know that this is untrue. The ancient Romans, Chinese, Egyptians, the Maya and the Incas, didn't practice democracy, or Christianity for that matter, and they managed to create civilizations that were vigorous, civilizations that we admire. North America defends democracy as the cornerstone of social, religious, and political enlightenment because it is obliged to think well of itself and its institutions.

So, in North America—according to western orthodoxy—you had Europeans who were enlightened and Indians who were not. For the first century or so, the two groups killed each other. Not all the time, of course. In between depredations and deprivations,

Europeans and Indians found time for commerce. The French traded with tribes such as the Huron, while the English traded with tribes such as the Mohawk, and for the next two hundred years or so, the two groups traded and fought, fought and traded. When the dust cleared from the so-called Seven Years' War, the American Revolutionary War, and the War of 1812, what had been, according to William Bradford, "a hideous and desolate wilderness, full of wild beasts and wild men" was now two nation states, Canada and the United States, all clean and spanking new.

That's not quite true. While the United States became its own nation in 1776, Canada had to wait another ninety-one years for nationhood to become official. Of course, that didn't stop Great Britain, the United States, and the geographical lump that would later become Canada from drawing an imaginary political line from the Atlantic, along the St. Lawrence, ziggy-zag through the Great Lakes, across the prairies, over the Rockies, all the way to the Pacific Ocean and agreeing that all of the land north of the 49th parallel (more or less) would be the property of England cum Canada, and all of the land south of the 49th parallel (more or less) would belong to the United States. Trees, lakes, rivers, mountains, swamps, deserts, bays, islands, animals, plants, birds, minerals.

Indians.

Indian–White relations were originally constructed around the concerns of commerce—the fur trade being a prime example—and military alliances. In these matters, Native peoples understood themselves to be sovereign, independent nations, and in early land and treaty negotiations, they were treated as such. But by the late 1700s, as European military forces gained the upper hand, Whites began to reimagine the place of Indian nations in North America. In the U.S. Articles of Confederation, the federal government gave itself the exclusive right to regulate "the trade and managing all affairs with the Indians." This power was repeated in the 1790 Trade and Intercourse Act, which further refined "trade" and "affairs" to include the purchase and sale of Indian land. The intent of these two pieces of legislation was clear. Whatever powers states were to have, those powers did not extend to Native peoples.

Beginning in 1823, there would be three U.S. Supreme Court decisions—*Johnson v. McIntosh, Cherokee v. Georgia, Worcester v. Georgia*—that would confirm the powers that the U.S. government had unilaterally taken upon itself and spell out the legal arrangement that tribes were to be allowed.

I'm always looking for the funny bit in the historical record, the ironic slant, the chuckle, something to make a dull subject interesting, something to make a boring discussion lively. But there really isn't much of anything that could be described as delightful in these three decisions, so we might as well get to it.

1823. *Johnson v. McIntosh.* The court decided that private citizens could not purchase land directly from Indians. Since all land in the boundaries of America belonged to the federal government by right of discovery, Native people could sell their land only to the U.S. government. Indians had the right of occupancy, but they did not hold legal title to their lands.

1831. *Cherokee v. Georgia.* The State of Georgia attempted to extend state laws to the Cherokee nation. The Cherokee argued that they were a foreign nation and therefore not subject to the laws of Georgia. The court held that Indian tribes were not sovereign, independent nations but domestic, dependent nations.

1832. *Worcester v. Georgia*. This case was a follow-up to *Cherokee v. Georgia*. Having determined that the Cherokee were a domestic, dependent nation, the court settled the matter of jurisdiction, ruling that the responsibility to regulate relations with Native nations was the exclusive prerogative of Congress and the federal government.

These three cases unilaterally redefined relationships between Whites and Indians in America. Native nations were no longer sovereign nations. Indians were reduced to the status of children and declared wards of the state. And with these decisions, all Indian land within America now belonged to the federal government. While these rulings had legal standing only in the United States, Canada would formalize an identical relationship with Native people a little later in 1876 with the passage of the Indian Act. Now it was official. Indians in all of North America were property.

When she read the passage above, Helen was concerned that the word "property" might imply that I was suggesting that Indians were slaves. That's not accurate. We were more like . . . furniture.

The three U.S. court cases, along with Canada's Indian Act, were not random, stand-alone decisions. They were part of a coordinated undertaking to organize Indians. Even though disease and conflict had dramatically reduced the tribes, there were still, in the minds of policy makers, too many Indians. Too many Indians, too many tribes, too many languages. Indians were a great, sprawling mess. What was needed was a plan to give this snarl of cultures a definitive and manageable form. So, out of ignorance, disregard, frustration, and expediency, North America set about creating a single entity, an entity that would stand for the whole.

The Indian.

Or as J. R. R. Tolkien might have said, "One name to rule them all, One name to find them, One name to bring them all, and in the darkness bind them."

No one really believed that there was only one Indian. No one ever said there was only one Indian. But as North America began to experiment with its "Indian programs," it did so with a "one size fits all" mindset. Rather than see tribes as an arrangement of separate nation states in the style of the Old World, North America imagined that Indians were basically the same. Sure, Mohawk were not Apache, Cherokee were not Cheyenne, but the differences among Native peoples were really just a matter of degree.

All for one. One for all.

Now the only real question was what to do with this Indian. What could North America expect of this Indian? What might be this Indian's place, if any, in the new order? With the proper guidance, what might this Indian become? These questions and their answers would form the backbone of what we call "Indian Policy."

Prior to the 1800s, military action had been, by default, Indian policy in North America, but in the nineteenth century, gunboat diplomacy was augmented by treaties, removals, and relocations, all bundled into a package that we will call Plan A. Plan A wasn't so much a coherent undertaking as it was a series of speculations about how to shuffle Indians out of the way of White settlement and economic development.

Plan A was also a pattern. Someone would start a conflict—it didn't matter who—and the military would come to the rescue. A treaty would be negotiated in which Native people, if they were fortunate, were forced to give up a portion of their land but allowed to keep the remainder and stay where they were. If they were unfortunate, tribes and bands were forced to give up all of their land and move elsewhere to a location chosen for them.

During the colonial period, European powers signed over 1,500 such treaties with Native people, while, on their own, the United States and Canada signed well over 500. In the United States, the first treaty was signed with the Delaware in 1778, and the last one with the Nez Perces in 1868. Treaty-making in the United States was eliminated by statute in 1871, which, coincidentally, was the same year that Canada *began* signing treaties, starting with the eleven Numbered Treaties that dealt with First Nations bands in Alberta, British Columbia, Manitoba, Ontario, Saskatchewan, and the Northwest Territories. The last of the so-called "historical" treaties was signed in 1923 with the Chippewa and Mississauga First Nations, while the last "modern" treaty was signed in 2000 with the Nisga—though, given the number of outstanding Native land claims, there may well be more treaties on Canada's horizon.

Peace treaties should have been the answer to Indian–White conflict, but as Vine Deloria Jr. points out, "America has yet to keep one Indian treaty or agreement." Sweeping generalizations are always suspect, but I'm not sure that Deloria is wrong. I have no idea what Deloria thought of Canada's record of keeping its promises to Native people, but I doubt he would have been impressed.

More than one scholar has argued that treaties were never meant to be long-standing agreements, that they were simply expediencies of the moment. Indians were dying, so the wisdom of the day argued. In fifty or a hundred years, Native people would be gone, and the gnarly, logistical questions that the terms of the treaties might raise in the long term would be resolved

naturally through attrition. In the meantime, however, the combination of military action, treaties, and the myth of Native
extinction was not working fast enough to keep pace with the
demand for space. Even though they had ceased to be a military
threat, even though they had been forced to give up vast tracts of
land, Indians were, through no fault of their own, still in the way.

Still inconvenient.

The official rationale for removal and relocation was Indian
welfare. Removing Indians from the path of White settlement
would reduce the potential for conflicts. Separating Indians from
Whites would limit the occasions for racism. Removal and relocation would limit the availability of White vices such as alcohol.
Out of sight of Whites and away from the corrupting influences
of White culture, Indians would be able to maintain their own
cultures in peace.

Oh, and by the way, Indians had more land than they needed,
more land than they knew what to do with, more land than they
deserved.

The assault on Aboriginal land was greater in the United
States, where the flow of settlement had assumed the proportions
of a tidal wave. In 1763, the British tried to control this tsunami
with a proclamation that forbade White settlement west of the
Appalachians. This line was not intended to be a permanent
boundary. Rather it was a stratagem to maintain the peace with
the tribes between the Appalachians and the Mississippi, while
at the same time allowing for the slow and orderly settlement of
the trans-Appalachian west. But by 1763, it was already too late
for such lines and such cautions. The boundary had already been
breached, with more settlers pouring in all the time. Since no

politician wanted to alienate western voters by trying to evict them, it was decided that the best course of action would be to move Indians to another place.

Just not here.

In the United States, sentiment for forcing Indians out of areas that Whites wanted was as old as the first colonies, but it got its legislative legs in the early 1800s with Thomas Jefferson. In 1802, Georgia was asked to cede the western portion of its lands to the federal government. Georgia agreed to the deal, but only with the stipulation that the federal government secure and turn over title to the state of all lands held by Indian tribes within Georgia's new boundaries. In 1803, Jefferson drafted a constitutional amendment that authorized Congress to trade land west of the Mississippi, bought from France in the Louisiana Purchase, for land that the tribes held in the east. The amendment was never submitted for ratification, but in 1804, Congress passed legislation that authorized the president to pursue such a policy. And the sooner, the better.

Tribes were not particularly keen on moving anywhere, but there was no mistaking the intent of Whites and their government. In 1804, Henry Harrison, the governor of Indiana, "negotiated" a treaty with a small contingent of Sauk chiefs who had come to discuss the fate of a Sauk warrior accused of killing three settlers. Harrison offered to release the man if the Sauk would compensate the families of the slain settlers, which wasn't a problem since this was Sauk custom anyway. But Harrison wanted more. He also insisted that the Sauk sign a removal treaty that ceded all of the tribe's land in Illinois and Wisconsin. Various stories have Harrison intimidating the men or getting them drunk until he had their names on his treaty. The fact that the

Sauks who signed the treaty had no authority to do so didn't bother Harrison or the politicians in Washington in the least.

In fact, scenarios such as this were commonplace, coercion coming in a variety of forms and flavors. If a tribe or a band refused to sign a removal treaty, government officials would find a few members who could be convinced to sign, and then the treaty would be applied to the entire tribe. Native people opposed to such treaties and tactics were frequently threatened with military action. Annuity payments from a previous treaty would be withheld to force compliance. A food source such as the buffalo would be driven off or destroyed in order to bring Indians to heel. These were some of the methods used to bully the Choctaw into the Treaty of Doak's Stand in 1820 and to force Big Bear's Cree to sign Treaty Six in 1876.

Removal, as national policy, began in the United States when the Removal Act was signed into law by Andrew Jackson in 1830. That same year, in his second annual address to Congress, Jackson justified the policy, saying, "Toward the aborigines of the country, no one can indulge a more friendly feeling than myself, or would go further to reclaim them from their wandering habits and make them a happy, prosperous people."

And then he asked the rhetorical question to which all of White North America knew the answer.

"What good man would prefer a country covered with forests and ranged by a few thousand savages to our extensive Republic, studded with cities, towns, and prosperous farms, embellished with all the improvements which art can devise or industry execute, occupied by more than 12,000,000 happy people, and filled with all the blessings of liberty, civilization, and religion?"

Well, since you put it that way.

The U.S. government may have been slow to react to Hurricane Katrina when it hit the Gulf coast in 2005, or to British Petroleum's massive oil spill in 2010, but in 1830 they wasted no time implementing Indian removal legislation. Almost as soon as the bill had left the building, the Choctaw were hustled out of Alabama, Mississippi, and Louisiana and packed off to Indian Territory. That same year, 1831, the Shawnee were dragged out of Ohio. The following year, the Ottawa and the Wyandot followed, leaving Ohio free of Native people. In short order, the Creek, the Chickasaw, the Cherokee, and portions of the Seminole were shipped west. By 1840, the majority of the tribes east of the Mississippi had been moved west of the river into what would eventually become Oklahoma.

The Cherokee call the removal from Georgia *nunna daul isunyi* or "the trail where they cried." Out of some 17,000 Cherokee, over 4,000 died on the trail. Some historians claim the numbers were higher. Some claim they were lower. Whatever the actual number was, the Trail of Tears was, arguably, the largest massacre of Native people in North American history.

A Twin Towers moment.

Choctaw, Chickasaw, Creek, Seminole, Cherokee, Shawnee, Ottawa, Potawatomi, Sauk and Fox, Osage, Kickapoo, Wyandot, Ho-Chunks, Kaskaskia, Peoria, Miami, Delaware, Illinois, Modoc, Oto, Ponca, Seneca, Cayuga, Tuskegee, Quapaw. These are the names of a few of the tribes that were removed from their homelands during the middle of the nineteenth century. What you can't see by reading about these removals is that these were massive upheavals that, in many cases, broke the backs of the communities.

No one has exact figures on how many Native people were relocated during the years that removal was national policy, but for the Choctaw, the Creek, the Chickasaw, the Cherokee, and the Seminole alone, the number was probably between 75,000 and 100,000. How many people were lost in these relocations? No one knows. At the time, no one really kept track. No one much cared. No one really cares now.

Oh, sure, the tribes care. But they're biased.

Canada didn't have an Indian removal policy, certainly not in the same way or on the same scale as their cousins to the south. However, the government did tinker with what it liked to call "relocations," the moving of families, groups, and small bands from one place to another for a variety of reasons. In the States, removals were part of a national strategy to move Native people off prime land and push them out of the way of White settlement. In Canada, relocations were employed ostensibly to further the official goals—protection, civilization, and assimilation—of Canadian Native policy.

The 1996 Report of the Royal Commission on Aboriginal Peoples summed up relocation policy nicely:

Government administrators saw Aboriginal people as unsophisticated, poor, outside modern society and generally incapable of making the right choices. Confronted with the enormous task of adapting to "modern society," they faced numerous problems that government believed could be solved only with government assistance. If they appeared to be starving, they could be moved to where game was more plentiful. If they were sick, they could be placed in new communities where health services and amenities such as sewers, water and electricity were available. If they were thought to be "indolent," the new communities would provide education and training facilities, which would lead to integration into the wage economy. If they were in the way of expanding agricultural frontiers or happened to occupy land needed for urban settlement, they could be moved "for their own protection." And if their traditional lands contained natural resources—minerals to be exploited, forests to be cut, rivers to be dammed—they could be relocated "in the national interest."

The majority of relocations in Canada began in the 1940s, almost a century after the mass removals of Native people in the United States. You might have thought that by then the government would have learned something about such programs and policies, but perhaps the old adage is true after all: "Those who do not understand the lessons of history are doomed to repeat them."

After watching what has happened over the past fifty years in Vietnam, Iraq, and Afghanistan, and seeing the money that is to be made from such ventures, I wonder if that adage should have a corollary: "Those who understand the lessons of history are only too happy to repeat them."

Still, a hundred years *is* a long time. There was no particular reason for the Canadian government to remember what had happened to the Cherokee in the 1840s. After all, most governments can't remember the promises that got them elected. A hundred years? In political terms, that's when dinosaurs ruled the planet.

I said that the majority of relocations in Canada began in the 1940s. And that's true. But practice for what would later become unofficial policy began much earlier. In 1836, the Governor

General of Canada, Francis Bond Head, came up with the paternalistic notion that Indians needed to be protected from White
vices. The most effective way to accomplish that, he decided, was
to move them far away from White settlement. So, in 1836, at
the same time that Georgia was getting ready to evict the
Cherokee, Head forced the surrender of some 600,000 hectares
of land south of Owen Sound, Ontario, that was held by the
Newash and Saugeen bands of the Ojibway. The Ojibway were
moved to what is now the Bruce Peninsula with the promise that
the area would be protected from White encroachment.

Forever.

Twenty years later, the Newash band was forced to give up its
4,000-hectare reserve once again to make way for more White
expansion. This was followed by further "surrenders" in 1851,
1857, and 1861 as the Ojibway in the area were pushed onto
smaller and smaller parcels of land.

"Forever," it turned out, was a conditional rather than an absolute concept.

Farther to the west, the Songhees of Vancouver Island were
being beguiled with the same adverb. In 1850, James Douglas,
Chief Factor of the Hudson's Bay Company, signed a treaty with
the Songhees in which the band gave up a large parcel of land in
exchange for a smaller parcel that was to be held in perpetuity
for them and their descendants.

Forever. Again.

By 1859, the folks living in Victoria had become annoyed with
Indians living next door and began suggesting that the Songhees be
moved. Douglas, to his credit, objected, but after he retired in
1864, enthusiasm for relocation gathered strength and momentum.

Finally, in 1911, the federal and provincial governments reached an agreement among themselves to move the Songhees to a reserve near Esquimalt. After all, the Songhees, according to the wisdom of the time, were only occupying the land. They didn't really own it. They hadn't improved it. They didn't appreciate its real value. Ergo, they didn't deserve it.

Ergo. There's nothing like a little Latin to brighten a logical fallacy.

In 1935, the Métis of Ste. Madeleine in Manitoba were confronted by the Prairie Farm Rehabilitation Act, which allowed the government to turn farmland into pasture land in an attempt to control soil erosion in the prairies. Under the act, when pastures were created and people displaced, farmers were supposed to be compensated and relocated to other lands close to the lands that had been lost. But, technically, that applied only to farmers whose tax payments on the land were up to date. While the Métis had been living at Ste. Madeleine and working the land since around 1900, under the Prairie Farm Rehabilitation Act they did not have the same legal standing as their White neighbors. In spite of their tenure on the land, they were deemed squatters and evicted with little fanfare. Their houses were burned to the ground, and their community was destroyed. No compensation. No land to replace the land that had been lost. The Métis of Ste. Madeleine weren't relocated. They were simply removed.

But in 1942, about 2,000 Mi'kmaq living in some twenty scattered locations in Nova Scotia *were* relocated. The government decided to concentrate all the Mi'kmaq in the two largest settlements at Eskasoni and Shubenacadie. As the Mi'kmaq were mostly Catholic, the government enlisted the Church's support in its relocation plan. The Church was only too happy to help sell the idea of relocation, since concentrating the Mi'kmaq would make the Church's work in religious instruction and assimilation considerably easier. The Mi'kmaq at Eskasoni and Shubenacadie weren't keen about a large influx of new residents, and the Mi'kmaq who were to be relocated weren't keen on moving. Both groups complained, sent letters of protest, and petitioned the government to reconsider.

Which was more or less like throwing mud at a wall.

Of course, the Mi'kmaq were "consulted." After all, Canada is, according to Canada, a just society. There were meetings. Government officials, armed with maps and charts and pie graphs, flew in to talk with Native people about a new future. The officials, sometimes with a respected member of the community at their side, sometimes with a local cleric in tow, coaxed, argued, cajoled, badgered, pleaded, and, on occasion, threatened. Sometimes relocation agreements were signed, and sometimes they weren't. The only constant in the process was that, long before the government ever raised the question of relocation with the people themselves, Ottawa had already decided what it wanted to do, had already decided what would be best for the Department of Indian Affairs, had already decided that what Natives wanted or what Natives thought wasn't terribly important and would have little or no bearing on the final outcome of the "negotiations" and "consultations."

Was relocation—or, as the government called it, "centralization"—going to be good for the Mi'kmaq? That was never really the question. We do know that the government was looking for ways to cut costs, and the centralization of the Mi'kmaq made sense from an administrative point of view. As for the promises of houses, jobs, and a better future?

Relocation of the Mi'kmaq began in 1942. By 1944, only ten new houses had been built at Eskasoni and Shubenacadie. By 1946, many of the families who had been moved to the two reserves were still living in tents. By 1948, unemployment at Eskasoni and Shubenacadie was rampant, even for the original residents, and the entire community was on welfare. By 1949, the government finally admitted that relocation hadn't been the money-saver they'd hoped it would be and shut the program down, leaving the Mi'kmaq worse off than they had been before the program began.

Mind you, these lessons didn't seem to alter the general thinking in Ottawa, and in the 1950s and the 1960s, the Canadian government pressed ahead with its dubious ideas on relocation. In short order, the policies were inflicted on the Inuit at Hebron and Nutak in Labrador, the Sayisi Dene in Manitoba, a number of the Yukon bands—Aishihik, Champagne, White River, Ross River, and Pelly River—the Gwa'Sala and the 'Nakwaxda'xw of British Columbia, and the Mushuau Innu of Davis Inlet, Labrador.

You know what they say. If at first you don't succeed, try the same thing again. Sometimes this effort is called persistence and is the mark of a strong will. Sometimes it's called perseveration and is a sign of immaturity. For an individual, one of the definitions of insanity is doing the same thing over and over again in the same way and expecting different results. For a government, such behavior is called . . . policy.

Nothing to worry about, really. But if we ever get to the stars and find a new world that can support our version of life, and we decide to terraform the place, it would be best to keep the Department of Indian Affairs and the Bureau of Indian Affairs as far away from that planet as possible.

The removals of the Saugeen, the Songhees, and the Métis of Ste. Madeleine were early examples of pushing Native peoples out of the way. But because most reserves were not in close proximity to White settlement, such removals, in Canada at least, were not the rule.

It wasn't until after World War II, as the economy began to heat up, that Indians across North America found themselves being moved and relocated once again, this time to make way for large-scale industrial projects. In particular, hydroelectric projects.

From British Columbia to Pennsylvania, from Saskatchewan to the Missouri River, from the Northwest Territories to Arizona, from Quebec to Washington, from Labrador to California, North America began building dams. Many of these dams were built on Indian land. The Army Corps of Engineers, in particular, was able to determine with amazing regularity that the best sites for dams just happened to be on Indian land. Even when there were more suitable non-Native sites available.

Dams in the United States and Canada destroyed Aboriginal hunting and fishing resources, flooded villages and sacred sites, and forced the relocation of Native people. One of the jokes that went around Indian country in the early 1960s, when the Kinzua Dam was being built in Pennsylvania, was that if Custer had brought along two or three Army Corps engineers, they would have built a dam across the Little Bighorn, drowned the Lakota and the Cheyenne, and made enough off the waterfront lots to pay for Custer's entire campaign.

Helen tells me that I need to balance my generalizations with some examples. Luckily, I can do that.

Initially authorized by the Flood Control Act of 1944, the Pick–Sloan Plan for flood control and navigation on the Missouri River created a system of dams and reservoirs on the backs of over two dozen tribes whose lands lay along the river in the Missouri River basin. None of the tribes was consulted about the project. The Army Corps of Engineers simply ignored the various treaties that were in effect, acquired the land through *eminent domain*, and built the dams. While the Pick–Sloan Plan affected some 23 reserves, forced the relocation of over 1,000 families, and flooded about 155,000 acres of Indian farmland, the plan somehow avoided flooding any of the non-Indian towns along the Missouri.

In 1967, construction began on the hydroelectric project at Churchill Falls in Newfoundland in spite of the objections of the Innu, who lost over 1,900 square miles of traditional hunting and trapping land to the subsequent flooding.

The 1971 James Bay project on La Grande River in north-western Quebec, in violation of earlier treaties with the Cree and Inuit, flooded over 11,500 square kilometers of Aboriginal land and forced the relocation of a number of Native villages. Apologists for Quebec and Ottawa like to point out that, in 1975, the Cree and the Inuit freely relinquished their claims to the land that was to be flooded when they signed the James Bay and Northern Quebec Agreement, for which they received exclusive hunting and fishing rights to a large block of replacement land, along with $250 million in compensation. The agreement has been hailed as a model for "White–Aboriginal co-operation," though it's difficult to see the cooperation. The

Cree and the Inuit were not consulted about the project. Their strong objections to the project were not considered. Quebec and Ottawa didn't give a damn what the Cree and the Inuit thought or wanted. And the agreement that was signed in 1975? Well, that wasn't a negotiation so much as it was the Cree and the Inuit making the best of a bad situation.

Enough examples. You can look up Kemano and the Cheslatta, Grand Rapids and the Chemawamin, Glen Canyon and the Navajo, Warm Springs and the Pomo, Shasta and the Winnemem Wintu, and the constricting of the Columbia River on your own. If you're so inclined.

What needs to be said is that removals and relocations, as federal policies in both countries, allowed Whites to steal Aboriginal land and push Native people about the countryside. I know this sounds harsh, and, although it's accurate, I have to concede that if theft is legally sanctioned, it is no longer theft. So I should probably apologize for using the verb "to steal."

"To appropriate" might be more generous and less inflammatory.

Moving Indians around the continent was like redecorating a very large house. The Cherokee can no longer stay in the living room. Put them in the second bedroom. The Mi'kmaq are taking up too much space in the kitchen. Move them to the laundry. The Seminoles can go from the master bedroom into the sunroom, and lean the Songhees against the wall in the upstairs hallway. We'll see if that works. For the time being, the Ojibway, the Seneca, the Métis, and the Inuit can be stored in the shed behind the garage. And what the hell are we going to do with the Blackfoot, the Mohawk, the Arapaho, and the Piaute?

Do we have any garbage bags left?

Of course, moving Indians around was not enough. Native people were always in the way, always under foot. God knows North America spent a great deal of time and money—Allotment in 1887, Termination and Relocation in the 1950s, Termination once again in the late 1960s, but this time in Canada—trying to find places to put them. But such efforts never seemed to suffice. Even after all the tribes had been moved out of that metaphorical house and into that metaphorical shed, Indians were still in the way. Worse, they were still Indians. While many Native people spoke English, while many had converted to Christianity, while many were small business entrepreneurs, Native culture remained alive and well in North America. Removal and Relocation had been effective in displacing and disrupting the lives of Native people and taking their lands, but these policies and practices had not been the answer to the Indian Problem.

Still, North America was nothing if not resilient. Plan A hadn't worked. Time for Plan B.

5

WE ARE SORRY

Where do you begin telling someone their world is not the only one?

—Lee Maracle, *Ravensong*

Whenever someone says "Plan B," I'm instantly reminded of that wondrously horrid movie that Ed Wood wrote and directed back in 1956.

Plan 9 from Outer Space.

The film was shot in just five days and cost less than $20,000 to make, much of the capital coming from a group of Baptist churches. How Wood got these folks to invest in a horror/science fiction movie is a mystery, although the best story has him convincing the clergy that if *Plan 9* was successful, the profits could be used to make twelve movies, about the lives of each of the apostles. In any case, the churches took their role as investors seriously, insisting that the original title, *Grave Robbers from Space,* be changed, that any dialogue they considered profane be removed, and that all the members of the cast be baptized. The part about baptism is probably apocryphal, but had it been a deal-breaker, Wood would, no doubt, have obliged.

In the film, aliens try to stop human beings from creating a doomsday weapon that will destroy the universe. In 1980, Michael Medved hailed *Plan 9* as the worst film ever made, but when I look at the movie with its cheap sets, its dreadful script, its pedestrian acting, its incompetent direction, and its rumors of mandatory conversion, it reminds me a great deal of North American Indian policy.

Indeed, North American Indian policy in the last half of the nineteenth century had many of the qualities of a bad movie. It was a low-budget affair with a simplistic plot: politicians, soldiers, clerics, social scientists, and people of unexamined goodwill dash about North America, saving themselves from Indians by saving Indians from themselves. But, unlike *Plan 9 from Outer Space*, Plan B didn't include the option to get up and leave the theater.

For 250 years, Whites and Indians had fought as enemies, had fought as allies, had made peace, had broken the peace, and had fought each other again. But when Great Britain, France, and the newly formed United States sat down in 1783 to hammer out the details of the Treaty of Paris that would officially end the American Revolution, Native people, who had fought alongside both England and the colonies, were neither invited to the negotiations nor mentioned in the treaty itself.

So long and thanks for all the fish.

Indians *were* mentioned in the Treaty of Ghent, which tidied up the War of 1812. Article Nine specified that the United States cease all hostilities toward the "Nations of Indians" and restore to the tribes all the "possessions, rights, and privileges which they may have enjoyed or been entitled to in one thousand eight hundred and eleven previous to such hostilities." The Americans more or less forgot about this particular article as soon as they signed the treaty, but anyone watching the film shouldn't have been surprised.

Throughout the history of Indian–White relations in North America, there have always been two impulses afoot. Extermination and assimilation. Extermination of Native peoples, especially in the early years, was not considered "genocide"—a term coined in 1944 by the legal scholar Raphael Lemkin—so much as it was deemed a by-product of "manifest destiny"—a term struck in the 1840s when U.S. Democrats used it to justify the war with Mexico. Extermination was also seen as an expression of "natural law," a concept conceived by Aristotle in the fourth century B.C. and used by the Spanish humanist Juan de Sepúlveda in the sixteenth as a legal justification for the enslavement of Native people in the Caribbean and Mexico.

The means of extermination didn't much matter. Bullets were okay. Disease was fine. Starvation was acceptable. In the minds of many, these were not so much cruelties as they were variations on the principles underlying the concept "survival of the fittest," a phrase that Herbert Spencer had fashioned in 1864 and that would become synonymous with Charles Darwin's theory of natural selection.

The second impulse, assimilation, argued for salvation and improvement. One of the questions that the Spanish worried over was whether or not Indians were human beings. This was the subject of the great debate organized by the Vatican in Valladolid, Spain, in 1550 and 1551 where the cleric Bartolomé de las Casas maintained that Indians had souls and should be treated as other free men, while the aforementioned Juan de Sepúlveda made the case on behalf of land owners, arguing that Indians did not have souls and were therefore natural slaves. De las Casas's position carried the day, but the "Indians have souls" argument provided no more than a philosophical victory and had no effect on the day-to-day actions of Spanish colonists in the New World, who continued to use Indians as slaves to run their plantations.

Neither the English nor the French spent any time with this question. For these two groups, Indians were simply humans at an early point in the evolution of the species. They were savages with no understanding of orthodox theology, devoid of complex language, and lacking civilized manners. Barbarians certainly, and quite possibly minions of the devil. But human beings, nonetheless. And as such, many colonists believed that Native people could be civilized and educated, believed that there was, within the Indian, the possibility for enlightenment.

Extermination dominated the early contact period, assimilation the latter, until finally, in the nineteenth century, they came together in an amalgam of militarism and social theory that allowed North America to mount a series of benevolent assaults on Native people, assaults facilitated by force of arms, deception, and coercion, assaults that sought to dismantle Native culture with missionary zeal and humanitarian paternalism, and to replace it with something that Whites could recognize.

These assaults came singly, in partnerships, and from various angles. In general, settlers and missionaries of one flavor or another led the way, taking turns leapfrogging each other into the "wilderness." In Canada, it was the French and the Jesuits, followed by the English and Anglicans, Methodists, and Presbyterians. In the American northeast and along the Atlantic coast, it was the English and the Puritans, Methodists, Baptists, and Presbyterians, with a smattering of Quakers and other nonconformists working out of Rhode Island. In the southeast, it was the Spanish and the Jesuits and the Franciscans. In the far west, along the Pacific coast, it was the Spanish and the Franciscans, while, much later and farther north in California and up the Pacific coast, it was the Russians and the Orthodox Church.

Francis Jennings, in his book *The Invasion of America*, called Christianity a "conquest religion." I suspect this description is true of most religions. I can't think of one that could be termed a "seduction religion," where converts are lured in by the beauty of the doctrine *and* the generosity of the practice.

Maybe Buddhism. Certainly not Christianity.

Missionary work in the New World was war. Christianity, in all its varieties, has always been a stakeholder in the business of assimilation, and, in the sixteenth century, it was the initial wound in the side of Native culture. Or, if you want the positive but somewhat callous view, you might wish to describe Christianity as the gateway drug to supply-side capitalism.

George Washington and Henry Knox believed in the potential of Indians to become Whites, and they developed a six-point "civilizing" plan to accomplish this. Among other things, the plan called for impartial justice toward Indians, for the development of "educational" experiments to civilize Indian society, and for the prosecution and punishment of anyone who violated Native rights.

Impartial justice? Prosecute anyone who violated Native rights? I'm tempted to say something cranky and sarcastic, but I'm sure

Washington and Knox were serious. For his part, Knox argued for Native rights and for treating Indian nations as sovereign, foreign nations. Knox wrote Washington to say, "How different would be the sensation of a philosophic mind to reflect that instead of exterminating a part of the human race by our modes of population that we had persevered through all difficulties and at last had imparted our Knowledge of cultivation and the arts, to the Aboriginals of the Country." Knox goes on to say that "it has been conceived to be impractical to civilize the Indians of North America" but that "this opinion is probably more convenient than just."

While "impartial justice" and "protection of Native rights" proved to be empty rhetoric, the desire to find ways to civilize Indians had been an impulse from the beginning of European settlement. And while many of the civilizing programs in Canada and the United States were marked by education of one sort or another—farming for the men, domestic service for the women, along with a little reading, writing, and arithmetic—almost all of them were anchored in Christianity.

Teach Indians to fish, but teach them to be Christian fishers. And then you can sell them fishing gear.

The hope for Native peoples was that, with a little training and a push in the right direction, they would become contributing members of White North America. This was not to be a compromise between cultures. It was to be a unilateral surrender. Indians were to give up what they had and what they believed, in exchange for what Whites had and believed. The implication could not have been clearer. European culture, religion, and art were superior to Native culture, religion, and art, and the proof of that superiority could be found in the military might of Canada and America.

Whenever I think about this, I'm reminded of the television series *Star Trek* and, in particular, the Borg, whose battle cry, "Resistance is futile. You will be assimilated," could well have been spoken by John A. Macdonald and Andrew Jackson. Or Stephen Harper and George W. Bush.

While there are a great many places to start a discussion of assimilation, two excellent beginnings are in seventeenth-century Quebec and seventeenth-century New England.

Around 1637, the Jesuit Father Le Jeune set about building a Catholic Indian village along the St. Lawrence near Saguenay. He was aided in this effort by Noël Brûlart de Sillery, a Knight of Malta and a member of the Company of the Hundred Associates. The idea was to create a community of Native people who wished to be converted to Catholicism and who would be willing to give up their "nomadic" ways and take up farming. The village was named Sillery after its chief benefactor, and by 1647, there were around 167 Indians living there. However, European religion and farming were not as enticing as the Jesuits had hoped, and, by the winter of 1649, the population of Sillery was reduced to two men, both of them White. The Jesuits would continue to construct such villages in the hopes that Indians would come in out of the woods for the gifts of Christianity. And they did. But it's reasonably clear, from the historical record, that when Native people made use of these settlements, they did so primarily for food, for temporary shelter, and for protection from other tribes.

The Puritan cleric John Eliot, who was known as the "Indian Apostle," arrived in Boston in 1631. His mission was to convert Indians to his particular brand of Christianity, and, between 1645 and 1675, he was the leading force in the creation of what were called "praying towns." These towns, around fourteen in number, were situated on the outskirts of the Puritan settlements and functioned as halfway houses for Indians who were interested in converting. In these outposts between savagery and civilization, Native people were to be schooled in English, Christianity, and the norms of civilized society.

Praying towns weren't a bad idea, but because they sat between the forest and the Puritan towns, in what could be seen as an early American demilitarized zone, they became the target for tribes bent on pushing the colonists into the sea, as well as targets for colonists who didn't make a distinction between friendly Indians and their more hostile relatives. During the 1675 King Philip War, these towns were attacked by both sides, and, in October of that year, the praying Indians, who had pledged their loyalty to the Puritans but who were still seen as a threat, were shipped off to Deer Island in Boston Harbor. It was essentially a concentration camp, the first in North America, though sadly not the last. The war ended in 1676, but the "praying" Indians were kept on the island for another year.

By the way, Deer Island today is no longer an island. The Shirley Gut channel was filled in by a hurricane in 1938, and the island is now the site of the Deer Island Waste Water Treatment Plant, which treats the sewage from forty-three cities and towns in the area. Park lands surround the treatment plant, and there are walking trails, jogging trails, and picnic areas. So far as I know, there is no plaque or monument to commemorate the Christian Indians who were imprisoned there.

As an assimilation experiment, neither the Jesuit villages in Lower Canada nor the praying towns in New England worked out well. Still, they were a beginning in the business of assimilation and the precursors to later solutions.

By the late nineteenth century, the Indian Problem was still a problem. Yes, Indians had been defeated militarily. Yes, most of the tribes had been safely locked up on reservations and reserves. Yes, Indians were dying off in satisfying numbers from disease and starvation. Yes, all of this was encouraging. But, at the same time, Indians were still being Indians. How could this happen? How could Native cultures hold their own against the potency of western civilization? Or to put this question in the vernacular, why would anyone prefer a horse when they could have a 1957 Chevrolet two-door convertible with a 283 horsepower Super Turbo V8?

Unless, of course, you're a Ford person.

Sure, White culture might have seemed a bit on the stingy side, a little mean-spirited from time to time. Greedy. Pompous. But that was the practice of the thing, not what was preached. The Bible, it should be noted, has entire verses devoted to peace, goodwill, and sharing. Assimilation wasn't a bad thing in itself. It had just been poorly handled.

Speaking in 1892, at the Nineteenth Annual Conference of Charities and Correction, Richard Pratt, a fifty-two-year-old army captain, stood and told the audience how assimilation might be accomplished in a more humane and effective manner.

Education.

Pratt's plan was a simple one. North America would have to kill the Indian in order to save the man. "Kill the Indian in him, and save the man" was the exact quotation, and while it sounds harsh, it was an improvement on Philadelphia lawyer Henry

Pancoast's 1882 suggestion that "We must either butcher them [Indians] or civilize them, and what we do we must do quickly."

For Pratt, the problem of educating and civilizing the Indian was not race or some defect in the blood. It was environmental determinism. "It is a great mistake to think that the Indian is born an inevitable savage," said Pratt. "He is born a blank, like the rest of us. We make our greatest mistake in feeding our civilization to the Indians instead of feeding the Indians to our civilization."

Now, there's a pleasant thought.

In 1879 Pratt opened one of the first modern residential schools for Indians at the old Carlisle Army Barracks in Carlisle, Pennsylvania. Kill the Indian, save the man. Here, at last, was the answer to the "Indian Problem." Here, at last, was an effective blueprint for assimilation. Kill the Indian, save the man. A little late in being codified perhaps, but concise and elegant in its simplicity. If I had been Pratt, I would have been tempted to hang the slogan over the entrance to every residential school in Canada and the United States. "Kill the Indian, save the man." But I'd do it in Latin. To give it more import.

Intermino Indian, Servo Vir.

Although perhaps Dante's famous caution, *Lasciate Ogne Speranza, Voi Ch'intrate*, might have been more appropriate. And no less honest. Except it's Italian, rather than Latin. Not that any of the Native children who passed through the doors of residential schools would have noticed the difference. Or cared.

That was the trick, of course. When North America talked about the education and assimilation of Natives, it wasn't talking about adult Indians. Or as the Reverend E. F. Wilson, founder of the Shingwauk residential school in Sault Ste. Marie, Ontario, called them, "the old unimprovable people." North America had long ago given up on them. If education was going to make any inroads in Native communities, it would make them through the children.

The idea of educating Native children hadn't begun with Richard Pratt. Both the Catholic and Protestant churches had been conducting their own private wars for missions long before Pratt's Carlisle Indian Industrial School opened its doors. In 1885, J. A. Stephan, the Director of the Catholic Bureau, urged the immediate building of more Catholic schools on reservations: "If we do this, we do an immense deal of good, get the Indians into our hands and thus make them Catholics; if we neglect it any longer, the Government and the Protestants will build ahead of us schools in all the agencies and crowd us completely out and the Indians are lost."

Francis Paul Prucha, the Jesuit scholar and historian, talks about the conflict between Catholics and Protestants as they battled each other for schools on reserves and reservations in his book *The Churches and the Indian Schools, 1888–1912*. Reading Prucha's book, which is rich in its referencing of primary sources, leaves one with the distinct impression that the main concern of the Catholic and Protestant missions was not so much Native education as it was outdoing each other in the race for Native converts.

Schools came in a variety of configurations. The early schools were mostly day schools located on reserves and reservations where Indian children remained in contact with their family and culture. However, almost immediately, these proved to be ineffective. So long as the children could stay in their communities, any progress with assimilation was blunted by the strength of Native culture.

The second group of schools was day and residential schools located near reservations and reserves, and developed, in part, to limit the access of Native children to their families and communities. Francis Xavier, the cofounder of the Jesuit Order, is supposed to have said, "Give me a child until he is seven and I will give you the man," but, frankly, any fool could have figured that one out. It's what advertising is about, the training of generations of consumers who will remain loyal to particular products. And whether you like the idea or not, religion and culture are products. Just like hot dogs and frosted cereals.

From the standpoint of the churches, limiting a child's access to his or her culture, limiting the influence of the "old, unimproved people," made a great deal of sense. Why give children choices when it would only confuse them? Why have them exposed to traditional beliefs when the goal of the schools was the Christianizing and civilizing of Native youth? The off-reserve day and residential schools were more effective in controlling access to family and community than the schools on the reserves, but only by degrees.

And then, in 1879, along came Richard Pratt and the Carlisle Indian Industrial School.

Carlisle was the first truly off-reservation, residential school. As an officer in the U.S. Army, Pratt had a long history with Native people. He had fought against the tribes of the southwestern plains. He had been in charge of the Fort Marion prison in St. Augustine, Florida, where seventy-one Indian prisoners were sent in 1875. It was at this prison that Pratt began considering how Native people might be assimilated, and it was this history and his experience as a soldier and a warden that he brought with him to Carlisle.

The Carlisle model called for schools to be situated as far away from Native communities as possible. The model insisted that personal contact between parents and students be greatly reduced or eliminated altogether. It prohibited the practice of Native traditions and the speaking of Native languages. The children were taught to read and write English, encouraged to join a Protestant Christian denomination, and given vocational training in such matters as farming, baking, printing, housekeeping, cooking, and shoemaking. License plates.

I'm kidding about the license plates, but depending on your sensibility, the Carlisle model resembled either a military camp or a prison. Or both. And by 1909, there were some 25 schools based on the Carlisle model in operation in the United States, along with 157 on-reservation boarding schools and 307 day schools.

When I was fifteen, I wound up at a Catholic boarding school in Sacramento, California, run by the Christian Brothers. As a teenager, I can remember being something of a problem. I didn't have a father, and I think my mother worried that my delinquencies resulted, in part, from a lack of male models and mentors. Looking at me through my mother's eyes, I can see how Christian Brothers would have seemed a good place for a boy such as me.

The school was a long list of regulations, which were enthusiastically and martially enforced, and it contained an assortment of miseries and indignities passed out like treats at a party. I had never been hit at home, but, at Christian Brothers, I got my knuckles cracked with a ruler for talking in class and swatted across the shoulders with a wooden pointer for having a smart mouth. I was whacked across the backs of my thighs for a variety of offenses and kicked once for not leaving the recreation room fast enough. But, all in all, it was minor stuff. Not much worse than you'd expect from a fraternity hazing. Or a mugging.

Then there was the food. Breakfast was, most often, a kind of grey, tasteless porridge, what Basil Johnston, in his residential school memoir *Indian School Days*, calls "sad ol' mush." Fred Lazenby, one of the guys at the school who seemed to enjoy getting into trouble most of the time, called our cuisine "shit on a shingle." Years later I would learn that "shit on a shingle" was a colorful metaphor for chipped beef on toast, but at the time, everyone thought that Fred was clever as hell. Except the Brothers. Nothing much amused them. Not the food. Certainly not us.

There was a great deal that I disliked about the school and not much that I remember with any fondness. But the one thing I do remember clearly from the two years I spent at Christian Brothers was the feeling of isolation and the sense of loss and abandonment. I knew my mother believed that I would get a good education, and I knew she wanted the best for me, and all I wanted to do was come home. The school was, at its best, a cold, dead place. I've tried to forget about the experience, but researching Native residential schools for this book has caused those memories to seep to the surface once again, and they taste just as bitter now as they did then. My mother was at home. My brother was at home. My grandmother was there, and so were my cousins and aunts and uncles. For the two years I was at the school, I couldn't help but think that I had done something wrong, something so very wrong that the only solution had been exile.

The truth is that my experiences have little in common with the experiences of the children who were dragged out of their homes across North America and incarcerated at residential schools. I hadn't been raised on a reserve. I spoke English. I wasn't seven or eight or nine. I wasn't beaten, though there were those "boxing matches" with Brother Arnold. I wasn't sexually abused. I wasn't one of the four boys who, in 1937, fled the Lejac residential school in British Columbia and froze to death within sight of their home community. On those occasions when I ran away from Christian Brothers, I simply snuck out of the dormitory, walked to the freeway, and hitchhiked the twenty miles home. I could have walked it. In California in 1957, the only perils I faced on my periodic escapes were too much sun and the concerns of a mother who loved me.

In my junior year, I returned to Roseville and public high school, and simply shoved Christian Brothers into the back of my mind where I couldn't see it. I know it's lurking in the shadows somewhere, but it no longer distresses me the way it did. One thing, though, is clear. Given my obvious lack of emotional fiber, I would never have survived Carlisle. Had I gone to that institution with Ernest White Thunder, Fanny Charging Shield, Susia Nach Kea, Nannie Little Robe, or Albert Henderson, I would have been buried with them in the school graveyard.

In Canada, residential schools began popping up in the 1840s, and by 1932, there were more than eighty schools in operation. Sixty percent of the schools were run by the Catholic Church, with another 30 percent run by the Anglican Church. The rest were run by other Protestant denominations, such as the Presbyterians and the Methodists. In 1850, attendance at residential schools became compulsory for all children from the ages of six to fifteen. There was no opting out. Noncompliance by parents was punishable by prison terms. Children were forcibly removed from their homes and kept at the schools. As with their U.S. counterparts, schools insisted that the children not have any extensive contact with their families or home communities. Students were forbidden to speak their languages or practice any part of their culture.

The schools in both countries were, for the most part, over-crowded. Diseases flourished. Sexual and physical abuse was common. The children received neither proper nutrition nor proper clothing. In 1907, Dr. Peter Bryce submitted a report to Duncan Campbell Scott, the Superintendent of the Department of Indian Affairs, which set the mortality rate for Native students at residential schools in British Columbia at around 30 percent. The rate for Alberta was 50 percent. I'm not sure exactly how Scott reacted to the report, but, in 1910, he dismissed the high death rate at the schools, insisting that "this alone does not justify a change in the policy of this Department, which is geared towards the final solution of our Indian Problem."

Final solution. An unfortunate choice of words. Of course, no one is suggesting that Adolf Hitler was quoting Scott when Hitler talked about the final solution of the "Jewish problem" in 1942. That would be tactless and unseemly. And just so we're perfectly clear, Scott was advocating assimilation, not extermination. Sometimes people get the two mixed up.

In 1919, Scott abolished the post of Medical Inspector for Indian Agencies. Perhaps the position fell to budget cuts. Perhaps Scott and his department were still stinging from Bryce's report and decided that the best way to deal with mortality figures was not to keep them.

In 1926, the U.S. Secretary of the Interior, Hubert Work, com-missioned a survey that looked at the general condition of Indians in the United States. Lewis Meriam, a Harvard graduate with a law degree from George Washington University and a doctorate from the Brookings Institution, led the investigation. Meriam and his team spent some twenty months travelling to reservations, talking with people in the field, examining the whole of Indian Affairs, and writing a comprehensive report on the subject.

The Problem of Indian Administration.

In the 847-page report, which was cowritten by Henry Roe Cloud (Winnebago) and released in 1928, Meriam says candidly, "The survey staff finds itself obliged to say frankly and unequivocally that the provisions for the care of Indian children in boarding school are grossly inadequate." The report goes on to describe the diet at the schools as "deficient in quantity, quality, and variety," and insists that the "per capita of eleven cents a day" per student is insufficient.

Diseases such as tuberculosis and trachoma were rampant. Dormitories were overcrowded "beyond their capacities." Medical services were not up to a "reasonable standard." Nor were the children getting much of an education. "The boarding schools are frankly supported in part by the labor of the students," noted the report. "Those above the fourth grade ordinarily work for half a day and go to school for half a day. A distinction in theory is drawn between industrial work undertaken primarily for the education of the child and production work done primarily for the support of the institution." The question, says the report, "may very properly be raised as to whether much of the work of Indian children in boarding school would not be prohibited in many states by the child labor laws . . ."

As for the "industrial" training that the children received, which was supposed to allow them to move effortlessly into

White society and find work, the Meriam Report cautions that "Several of the industries taught may be called vanishing trades and others are taught in such a way that the Indian students cannot apply what they have learned in their own home and they are not far enough advanced to follow their trade in a white community in competition with white workers."

Of the residential school system in general, the report was succinct and to the point: "The first and foremost need in Indian education is a change in point of view. Whatever may have been the official governmental attitude, education for the Indian in the past has proceeded largely on the theory that it is necessary to remove the Indian child as far as possible from his home environment, whereas the modern point of view in education and social work lays stress on upbringing in the natural setting of home and family life. The Indian educational enterprise is peculiarly in need of the kind of approach that recognizes this principle, that is less concerned with a conventional school system and more with the understanding of human beings."

Overall, the Meriam Report was extremely critical of the federal government and its failure to protect the rights of Natives as well as tribal land and tribal resources. Perhaps that is why, in the eighty-three years since the report was filed, the United States has never commissioned another study of its kind. Why would the government spend money, one could argue, to ask questions to which it already knows the answers?

Canada waited until the 1960s to ask the same question of Indian policy that their American cousins had asked thirty-eight years earlier. The Hawthorn Report, which was published in 1966 and 1967, looked at "the contemporary situation of the Indians of Canada with a view to understanding the difficulties they faced in overcoming some pressing problems and their many ramifications." The "problems," according to the report, were the "inadequate fulfillment of the proper and just aspirations of the Indians of Canada to material well being, to health, and to the knowledge that they live in equality and in dignity with the greater Canadian society."

The report was a well-researched, conscientiously written document, whose preamble was careful to stress that the researchers did not believe that "the Indian should be required to assimilate, neither in order to receive what he now needs nor at any future time." Indeed, the framers of the report were explicit in pointing out that "it is our opinion that the retention of these identities is up to the Indians. No official and perhaps no outside agency at all can do that task for them. Whether or not, and to what extent, Indians remain culturally separate depends on what it is worth to them."

I have no quarrel with this basic premise, that the retention of our identities is up to us. Still, it is a strikingly disingenuous argument in that the report makes little mention of the myriad of ways in which Canadian Indian policy has *discouraged* Indians from pursuing traditional goals and aspirations and continues to push us up the cattle chute of capitalism.

But let's put the philosophical sophistries to one side for the moment. While the report was awash in generous language and fine recommendations, it was also narrowly focused on the economics of being Indian and the problems that bands and individuals have in measuring up to the expectations of Canadian capitalism. The per capita income of Indians in the 1960s, for example, was only $300, less than a quarter of the per capita income of non-Indians, while the average duration of employment for Native people was 4.8 months. Of the Sarcee and the Blood in Alberta, the report notes that while these bands have "ownership and access to a wealth of resources, as well as a metropolitan center which offers manifold job opportunities," they fail "to utilize these assets fully." For "northern Indians . . . any substantial improvement in the employment and income prospects . . . will be possible only with a large-scale migration to, and relocation in, areas offering opportunities for remunerative wage employment." Indians, the report laments, are not accustomed to jobs that "require regular hours, punctuality, and a highly mechanized routine of work." At every turn, the report posits White goals and standards as the measure against which Native people are to be measured and, in each instance, Indians are found wanting.

There were a host of recommendations that the Hawthorn Report put forth to try to close the gap between Native people and non-Natives. Many of them were reasonable, but what the report highlighted was that, in terms of economic development and economic sustainability, Canadian Indian policy had been a failure.

More to the point, the report revealed the logical fallacy that has haunted Indian history and policy in North America since contact—to wit, that all people yearn for the individual freedom to pursue economic goals. Indians are people, ergo, they want to make money and create wealth for themselves and their families.

In the 1950s and '60s, Helen's father, Bernard Hoy, my father-in-law, was an inspector for the Catholic Separate School Board in the Sudbury region. One of his duties was to look in on Catholic residential schools in northern Ontario. His memories of the schools were neither as damning as the Meriam Report nor as detailed as the Hawthorn Report. What he remembered were Native students who spent their classroom time in their seats looking out the window. "They didn't belong there," Bernard told his daughter.

He was right. But if they didn't belong there, where did they belong? Instead of trying to kill the Indian to save the child, North America might have gone into partnership with the various nations, and, together, they could have come up with an education plan that would have complemented Native cultures and, perhaps, even enriched White culture at the same time.

Just a thought.

Here's the irony. Native people have never been resistant to education. We had been educating our children long before Europeans showed up. Nor were we against our children learning about White culture. By the beginning of the nineteenth century, Natives and Whites had been living together in the same neighborhood for almost three hundred years. Like it or not. It made sense for Native people to know English and/or French. It made sense to understand how the European mind worked.

Education is generally described in terms of "benefits." But why, in the name of education, should we have been required to give up everything we had, to give up who we were in order to become something we did not choose to be? Where was the benefit in that?

Instead, North America decided that Native education had to be narrowly focused on White values, decided that Native values, ceremonies, and languages were inferior and had no value or place in a contemporary curriculum. This was the first abuse of the residential school system.

The second abuse was the unwillingness and inability of the governments of Canada and the United States, and the governing bodies of the various churches, to oversee the schools under their control.

The third abuse, once officials knew that health conditions and services were substandard, once they knew that disease was rampant, once they knew malnutrition was a problem, once they knew for certain that the children under their protection were being physically, mentally, and sexually abused, was their failure to act. They did nothing.

They knew, and they did nothing.

Richard Pratt was wrong. As it turned out, if you killed the Indian, you killed the Indian. A great many intelligent and compassionate people have called residential schools a national tragedy. And they were. But perhaps "tragedy" is the wrong term. It suggests that the consequences of residential schools were unintended and undesired, a difficult argument to make since, as Ward Churchill points out, the schools were national policy.

No one knows for sure how many Native children wound up at residential schools in the United States. Canada reckons their own numbers at about 150,000, so the tally for America would have been considerably higher. But for the children who did find themselves there, the schools were, in all ways, a death trap. Children were stripped of their cultures and their languages. Up to 50 percent of them lost their lives to disease, malnutrition, neglect, and abuse—50 percent. One in two. If residential schools had been a virulent disease, they would have been in the same category as smallpox and Ebola. By contrast, the 1918 Spanish flu, which killed millions worldwide, had a mortality rate of only 10 to 20 percent.

But for the sake of argument, let's say that the mortality rate was only 20 percent, one in five. And let's turn things around and ask a somewhat different question. What would have happened if the residential schools had been public schools instead? Schools in

Toronto, San Francisco, Vancouver, New York. What would have happened if the children who were dying were White? What would have happened if one of them had been your child?

Sure. It's a rhetorical question.

The end of the twentieth century and the beginning of the new millennium saw a rash of apologies from churches and governments. In 1986, the United Church of Canada formally apologized to Native people for the treatment Native children received at their schools. In 1991, the Missionary Oblates of Mary Immaculate offered their apology. In 1993, it was the Anglican Church's turn, and in 1994, the Presbyterian Church followed suit.

In 1988, then Minister of Indian Affairs Jane Stewart offered the first apology from the Canadian government. Twenty-one years later, in 2009, Pope Benedict XVI expressed "sorrow" to Assembly of First Nations delegates for the "deplorable" treatment of Aboriginal students at Catholic-run residential schools. But this was not an apology, nor was it a statement of responsibility. It was nothing more than a sympathetic lament.

Some of you might suppose that the Pope, who is also the CEO of one of the world's more profitable corporations with assets around the world, was worried that a formal apology might have been seen as an admission of guilt and would make the Catholic Church liable for damages, but that is not the case. While Protestant sects have national churches, Catholics do not. There is no National Catholic Church of Canada. There are simply franchises—dioceses, religious orders, and institutions—that are legally separate and legally protected from each other's liability. Even though the Vatican is in charge of all Catholic activity in the world, there is no way to hold the folks in Rome legally responsible for the abuses that happened at a residential school in the wilds of Canada, even if the Church knew about it, even if they did nothing to stop it, even if they condoned it as part of the process of assimilation.

Finally, in 2008, Prime Minister Stephen Harper stood up in the House of Commons and said that "assimilation was wrong, has caused great harm and has no place in our country." And then the Prime Minister of Canada said, "We are sorry." He said it in the House of Commons with Native people in attendance. And it was broadcast on national television.

I was in Ottawa the day before the apology was given. Native people and Native leaders from all over the country came to town to hear what the government had to say. Many of the people I talked to had been waiting a very long time to hear those words.

We are sorry.

The United States, on the other hand, has offered no such apology, though in December of 2009 the U.S. Congress did pass an official apology resolution, which President Barack Obama signed into law. But, aside from signing it, President Obama has done nothing else with it. I would have expected that, by now, his staff would have organized a public ceremony, that the White House would have invited Native people to come to Washington to hear the apology. Maybe Obama is waiting for the Pope to clear his schedule, so the two of them can apologize at the same time.

The Canadian apology, while heartfelt, was, in many ways, a stingy thing, limited only to the abuse that Native people had endured in the residential school system. There was nothing in the apology about treaty violations. Nothing about the theft of land and resources. Nothing about government incompetence, indifference, and chicanery. Nothing about the institutional racism that Aboriginal people have endured and continue to endure.

The American apology, by contrast, was a blanket apology that did not limit itself to residential schools or shrink from specifics. The Removal Act, the Trail of Tears, the Sand Creek massacre, Wounded Knee, the General Allotment Act, the theft of Indian land, and the mismanagement of tribal funds were all spelled out in the joint resolution.

"The United States, acting through Congress . . . acknowledges years of official depredations, ill-conceived policies, and the breaking of covenants by the United States Government regarding Indian tribes" and "apologizes on behalf of the people of the United States to all Native Peoples for the many instances of violence, maltreatment, and neglect inflicted on Native Peoples by the citizens of the United States."

As apologies to Native people go, the American one is impressive. Mind you, it was an amendment buried in the bulk of the 2010 Defense Appropriations Act, so many people might have missed it in the hustle and bustle of their daily lives. The best part, at least to my twisted way of thinking, is the disclaimer tagged on at the end of the resolution, which says, "Nothing in this Joint Resolution authorizes any claim against the United States or serves as a settlement of any claim against the United States."

The North American legal wiggle. Guilty but not liable.

This is not very charitable on my part. Neither country was under any obligation to apologize to Native people, and yet, they did. Given the good opinion that Canada and the United States have of themselves and their reputation in the world, these apologies must have been difficult, and a more generous person would credit the effort.

So, thank you. I really mean it. My only concern—and I hate to bring it up and spoil the moment—is that I'm not sure that the apologies that Canada and the United States gave to Native people in North America were entirely sincere.

Certainly they were heartfelt. The Prime Minister of Canada, Stephen Harper, was clearly moved when he gave the government's apology, and I'm sure that President Obama was pleased to have signed the joint resolution. More important, there were a great many Native people who appreciated the apologies, whose lives were vindicated by these public gestures of regret and contrition.

And yet I can't help but feel that there was something disingenuous in these gestures. Perhaps it was Canada's unwillingness to consider the *whole* of its history with Native people. Perhaps it was that moment, less than three months after Harper offered Canada's apology, when he stood up at the G20 Summit in Philadelphia and announced to the world that, as Canadians, "We have no history of colonialism."

Hello.

Perhaps it was America's rather belligerent disclaimer of any legal liability. Or perhaps it was simply the continued framing of North America's deplorable behavior as little more than a no-fault fender-bender.

A tense moment in the parking lot at the mall.

In real life, we expect apologies to be accompanied by a firm purpose of amendment. I'm sorry. It was my fault. I won't do that again. But in the political world, apologies seem to have little to do with responsibility, and it appears that one can say "I'm sorry" and "I'm not responsible" in the same breath. I mention this because, despite the apology, North America's paternalistic intervention in the lives of Native people continues unrepentant and unabated.

But, of course, there's a perfectly good reason for this intervention. Native people can't look after ourselves. We don't have the capacity to manage our own affairs. We don't know what's good for us. We haven't the level of sophistication to understand the workings of the contemporary world and to participate in a modern economy.

You've probably heard these concerns. I know I have. I've been told any number of times that we have to learn to stand on our own two feet and develop the skills necessary to manage on our own, without relying on government generosities.

In the same way that Air Canada, AIG, Bombardier, Halliburton, General Motors, and the good folks out in Alberta's Tar Sands Project manage on their own, without relying on government handouts.

I suppose I could have mentioned Enron, World Com, Bre-X, and Bear Stearns as well, but these disasters were more greed than incompetence. Weren't they? Though I suppose the one does not preclude the other.

So, if I've got it right, while North America is reluctant to support the economic "incompetence" of Native people, it is more than willing to throw money at the incompetence of corporations. And why not? After all, if we've learned nothing in the past century, we should have learned that government support of big business is capitalism's only hope.

To be fair, some of the big boys did not wait for the government to step in with its bag of taxpayer money. During the financial meltdown in the United States, Goldman Sachs busied itself bundling mortgage stocks that the company knew were worthless and selling them off to unsuspecting investors. Lead plated to look like gold. And then the company helped itself to some $12.9 billion of public bailout money and promptly paid its executives large bonuses for their good work and business acumen.

Perhaps this is the kind of economic sophistication that North America wants Native people to learn.

But we've gotten ahead of ourselves. We need to find our way back to the nineteenth century. And, as luck would have it, we can get there from here.

6

LIKE COWBOYS AND INDIANS

For American Indians, injustice has been institutionalized and is administered by federal and state governments.

—Leslie Silko, *Yellow Woman and a Beauty of the Spirit*

And here we are: 1887.

In Canada, there was a federal election that year, and the Conservatives under John A. Macdonald retained power. Some of Macdonald's support surely came from his decision, two years earlier, to hang the Métis leader Louis Riel, though he probably lost votes in Quebec for this unnecessary act of hubris. The numbered treaties were underway, but none was signed that year. In British Columbia, delegates from the Commission of Enquiry into the Conditions of the Indians of the Northwest Coast were sent to meet with the Tsimshian and Nisga with instructions to assert Crown ownership of the land and to dismiss any claims of

Indian title. The one bright spot was the birth of the Onondaga long-distance runner Tom Longboat.

In the States, fifteen-inch snowflakes fell on Fort Keogh in Montana. In Punxsutawney, Pennsylvania, the first-ever Groundhog Day was observed. In May of that year, Buffalo Bill's Wild West Show opened in London as part of Queen Victoria's Jubilee. Sitting Bull was not with the show, though he had been the year before. Black Elk, the Lakota medicine man who would later share his vision with the poet John Neihardt, did make the Queen's party. But when the show wrapped up in Manchester, Black Elk missed the boat home and wound up stranded in Europe for two years, working for Mexican Joe's Wild West Show.

That year, 1887, was also the year in which the U.S. Congress passed the General Allotment Act.

By 1887, Native people in North America had already spent the last 280 years laid up with European colonialism, a condition much like malaria. Malaria, in case you've forgotten, is an infectious disease that sickens and kills millions of people every year. The disease causes fever, headaches, retinal damage, shakes, vomiting, anemia, and convulsions. Children who contract malaria can suffer severe brain damage. The disease is incurable. There is a vaccine that works on mice, which is great if you're a mouse. My brother Christopher got malaria when he was in Vietnam, and he can tell you all about it.

It's a remarkable disease. Like colonialism, it can lie dormant for years. And it can flare up at any moment.

In 1887, it flared up again.

The General Allotment Act, also known as the Dawes Act, would be Washington's new and improved effort at assimilating

Indians. Removal and relocation hadn't been as successful as had been hoped. Nascent residential schools might prove to be the answer to the "Indian Problem," but educating and assimilating children would take one or two generations, and delayed gratification is not a North American trait.

When I imagine this historical moment, I can see politicians, reformers, and the general public standing at the borders of reservations across America with their placards and signs, holding hands, and chanting:

"What do we want?"

"Assimilation."

"When do we want it?"

"Now."

Since the arrival of Europeans, private ownership of land has been one of the cornerstones of non-Native society and economy. Land, to the European mind, gave an individual station within society and was a certain source of wealth. Land could be bought, sold, and traded with more assurance than currency.

Indians, through inclination and treaty, held land in common, and when people of goodwill gathered together in Washington and at places such as the Lake Mohonk resort in southern New York to plan the future of Native people, they decided that land was too important to be left in the hands of a community that had no real sense of its value.

"While the Dawes Bill will change the Indian's legal and political status, it will not change his character. The child must become a man, the Indian must become an American; the pagan must be new created a Christian. His irrational and superstitious dread of imaginary gods must be transformed into a love for the All-Father;

his natural and traditional hatred of the pale-face into a faith in Christian brotherhood; his unreasoning adherence to the dead past into an inspiring hope in a great and glad future." This was the conclusion that the Friends of the Indian came to when they met for their annual meeting at Lake Mohonk in October of 1886.

All these imperatives, all these insistences, and not one voice in the room took a moment to ask, "Why?" "Why?" was not a question anyone asked of assimilation. The only proper question was, "How?"

And, in 1887, the answer was allotment. Reservations, which had seemed a good idea earlier, were now decried as an affront to Christianity and capitalism. Indian agents and church officials complained that so long as Indians were allowed to live on reservations, they would retain their pagan customs and cultures. So long as Indians were allowed to hold land in common, they would lose the advantages that free enterprise offered.

The General Allotment Act directed the government to break reservations into individual pieces. As a general rule, each head of household received an allotment of 160 acres. Single Indians over the age of eighteen and orphans under the age of eighteen got 80 acres, while minors under the age of eighteen got 40 acres. The federal government would hold each allotment in trust for a period of twenty-five years, during which time the allotments could not be sold and were tax-free. Each allottee lost their treaty status but was given U.S. citizenship.

Rather similar to a "kiddie-deal" at a fast food outlet. Order the burger, fries, and a drink, and the citizenship is free. Whether you want it or not.

At the end of the twenty-five-year trust period, each allottee would own their own allotment free and clear, and Indians, who had been communal members of a tribe, would now be individual, private land owners. Reservations would disappear. Indians would disappear. The "Indian Problem" would disappear. Private ownership of land would free Indians from the tyranny of the tribe and traditional Native culture, and civilize the savage.

What's not to like?

Instead, what allotment did was liquidate all of the reservations in Indian Territory (present-day Oklahoma), along with the land base of many of the tribes in Kansas, Nebraska, North and South Dakota, Wyoming, Montana, New Mexico, Oregon, and Washington, and give the surplus land to White settlers and business interests.

You might wonder where this "surplus land" came from. Okay, let's create a hypothetical example, and we'll work with nice round numbers to keep the math simple. Say you're an Indian. Your tribe has a population of a thousand other Indians, and the community holds three hundred thousand acres of land in common. Allotment comes along, and the tribe's land is divided up. You would expect that the government would divide one thousand into three hundred thousand and come up with three hundred acres per Indian.

But that's not what happened. Three hundred acres, the government decided, was too much land for an Indian. One hundred and sixty acres was more than enough. One hundred and sixty acres was plenty. And, after you allowed multiplication and subtraction to work their magic, the tribe wound up holding onto just one hundred and sixty thousand acres of their original three hundred thousand acres, while the government miraculously came away from the exercise with one hundred and forty thousand acres of "surplus" land.

The actual size of each allotment varied with tribes and the land they held, but in almost each instance, Indian land went in one end of allotment and surplus land came out the other. Native people, who had held title to some 138 million acres in 1887, saw that figure reduced to around 48 million acres, much of it desert.

Then, in 1934, allotment, as U.S. government policy, was repealed, and colonialism went into a brief remission.

In Canada in 1934 the Dionne Quintuplets were born, marking the period, but aside from that, and the births of Jean Chrétien, Peter Gzowski, Leonard Cohen, and novelist Rudy Wiebe, it wasn't a particularly exciting year. In the United States, Donald Duck appeared for the first time in a cartoon called "The Wise Little Hen." John Dillinger, Bonnie Parker, and Clyde Barrow were killed in shootouts with FBI agents, and Alcatraz became an official Federal Bureau of Prisons prison.

And in Washington, the Indian Reorganization Act was passed.

When Franklin D. Roosevelt became president in 1933, his administration quickly put together a series of programs that were to lift America and Americans out of the depths of the Great Depression. At the same time, he appointed John Collier to the post of Commissioner for the Bureau of Indian Affairs. Collier was a rare politician, a social crusader who rejected the forced assimilation of Indians and argued instead for a form of cultural pluralism whereby Indians could speak their languages and practice their religions without government interference. More important, Collier understood that if tribes were to maintain their traditions, they would have to maintain their land base.

It was under Collier's leadership, with Roosevelt's blessing, that the 1934 Indian Reorganization Act (IRA), or the Wheeler–Howard

Act, became national policy. In many ways, the legislation was a departure from previous programs and represented a positive shift in government thinking. Most important, it ended allotment as official policy and slowed the erosion and theft of Indian land by extending trust protection indefinitely. It allowed that surplus lands created by the allotment process might be returned to tribes. The IRA even created a fund, not to exceed two million dollars a year, to buy back lands that had been lost.

The act looked good on paper, and it *was* a reprieve from the programs that came before it. And to give Collier his due, his administration was more actively committed to the protection of Indian rights and lands than any before or after him.

As Commissioner of Indian Affairs, Collier could influence policy and he could advocate for Native people, but he could not control what the government actually did. While the Indian Reorganization Act "allowed" that Native people might control their own destinies, the reality was that all of the major decisions were still left firmly in the hands of the government.

I have a soft spot in my heart for John Collier, but for all his determination and reasonable ideas, he was not destined to prevail. While Collier was able to slow the destruction, he was up against a political cabal that was not about to let one man change the "proper" course of government Indian policy.

The Indian Reorganization Act was officially in effect for about nineteen years. But that's misleading. With the beginning of the Second World War in 1939, Indians, in both the United States and Canada, vanished from their respective governments' agendas. Canada declared war on Germany in 1939. America officially came on board in 1941. By the time the conflict ended in 1945, the small "generosities" that had been allowed in the Indian Reorganization Act were clawed back, and colonialism, which had been dormant, came back with a fierce virulence.

It came back in the guise of another new and improved government program.

This midcentury version of colonialism was called "termination," and it became official U.S. government policy in 1953 with the passage of House Concurrent Resolution 108. HCR 108 declared the intent of the United States to abrogate all treaties that it had made with Native people and abolish federal supervision over tribes. The resolution called for the immediate termination of the Flathead, the Klamath, the Menominee, the Potawatomi, and the Turtle Mountain Chippewa, along with all the tribes in Texas, New York, Florida, and California. Passed at the same time, Public Law 280 allowed a number of states to assume control of Indian reservations.

And that was that. No treaties. No reservations. No Indians. Problem solved. Again.

For the next thirteen years, termination worked its way through America like a plague. Before the policy was officially ended in 1966, 109 tribes had been terminated and another million acres of Indian land was lost.

Canada tried its hand at termination three years after the United States gave it up. In 1969, Pierre Trudeau and then Minister of Indian Affairs Jean Chrétien released the 1969 White Paper, which, had it become law, would have been a first step in abrogating treaties, eliminating Indian status, and effectively breaking up the land base of every Native tribe in the country.

I know what Ottawa's political managers were thinking. They were thinking the same thing their American cousins had thought.

The Indian business was complex and difficult. Indians and treaty rights were irrelevant in a modern world. Treaties were an instrument between sovereign nations, and Ottawa decided it was now unwilling to deal with such sovereign nations, even though treaties were the way in which Canada and Native people had always conducted their business.

So, in terms of government action, government policy, and Indians, one could argue that the twentieth century was just like the nineteenth, was just like the eighteenth. Business as usual. But there was something else afoot. After five hundred years of being legislated, policied, and programmed out of existence, Native people began to say, rather loudly, "Enough." Sure, we were worn out by the centuries of exploitation, neglect, mistreatment, and oppression, but by the 1960s, we were also angry as hell.

I say "we" in the generous sense of the word. I wasn't even in North America. In 1964, I had signed on with a tramp steamer out of San Francisco and worked my way across several oceans to New Zealand. I worked in that country as a deer culler, a beer-bottle sorter, and a photographer. I might have stayed, but I had entered New Zealand on a thirty-day tourist visa, and after I'd lived and worked there for about a year, immigration noticed that, while I had arrived, I hadn't left.

I was in Auckland when I got a phone call. A fellow with a very British accent asked me if I was aware that I had been in the country for almost a year on a thirty-day visa. I told him I was aware of this. Had I been working? he wanted to know. A little, I told him.

"When might we expect you to leave?"

As I said, I liked New Zealand, and I was keen on staying longer, so I asked if there was a way I could apply for an immigration visa.

The immigration man said that this wasn't normally the way it was done, that one generally applied for such a visa before arriving in the country.

"But I shall look into the matter," he told me.

In the meantime, he wanted some particulars. And then he read off a list of items. Height, weight, color of eyes, color of hair. Race.

"Six-foot-six, two hundred and fifty pounds, brown, black. Indian."

There was a long pause and then the immigration man said, "Oh dear, I'm afraid we can't accept an immigration application from you."

I was somewhat taken aback. "Why not?" I wanted to know.

"Well," said the immigration man, "we don't accept immigration applications from Indians."

I tried to imagine just how many immigration applications New Zealand could possibly get from Indians in any given year. So I asked. "How many immigration applications do you get from Indians?"

"Thousands," said the immigration man. "Thousands."

The Cree were a good-sized tribe. So were the Navajo and the Lakota. There were lots of Native people in Oklahoma, Alberta, Minnesota, Saskatchewan, the Dakotas, and British Columbia who might want to settle down in New Zealand. "These Indians," I asked, "where are they coming from?"

"New Delhi," said the immigration man. "Bombay."

"Ah," I said. "Wrong Indians. I'm North American Indian."

There was another long pause. "What?" said the immigration man. "You mean like cowboys and Indians?"

I didn't get a visa. I left New Zealand, went to Australia, worked there for a couple of years, and in 1967, I returned to

California. By the time I arrived home, the Vietnam war was in full swing, while throughout North America, marginalized groups were taking to the streets to protest both the war and the institutions and the social structures that assisted the rich in the accumulation of wealth and power, that kept the poor knee-deep in poverty, and that allowed racism to flourish. In Canada, Quebec separatism was gathering strength, but the country's focus was on celebrating the centenary. In Montreal, Expo 67, the most successful of the world fairs, opened its doors.

That year, 1967, was the one historian Pierre Berton called "Canada's last good year."

In the United States, 1967 wasn't quite so dazzling. Well, there was the whole hippie thing. Flower power, free love, tie-dyed T-shirts, Haight-Ashbury, drugs and communes and young men and women dressed up as Day-Glo Indians. I guess that was *somewhat* dazzling. But by 1968, the dazzle had begun to fade.

That year saw the assassination of Martin Luther King in April and the assassination of Robert Kennedy in June. In August, at the Democratic Convention in Chicago, police clashed with demonstrators opposed to the war and determined to end it. Meanwhile, in Canada, in June of that year, separatists rioted in Montreal on Saint-Jean-Baptiste Day, while politicians in Ottawa passed the Criminal Law Amendment Act, which decriminalized homosexuality and allowed abortions and contraception. This was the bill that Pierre Trudeau defended by saying that "there's no place for the state in the bedrooms of the nation." In that year, Leonard Marchand became the first Status Indian to be elected to the House of Commons.

It was also the year that N. Scott Momaday (Kiowa–Cherokee) won the Pulitzer Prize, the first and only Aboriginal author to do so, while in Minneapolis, Minnesota, the American Indian Movement (AIM) was slouching towards Wounded Knee.

For me, 1968 was the year I enrolled at Chico State University, in Chico, California, and became involved in Native activism. There were hardly any Indians on campus. The only other Native I remember was a Mohawk, an artist named Richard Glazer Danay. Richard and I got together with a professor from the Anthropology department to form what I think was the first Indian organization on that campus. But my memory for those years is terrible. The only thing I remember with any real clarity is a survey.

Neither Richard nor I had any idea how many Indian students were on campus, but, in 1969 or 1970, the registrar's office included a brief survey in the packets of all incoming students that allowed them to declare ethnicity. When the surveys came back, there were about sixty incoming students who had marked the "Indian" box. I was ecstatic. I had been hoping Chico State might have a dozen Indians, and here we were with five times that many. So Richard and I began calling the students to say hello, to welcome them to Chico, and we discovered that the vast majority of the students who had marked "Indian" in the box were not Indian at all. "I'm not actually Indian," one student told me, "but I support you guys one hundred percent."

That was the way it was in the late '60s and early '70s in North America. Everyone wanted to be an Indian. Even the Indians.

In 1969, many Native people weren't really aware of what was happening in Indian country. Those of us on campuses throughout North America liked to believe that we were up to date, but our knowledge was limited by our background and experience. Universities didn't offer "Indian" courses. We knew what we knew in bits and pieces, and I suspect that this was equally true for Indians on reservations/reserves, in cities, and in rural areas. Momaday winning the Pulitzer in 1968 was certainly a source of pride, but I'm not sure many Native people actually read *House Made of Dawn.* The book we did read was Vine Deloria's *Custer Died for Your Sins* (1969). We knew about AIM, of course, without knowing exactly what the organization did. Indian role models were few and far between. In 1969, they were the usual suspects, individuals who were—for one reason or another—on public display in the consciousness of White North America. Sitting Bull, Louis Riel, Crazy Horse, Big Bear, Jim Thorpe, Tom Longboat, and Billy Mills.

Then, on November 20, 1969, eighty-nine American Indians from a variety of tribes set sail from Sausalito, a boutique town for wealthy folk just across the bay from San Francisco, and took over the defunct federal prison known as Alcatraz. Or "the Rock."

It wasn't the first time Indians had been on the island. Native oral stories from the area tell of Alcatraz as a place where people gathered bird eggs and as a sanctuary to escape the Franciscan monks, who used Indians in California as slave labor in the building of their missions. Some of the tribes in the area regarded the island as a holy place. Others avoided it altogether.

Whatever else the island might have been, by the early 1860s Alcatraz was a prison, and in 1895 the U.S. government shipped nineteen Hopi Indians to the Rock. An article in the *San Francisco Call* reported that the Hopi had been arrested because "they would not let their children go to school."

A capital offense, to be sure.

The *Call* went on to assure its readers that the Hopi (whom the paper had earlier misidentified as "murderous-looking Apaches") were not badly treated. "They have not hardship," said the paper, "aside from the fact that they have been rudely snatched from the bosom of their families and are prisoners and prisoners they shall stay until they have learned to appreciate the advantage of education."

Exactly what that advantage was, the paper did not say.

The Hopi, by the way, weren't the first Indian prisoners on the island. In 1873, a Native man named Paiute Tom was sent to Alcatraz from Camp McDermit in Nevada. He didn't stay long. He was shot dead by a guard two days after he arrived. In that same year, two Modoc, Barncho and Sloluck, were sent to the Rock. In 1874, Native rights activist Sarah Winnemucca's brother Natchez (Paiute) spent a couple of less-than-pleasant weeks in the prison, while a Chiricachua Apache chief named Kaetena wound up on the island in July of 1884, courtesy of the old Indian fighter General George Cook.

Nor was the 1969 occupation the first time Native people had "captured" Alcatraz. In 1964, a group of Lakota had landed on the island and claimed it in a peaceful demonstration. They were removed by federal marshals before the day was out.

So, even before the armada landed on the island in 1969, Alcatraz and Indians already had a long and mixed history together. Still, the 1969 event was an electrifying moment. Talking about taking action was one thing—and there had certainly been enough talk. Actually doing something was another thing altogether. Action. The takeover of Alcatraz was action.

That is not to say that the takeover was the most well-organized action. No one, it seemed, had thought much about the matter of clothing, food, blankets, toilet paper, potable water, items that might be needed for an extended stay on the Rock.

From an aesthetic point of view, Native people would have been hard put to come up with an uglier or bleaker piece of geography to occupy. Weather on the island could be windy, cool, warm, clear, foggy, and rainy all on the same day. The Rock was grey, the buildings were grey, the sky was grey, the ocean was grey. Even in bright sunshine, even without being locked up in a cell, Alcatraz was depressing.

Several clever protesters suggested that the reason Indians took Alcatraz was because it looked and felt so much like a reservation. In fact, as Helen reminded me, the original "Alcatraz Proclamation" listed the similarities:

1. It is isolated from modern facilities, and without adequate means of transportation.
2. It has no fresh running water.
3. It has inadequate sanitation facilities.
4. There are no oil or mineral rights.
5. There is no industry, and so unemployment is great.
6. There are no health-care facilities.
7. The soil is rocky and non productive, and the land does not support game.
8. There are no educational facilities.
9. The population has always exceeded the land base.
10. The population has always been held as prisoners and kept dependent upon others.

On the positive side, Alcatraz did have some lovely rock pools and a resident colony of western gulls, cormorants, and egrets. More than that, the views of the San Francisco skyline and the Golden Gate Bridge were to die for.

Still, it was an island, which meant that people and goods had to be ferried across San Francisco Bay by boat. And because it was an island, and a small one at that, it should have been an easy matter for the authorities to seal it off, cut the water and power, and force the Indians off the Rock before the second week was out.

But that's not what happened. Maybe it was the times. Maybe it was the crazy magic of San Francisco. Maybe people were looking for a diversion to take their minds off the war in Vietnam and the My Lai massacre. Maybe it was a little of all of these. Whatever the reason or reasons, Alcatraz became an instant *cause célèbre*. While the Indians were struggling with organizing and outfitting the occupation, while the government was trying to come up with a plan to evict the "pesky redskins," famous people were lining up to visit the island. Hollywood stars such as Jonathan Winters, Jane Fonda, Marlon Brando, Anthony Quinn, Buffy Sainte-Marie, Dick Gregory, and Candice Bergen came to Alcatraz to show their support. Many gave money. No one knows how much money came to the occupation. Records of donations were not all that tidy. Horace Spencer, who sat on the Alcatraz council, estimated the amount of money donated at between twenty dollars and twenty-five million.

Ironically, Alcatraz the media event was, in many ways, more successful than Alcatraz the occupation. In spite of problems with resources, in-fighting, and the constantly changing population, the occupation lasted almost nineteen months. But it was effectively over much earlier than that. There were too many people on the Rock, and there were too few. Some were committed, some were looking for a free lunch. Even with the adrenaline of enthusiasm, the environment was harsh, the conditions austere. There was no consistent plan, no consistent leadership, no continuity. The media quickly tired of the event in the way that the media always tire of such things, and many of the celebrities who had flocked to Alcatraz found other worthy moments and other worthy causes that held the promise of network coverage and camera crews.

This is not to impugn, in any way, the commitment of people such as Richard Oakes, LaNada Means, Stella Leach, Joe Bill, John Trudell, Ed Castillo, Denise Quitaquit, and Ross Harden. The occupation simply had too many loose ends and loose cannons to succeed.

And yet succeed it did. Not in its attempt to occupy the island and turn the facilities into a cultural park, or an institution for Native American Studies, or a spiritual gathering place, or an Indian foundation for ecology. Rather, the occupation turned Alcatraz into an emblem of Native resistance and pride.

Vine Deloria Jr. said it well: "Alcatraz was a big enough symbol that for the first time this century Indians were taken seriously." Certainly the episode caught the government's attention, though I suspect that Alcatraz was forgotten a month after the island was cleared. But I like to imagine that Deloria wasn't talking only about the politicians in Washington. I like to imagine that he was talking about Native people taking ourselves seriously, that for perhaps the first time in a long time, we were able to see what might be possible with imagination, commitment, and a little organization.

The occupation of Alcatraz ended on June 10, 1971, when police and federal agents removed the last fifteen people from the Rock.

Whenever I'm out in California and cross the Golden Gate and look down on Alcatraz, I imagine how it might be if we went back there with better advance planning. We'd bring plenty of food and water this time. Solar panels, generators, stoves, pots and pans, utensils, composting toilets, toilet paper, sleeping bags and blankets, computers, a video camera, a short-wave radio, cellphones. We'd make sure our community included at least one doctor, several nurses, an electrician, a plumber, a carpenter, storytellers and artists, a mediator to help with any conflicts that might arise, an embedded journalist to handle the publicity and news releases, a big drum, and someone with a guitar, who could sing Don Ross, Robbie Robertson, and Buffy Sainte-Marie.

We'd probably need a lawyer, and if we couldn't endure living alongside the real thing, we could get an actor such as Wes Studi to play the part. Oh, and lots of large-print books.

Retired Indians. That's the key to a new occupation. Assault Alcatraz with senior citizens. Native elders. Those of us who have nothing better to do and are looking for a good story that our children can tell our grandkids. Young people are too busy to sit around on a large, grey rock in the middle of a large, grey bay. They have their lives to live, families to raise. A second occupation of Alcatraz is a job for the bucket-list brigade. Sure, there'd be some physical labor involved, some exertion, but with any luck, no one would have a heart attack or break a hip, and Hollywood might even make a movie about us.

I wonder who they'd get to play me.

Deloria was right. Alcatraz's value was largely symbolic. But it also revealed the complex of fault lines in Native–White relations, and almost before the aftershocks of the occupation had settled, new tremors began rattling doors and breaking windows across North America. The epicenter for much of this seismic activity was the American Indian Movement. AIM had been a part of the Alcatraz occupation, and in November of 1970, while the Rock was still in full swing, AIM staged a Thanksgiving Day protest, taking over Plymouth Rock in Massachusetts and painting it red. Then, with Alcatraz in the rear-view mirror for less than a month, AIM showed up at Mount Rushmore on July 4, 1971, as uninvited and unwanted guests at America's Independence Day celebrations.

There is no precise way to describe AIM. The original organization was formed in the summer of 1968 in Minneapolis, ostensibly to deal with police brutality against Native people in the Twin Cities area. Under the initial leadership of Native activists such as George Mitchell (Ojibway), Dennis Banks (Ojibway), and Clyde Bellecourt (Ojibway), AIM organized Indian patrols to shadow the police and to monitor their activities and conduct. As well, it helped to develop alternative schools—the Little Red Schoolhouse and Heart of the Earth—for Native children, many of whom were having a difficult time in public schools, and lobbied for programs on behalf of Native families who had been forced into the Twin Cities as a result of relocation.

I don't know that the leaders of AIM ever imagined the organization to be a knight on a horse roaming the countryside in search of dragons. And even if they *had* thought of themselves as a paramilitary unit, a flying squad, as some have claimed, they were inadequately trained, badly coordinated, and poorly armed. AIM was, from the beginning, a loosely managed group of Native men and women who had simply had enough, who decided, given the choice between doing nothing or acting, that they would act.

As it turned out, how AIM would act and where was determined by circumstances not necessarily of its making. None of

AIM's major confrontations and occupations was planned as such. Each began as an attempt to remedy an injustice and/or to garner some on-camera publicity. When these protests escalated into violence, as a number of them did, governmental antipathy and blinkered law enforcement were as responsible for what followed as was AIM. Sometimes more so.

In February of 1972, AIM went into Gordon, Nebraska, to protest the death of a fifty-one-year-old Native man, Raymond Yellow Thunder. Yellow Thunder had been kidnapped by four White men and a White woman, who stripped him of his pants, took him to the Gordon American Legion Hall, and shoved him, half-naked, out on the dance floor. Yellow Thunder was drunk at the time. So were his assailants. Afterward, they took the older man outside and beat him. The whole thing was supposed to be a joke. It was a Saturday night, after all. What better way to celebrate than to grab a couple of drinks, assault an Indian, have a good laugh? No harm done.

Eight days later, Yellow Thunder's body was found in the cab of a pickup truck on a used car lot. Cause of death was determined to be a cerebral hemorrhage.

The Sheridan County Attorney called the affair a cruel practical joke. AIM called it murder, and they demanded and got a full investigation, which included a second autopsy. Melvin and Leslie Hare, the brothers who had done the lion's share of the beating, were arrested, tried, convicted of manslaughter, and sentenced to one year in prison.

One year.

I know it doesn't seem like much of a sentence, but, according to the oral history in the area, the Hares were the first White men to be convicted of killing an Indian.

In the fall of 1972, AIM, along with the National Indian Brotherhood, the National Indian Youth Council, and five other Native groups, organized the Trail of Broken Treaties, a car caravan that travelled from the west coast to Washington, D.C., to lobby for Native sovereignty and treaty rights and to call attention to the problems of poverty on reserves and reservations.

The caravan, about a thousand strong, arrived in Washington in early November, about a week before the presidential elections. Arrangements to house the protesters were supposed to have been in place, but either through poor planning or government duplicity, housing never materialized. Tired and angry, the protesters marched on the Bureau of Indian Affairs building and took it over. For the next seven days, frustrated Indians ransacked the building.

I was in Salt Lake City at the time, working as the Counselor for Indian Students at the University of Utah. The Native community in town met with the Trail of Broken Treaties when the caravan came through. Some of us provided overnight housing for the people. Others provided supplies—blankets, sleeping bags, canned goods—for the long trip east. Everyone offered support and encouragement.

At first none of us wanted to believe the reports of vandalism. Destroying BIA files might have had some symbolic power, but the loss of those records also had the potential to hurt tribes, to set them back in their negotiations with the government, to allow Washington to drag its feet. The damage didn't make much sense. And when the media in Salt Lake came calling to get our views on the matter, we all mumbled supportive platitudes about Native rights and government deceit, but privately, among ourselves, we thought the destruction had been stupid.

Sure, we understood rage, but the vandalism was still stupid.

Many years later, at a conference in Phoenix, I ran into a guy who had been in the BIA building during the occupation. I made the mistake of sharing my opinion about the destruction, and we almost wound up in a fight. "You weren't there," he told me, "so you don't get it. You didn't see the files. Our lives were in those files. The bastards had us locked up in folders."

We didn't come to any agreement, but he was right about one thing. I wasn't there.

And I wasn't in Custer, South Dakota, either.

On January 20, 1973, Darld Schmitz and Wesley Bad Heart Bull were in Bill's Bar in Buffalo Gap, a small hamlet some forty-two miles southeast of Custer. It was a Saturday night. Both men had been drinking. Schmitz was particularly offensive, bragging that one day he would "get himself an Indian." Words were exchanged between the two men, and later, outside the saloon, Schmitz attacked Bad Heart Bull and stabbed him to death. Schmitz had threatened Bad Heart Bull inside the bar, shouting that he would "kill the son of a bitch." There were witnesses who heard the threat, and there were witnesses who saw Schmitz murder Bad Heart Bull. Schmitz even admitted to killing Bad Heart Bull.

But instead of being charged with first-degree or second-degree homicide, Schmitz was charged with second-degree manslaughter and immediately released.

On February 6, Dennis Banks and Russell Means, two of AIM's leaders, along with about eighty supporters, arrived in Custer in the middle of a blizzard to meet with County Attorney Hobart Gates. The charges against Schmitz, AIM argued, should be amended to first- or second-degree murder. Gates refused. In spite of all the evidence and the testimony of the witnesses, Gates saw the killing as a barroom brawl gone wrong. Gates's decision was met with outrage. Tempers flared. The police rushed in with nightsticks and tear gas. The Indians defended themselves with chairs and rocks and bricks, whatever happened to be at hand. And, in a flash, a full-scale riot, which lasted the afternoon, erupted inside and outside the courthouse.

About twenty-seven Indians were arrested, including Means and Sarah Bad Heart Bull, Wesley's mother, who was charged with "riot with arson." She would later be convicted and sentenced to one to five years in prison. Schmitz was charged with second-degree manslaughter and acquitted by an all-White jury. Sarah Bad Heart Bull served five months of her sentence. Schmitz spent part of one day in jail.

Twenty-one days after the confrontation in Custer, AIM and fifty-four cars filled with supporters left Calico, South Dakota, drove onto the Pine Ridge reservation, and took over the village of Wounded Knee. Pine Ridge was in the middle of a civil war that had many of the more traditional Lakota at odds with the tribal chairman, Dick Wilson, and his personal security force known as the "GOONs" (Guardians of the Oglala Nation). Even before AIM arrived, Pine Ridge was a divided, violent place where the per capita murder rate was higher than that of Detroit. Unnerving symbols of this division were the sandbags in front of the tribal council office and 50-caliber machine guns mounted on the roof.

AIM's appearance at Pine Ridge was not a surprise to anyone. The organization had been invited by a faction on the reservation to help them in the fight against Wilson, and the FBI had informants inside AIM. In his memoir *Wounded Knee: A Personal Account*,

Stanley Lyman, the Bureau of Indian Affairs superintendent at Pine Ridge, recalls asking U.S. Marshal Reese Kash how he knew so much about AIM's plans. Kash responded that their information came from "a very reliable source." So when AIM drove through Pine Ridge on February 27, federal marshals and FBI agents were waiting for them.

But instead of butting heads at the tribal council office, the fifty-plus cars in the AIM caravan drove right on by and took over the village of Wounded Knee.

Thus began the siege of Wounded Knee. At the height of the siege, the government had at its disposal some fifteen armored cars, over 100,000 rounds of M-16 ammunition, submachine guns, gas masks, bulletproof vests, sniper rifles with night scopes, and an unlimited number of federal marshals, FBI agents, military personnel, and local law enforcement.

The number of people inside Wounded Knee hovered around two hundred and fifty. By contrast with the government's arsenal, AIM had around thirty or forty weapons, mostly small caliber. The most potent piece was probably an AK-47 that belonged to a Kiowa from Oklahoma named Bobby Onco. If Dennis Banks's recollections are correct, Onco didn't have any bullets for the rifle, but was able to use the weapon as a prop to impress the media. Most of the other guns didn't have much in the way of ammunition either. No one had done any advance planning on securing the village or on what would be needed for an extended occupation. From a logistics point of view, Wounded Knee felt a great deal like Alcatraz, albeit without the waterfront setting and the great views.

But unlike Alcatraz, the general goodwill that had attended the Rock was not to be found at Wounded Knee. From the beginning, the media did not treat this occupation with the same grace and good humor. Celebrities did not flock to the Dakota plains to tour the encampment and show their support for the cause on the evening news. Money did not pour in, as it had in San Francisco. There was little of the magic that had been such a major component of Alcatraz. One newspaper story reminded its readers that South Dakota was not California. As though that needed saying.

Support for Wounded Knee was more grassroots, more militant. Almost immediately, all around North America, demonstrations and marches were organized to bring media attention to the occupation and to raise money. While the FBI and the U.S. marshals tried to cut the village off from the outside world, determined groups and individuals, Indian and White, made air supply drops from small planes and used the rutted South Dakota landscape—the arroyos and the coulees—to run the government lines and bring supplies into the village under cover of darkness.

Sometime during the occupation, I don't remember exactly when, there was a big rally on the steps of the Utah State Capitol in Salt Lake City in support of Wounded Knee. There were speeches, calls for action. A blanket was carried through the crowd to collect donations, and all of us tossed money and tobacco and food stamps on it. Then an older woman got up and asked the question that was asked again and again during this period of Indian history.

"Where are the warriors?"

Where are the warriors? Even now that call to arms heats my blood. It certainly did on that day in Salt Lake. When the rally ended, about a dozen men climbed into a van and three cars and headed east on highway 80. I was one of those men. As we drove into the mountains, as the passion of the moment cooled, I remember thinking that this was a mistake. I mean, I had a job. I had a wife and a baby. I was working with Indian students at the university. It wasn't as though I wasn't trying to do my part.

But then again, the people inside Wounded Knee probably had jobs, too. Many of them had children. I wasn't special. I was simply . . . safe.

When we crossed the border into Wyoming, we were stopped by the police. A warrior might have leaped into the van in Salt Lake City, but what jumped out was just a frightened twenty-nine-year-old university administrator. I had had some experience with police, but up to that moment, I had never had a gun pointed directly at me. Somehow the cops had known that we were coming. They asked questions about the rally in Salt Lake and about Wounded Knee. We said we were just sightseeing, and the police told us to "shut the fuck up." This comedy routine went on for most of an hour until a tow truck came along and took the van away.

After that, the police left. I must have seen them go, but I can't remember them leaving. Suddenly, they were just gone. We waited for a while by the side of that cold road, not sure what we were supposed to do. Then, we all squeezed into the remaining cars and drove home.

For seventy-one days, government forces on the perimeter of Wounded Knee and the Native people inside the village yelled at each other, threatened each other, tried their hand at negotiations, and shot at each other. When the occupation ended, one U.S. marshal, Lloyd Grimm, had been wounded, paralyzed from the waist down, and two Indians, Frank Clearwater and Lawrence Lamont, had been shot and killed by government snipers.

A great many people fixate on AIM as the first truly militant Native organization in North America. And they believe that AIM was concerned primarily with initiating confrontations and occupations at a national level, activities that would garner media coverage, activities that would give AIM an international profile and Aboriginal concerns a public face.

Both notions are true, and both are false. At the beginning of the nineteenth century, Opechancanough, Tecumseh and his brother Tenskwatawa, Pontiac, Osceola, and others led resistance actions long before AIM came along, actions that were far more intense and deadly. Nor was AIM the first pan-Indian organization in North America. The Society of American Indians was founded, ironically enough, on Columbus Day in 1911 by many of the Native intellectuals of the time: Dr. Carlos Montezuma (Yavapai-Apache), Charles Eastman (Dakota), Thomas L. Sloan (Omaha), Charles E. Dagenett (Peoria), Laura Cornelius (Oneida), and Henry Standing Bear (Oglala Lakota). For the next twenty years it was the main Indian lobby in the United States. In the 1930s the Society faded from public engagement, and the slack wasn't picked up until 1944, when the National Congress of American Indians was formed. While NCAI has been effective in many of its lobbying efforts—in 1954, it was successful in defeating legislation that would have allowed states to assume criminal and civil jurisdiction over Native people—like the Society of American Indians, it has tended to be conservative and conciliatory. At one point in the '60s, one part of its working slogan was "Indians Don't Demonstrate."

The "Indians Don't Demonstrate" sentiment did not endear the National Congress of American Indians to organizations such as the National Indian Youth Council (NIYC) and the Women of All Red Nations (WARN). NIYC was formed in 1961 at a conference in Chicago under the leadership of people such as Clyde Warrior (Ponca) and Mel Tom (Walker River Paiute). WARN was organized in 1974 under the leadership of Lorelei DeCora Means (Minneconjou Lakota), Madonna Thunderhawk (Hunkpapa Lakota), and Phyllis Young (Hunkpapa Lakota).

In many ways, both NIYC and WARN were as proactive on Native issues as AIM. During the 1960s, NIYC was involved with civil rights activities and was on the front lines of the Indian fishing-rights dispute in the Northwest. In the '70s, the Council assisted tribes who were trying to resist coal and uranium exploration and mining. At the same time, NIYC worked hard to improve access to education and job training and to encourage Native people to participate in the political process on their own terms. WARN was initially formed to support AIM, but it quickly expanded its activities, focusing their energies on Native civil rights and especially the rights of Native women and their families.

Still, for better and for worse, AIM was the organization that got most of the media attention. And it was this organization, and in particular its leaders, who took the brunt of law enforcement.

In Canada, Native political organizations began with the League of Indians of Canada in 1919. The League was founded by F. O. Loft (Mohawk) and was an extension of the American-based Council of Tribes. Its mandate was to encourage Ottawa to recognize Aboriginal land rights and to deal with the various grievances that Native people had with the federal government. While the League may have been a good idea, it wasn't widely supported by many tribes and was actively discouraged by the government.

In fact, Ottawa's dislike for such ideas was codified in 1927 when a provision was added to the Indian Act that forbade Native people from forming political organizations. Along with a provision that prohibited Indians from speaking their Aboriginal languages.

Blacks in the United States got the vote in 1870, though the Jim Crow laws in the South made participation in the political process virtually impossible. American women got the vote in 1909. Non-Native Canadian women got the federal vote in 1918. If Blacks and women could vote, Loft reasoned, then it might be time for Natives to have a political organization of their own.

It was an error in logic, of course, but you can see how Loft might have got the notion that equality was in the air.

So it shouldn't come as any surprise that the League of Indians of Canada didn't last very long. And given the generous attitudes and encouragements of the government, another Native political organization wouldn't be attempted until after World War II. Of course, Indian political organizations didn't disappear just because the government didn't like them. They went underground. One story I've heard is that at the beginning of some of these political meetings, to avoid the possibility of prosecution, the participants would sing "Onward Christian Soldiers." If anyone asked, they could say that they belonged to a Bible study group. I don't know if this is a true story, but I believe it. More than that, I like it. It makes us sound downright . . . subversive.

In 1945, Canada saw another short-lived attempt at a national organization, the North American Indian Brotherhood, which failed quickly, partly because it was seen as a parochial (Catholic) organization. Sixteen years later in 1961, the National Indian Council was formed. It was to include Status Indians, non-Status

Indians, and the Métis, but when these three groups failed to work together, the organization was split into two forums, the Native Council of Canada, which was to look after the needs of non-Status Indians and the Métis, and the National Indian Brotherhood, which was to look after the needs of Status Indians in Canada.

The Native Council of Canada didn't fare much better than the National Indian Council, and in 1983 the Métis separated from the Native Council of Canada and formed their own national organization, the Métis National Council. Even before that, the Inuit, in 1971, organized under the Inuit Tapirisat of Canada. The Inuit had not joined up with either the Native Council of Canada or the National Indian Brotherhood but had bided their time, forming their own organization to look after their specific needs. Then, in 1982, the National Indian Brotherhood broadened its mandate to try to include all Native people, changed its name to the Assembly of First Nations, and made itself over as a more representative national organization, even though, in the end, it really represented only Status Indians.

Not every band in Canada belongs to the Assembly of First Nations, just as not all tribes are members of the National Congress of American Indians. Still, these two organizations, for better and sometimes for worse, are the main players in North American Native politics.

And after all the dust had cleared from this shuffling and restructuring, Native people found themselves in the new millennium with the National Congress of American Indians on the American side of the line and the Inuit Tapirisat of Canada, the Métis National Council, and the Assembly of First Nations on the Canadian side.

As for AIM, while its influence was potent, its tenure was short-lived. By 1990, most of the leadership of AIM was either in jail or had had their lives destroyed by government sanctions, legal and illegal.

There are many people, Indians as well as Whites, who have little good to say about AIM, who continue to describe the leadership as thugs and criminals. Detractors point to the looting of the BIA building in Washington, D.C., the riot in Gordon, Nebraska, and the seventy-one-day occupation of Wounded Knee in the winter of 1973 as proof that AIM believed in violence and the destruction of property as legitimate responses to injustice.

Over the years, I've sat on panel discussions with such well-meaning people. Their default position is always that organizations such as AIM need to have more faith in the laws of the land and the judicial system. It's a great theory. Simple and elegant. I can see the attraction. It's the kind of theory that someone unfamiliar with Native history and the integrity of the justice system might consider proposing.

The idea that justice is blind and that everyone is equal before the law reminds me of a traditional story that I've heard over the years, in which Coyote tries to convince a band of ducks that he has their best interests at heart. Even if you don't know the story, the premise alone should make you chuckle.

Besieged by coyotes in Ottawa and Washington, Native people stopped asking for justice and began demanding it. Asking had gotten Indians little more than a paternalistic pat on the head. AIM and other activist groups were tired of begging, tired of being ignored. Were there ways to frame Native concerns other than with demonstrations, confrontations, and, on occasion, violence?

No.

I'm not trying to be provocative here. The fact is, the primary way that Ottawa and Washington deal with Native people is to ignore us. They know that the court system favors the powerful and the wealthy and the influential, and that, if we buy into the notion of an impartial justice system, tribes and bands can be forced through a long, convoluted, and expensive process designed to wear us down and bankrupt our economies.

Be good. Play by our rules. Don't cause a disturbance.

It's a fool's game. AIM and the other Native activist organizations knew this. Hell, any activist organization should know this. It's not a secret. But governments here and around the world also know that fear and poverty can hold an injustice in place in perpetuity, no matter how flagrant, no matter how obscene.

During the 2010 G20 Summit in Toronto, Canadian Prime Minister Stephen Harper said, "If the world's richest and most powerful nations do not deal with the world's hardest and most intractable problems, they simply will not be dealt with."

Turns out he wasn't being satiric. Which explains, I guess, why global warming, global poverty, and global conflict are all doing so well.

But enough. While pessimism and cynicism have been the salt and pepper in the stew that is Native–White history, there is no reason we can't change the recipe. We could, if we wanted, put the past behind us. We could say that today is a new day. We could, if we were so inclined, decide to start all over again.

Why don't we do that? What don't we give that a try?

7

FORGET ABOUT IT

In the Great American Indian novel, when it is finally written,
All the white people will be Indians and all the Indians will be ghosts.
—Sherman Alexie, "How to Write the
Great American Indian Novel"

Today is a new day. Let's enjoy it together.

This is a great sentiment. I like it. Maybe it is time for Native
people—such as me—to stop complaining about the past. Better
yet, maybe it's time to get rid of the past altogether.

How about 1985?

That was the year my second child was born. Let's draw a line
with that year. I'll gather up all of North American Indian history
prior to 1985, pile it in a field, and set it on fire. Get rid of everything. Massacres, deprivations, depredations, broken treaties,
government lies. Wounded Knee, 1890, where 487 well-armed

soldiers of the 7th Cavalry sat on a bluff with Hotchkiss guns and rifles and opened fire on an encampment of 350 Lakota. Depending on whom you choose to believe, somewhere between 200 and 300 Lakota were massacred, most of them women and children.

Forget about it.

Afterward, Congress awarded the Congressional Medal of Honor to twenty of the soldiers who had been involved in the massacre.

Forget about that, too.

Wounded Knee, 1890, can go on the pile. So can Wounded Knee, 1973, along with Louis Riel and the Trail of Tears. The mercury poisonings at Grassy Narrows. Residential schools. Removal. Termination. The slaughter of the buffalo. Kit Carson. John Chivington. Alcatraz. Wild West Shows. B-Westerns. The G-O road in northern California. The Tomahawk Chop. The Wisconsin fishing wars. The 1969 White Paper. Leonard Peltier.

I *would* like to pause for a moment and consider a pamphlet the Interstate Congress for Equal Rights and Responsibilities published. *Are We Giving America Back to the Indians?* consists of a series of questions and answers, a Socratic tour of Indian affairs, that leaves little doubt in the mind of the reader that Indians are a bunch of welfare bums living off generous government handouts, and that tribes are above the law and free to do whatever they want. "How do you define an Indian tribe?" the brochure asks. The answer: "It is a corporate entity run by a few individuals."

Silly me. I thought that was the general definition of government.

To the question "Why hasn't the Federal dole system brought about improvements within our Indian population?" the answer is,

"Because it is plain to close observers that these frequent doles have only increased the Indian people's ability to exist and sit on the sidelines of activity with plenty of time to ask for more."

To a question about the possibility of the federal expansion of the Uintah and Ouray reservation in Utah, the folks at the Interstate Congress for Equal Rights and Responsibilities respond that "we certainly don't want them [Utes] expanding their reservation boundaries unless they buy the land at fair market value from willing sellers. We want the Indians to own and supervise what is theirs, but we do not want them to assume authority over personal property that is not theirs."

I wonder if the Indians in question felt much the same way, that they did not want Whites expanding their boundaries unless they bought land at fair market value from willing Indians. In the early years of Indian–White relations, Native people saw land as a shared resource rather than as a commodity. Since then we've learned our lesson.

But the booklet was published in 1976, and although I'm angered by its blatant racism, into the fire it goes.

1985. Everything before that goes on the pyre. Everything before that is committed to the flames. Ashes to ashes.

And, in the spirit of generosity and new beginnings, and to show you I'm serious, I'll add Gustafson Lake (1995), the Mount Graham Observatory (1997), and Burnt Church (1999) to the pile even though they happened *after* my cutoff date. I'll even throw in the 1996 class-action lawsuit that Elouise Cobell (Blackfeet) filed against the U.S. Department of the Interior for the gross mismanagement of billions of dollars that never made it to the asset accounts of individual Native Americans. The case took fourteen years to settle and resulted in a $3.4 billion award against the U.S. government.

As a corollary, I'm even willing to admit that Native people have made some rather grievous errors, have had significant lapses in judgment. We've done a reasonably good job of injuring ourselves without the help of non-Natives. For instance, for decades we've beaten each other up over who is the better Indian. Full-bloods versus mixed-bloods. Indians on reservations and reserves versus Indians in cities. Status versus non-Status. Those who are enrolled members of a tribe versus those who are not. Those of us who look Indian versus those of us who don't. We have been and continue to be brutal about these distinctions, a mutated strain of ethnocentrism.

Helen, who happened to be looking over my shoulder as I was writing this, raised the issue of the Cherokee Freedmen.

I'd prefer to avoid that one, but because we're beginning anew, I'll touch on the highlights of the matter. Though "highlights" is most certainly the wrong term.

Since the mid-1800s, the Cherokee have been embroiled in a running political/economic/racial fight over who is a Cherokee and who is not, or, more properly, who is Cherokee enough to vote in the Nation's elections and to share in the tribe's assets.

The Cherokee participated in slavery. In 1835, there were over 1,500 African slaves within the Nation. When the Cherokee were forced to move to Indian Territory, many of the slaves went with them. Then, in 1866, after the Civil War, the Cherokee signed a treaty with the United States that, among other things, extended Cherokee citizenship to Cherokee slaves who had been freed by the Emancipation Proclamation. These former slaves, of African blood and African–Cherokee blood, are the Freedmen and were, according to the treaty, to have "all the rights of native Cherokees."

But many Cherokee have never been happy with the idea of Freedmen being members of the Nation, and in the 1970s, Ross Swimmer, Principal Chief of the Cherokee, issued an executive order that required all Cherokee Nation citizens to have a Certificate of Degree of Indian Blood (CDIB). There are three distinct groups in the Cherokee Nation: Cherokee by blood, Freedmen, and Whites who intermarried. The thrust of Swimmer's order was to make sure that the only group with voting rights was the Cherokee-by-blood group. This effectively disenfranchised the Freedmen.

In the late 1980s, Wilma Mankiller became Principal Chief and reaffirmed Swimmer's order on CDIBs and voting. But in 2004, Lucy Allen, a Freedman descendant, took the matter to the Cherokee Supreme Court, and the court, in a split decision, said that the descendants of Freedmen were, in fact, Cherokee, could apply to be enrolled, and should have the right to vote.

The reaction was immediate, and in 2006, the Principal Chief, Chad Smith, led a successful effort to change the Cherokee constitution and allow the Nation to restrict tribal membership and voting rights.

This has led to a series of cases currently before the courts, in which the Cherokee and the Freedmen continue to argue the matter. The Cherokee insist that, as a sovereign nation, the tribe has the power to set its rules of membership. This is absolutely true, and as it should be. But sovereignty and self-governance come with obligations, some legal, some moral. In the case of the Freedmen, while the 2006 vote to change the Nation's constitution was an affirmation of Cherokee sovereignty, it was also a vote on economics and race. The sad reality is that many Cherokee did not want to share tribal assets with the Freedmen, nor did they want Black people allowed in as full members of the Nation.

The Freedmen saga reminds me of the old adage that democracy has to be more than two wolves and a sheep voting on what to have for dinner.

I could say something mundane such as "this is an unfortunate chapter in Cherokee history," but that is such an overused phrase. Still, in our history, the Cherokee have looked smarter and behaved better.

And while we're on the subject of Native failings, I should probably own up to the alcoholism, drug abuse, poverty, crime, and corrupt leadership that plague many of the reserves and reservations. The news media have certainly been helpful in bringing these matters to public notice, and I salute the fifth estate for their simple-minded diligence. By now you should have some sense of the history that has made these such complicated problems. Nevertheless, the solutions, in the end, remain our responsibility.

Okay. All done.

But before we move on, I would like to remind everyone that, contrary to the stories that periodically appear in the newspapers and on the evening news chronicling Native poverty and despair, many of the tribes in North America are managing reasonably well. Some have developed strong economies. Of course, it helps if the tribe has natural resources, oil or coal or timber—the Cree at Hobbema, the Navajo in Arizona, Utah, and New Mexico, and the Alaskan tribes—or if the reservation is in an area that lends itself to tourism and eco-tourism, as with the Seminole in Florida.

In addition to the improvement in Native economies, Indians have also become more active in politics and the arts. Throughout North America, hundreds of Native organizations—grassroots, regional, national, and international—have come of age and are pursuing a variety of issues and concerns. Among these are the Native American Rights Fund, the Union of British Columbia Indian Chiefs, the National Aboriginal Achievement Foundation (now Indspire), the American Indian Policy Center, the Native Women's Association of Canada, the Minnesota Indian Affairs Council, the Native Council of Canada, the Indian Arts and Crafts Association, the National Association of Friendship Centres, the Inuit Tapirisat of Canada, the National Indian Child Welfare Association, the National Indian Women's Health Resource Center, and the Métis National Council.

We're cops, teachers, judges, writers, musicians, painters, soldiers, dancers, chefs, business men and women, pilots, architects, hockey players, singers. We're doctors, lawyers, and Indian chiefs. We're everywhere. Absolutely everywhere. Just a reminder of our cultural persistence and adaptation.

But enough of this boosterism. Let's get back to 1985 and our new beginnings.

By the way, this sloughing off of history is not an idea I came up with on my own. It is an approach to North American Native history that has been around for a while and appears to be gaining in popularity. One of the books that came out of the 2006 Mohawk land protest at Caledonia in Ontario, *Helpless! Caledonia's Nightmare of Fear and Anarchy and How the Law Failed All of Us* by *Globe and Mail* journalist Christie Blatchford, is a proponent of this style of scholarship.

Ignore the past. Play in the present.

In the introduction to the book, Blatchford writes: "This book is not about Aboriginal land claims. This book is not about the wholesale removal of seven generations of indigenous youngsters from their reserves and families . . . or the abuse dished out to many of them at the residential schools. . . . This book is not about the dubious merits of the reserve system which may better serve those who wish to see native people fail . . ."

Which raises the question, what *is* the book about?

As it turns out, the book is about the adverse effects that the occupation of the Douglas Creek Estates has had on the non-Native residents of Caledonia, the negligence of law enforcement in failing to protect the residents of Caledonia and their property, and the culpability of senior command officers and provincial politicians in not providing the necessary leadership.

Ignoring the past is certainly an expedient strategy. But without the long-standing Native land claim dating back to the 1700s, a claim that has been ignored and dismissed by Ottawa and the province, a standoff such as the one at Caledonia doesn't happen. Still, by uprooting itself from the landscape of history, the book is able to concentrate on the trees without having to consider the forest.

Using this approach as a template, one could write a book about the United States dropping two atomic bombs on Japan without having to mention World War II.

Still, a promise is a promise, so let's give our 1985 start date another try. And let's turn our attention to Canada. It's a great country, and for the period after 1985, Canada has most of the interesting stuff.

Bill C-31, for example.

If we really believe that we have moved beyond historical prejudices, if we believe we've left racism behind, then explaining Bill C-31 is going to be . . . difficult.

Bill C-31 is a piece of Canadian legislation passed in 1985 as an amendment to the Indian Act and designed to address the inequity that existed between Status Native men and Status Native women. Status is a Canadian concept. It does not exist in the United States. Indians in the United States have to deal with blood quantum, the amount of Native blood a person has—full, half, quarter, eighth, and on down the line—and with whether or not they are a card-carrying member of a federally recognized tribe. In Canada, Status Indians are simply those Indians who are recognized as Indians by the federal government. In general, Status Indians are also Treaty Indians, though there are reserves created by legislative action rather than by treaty and members of those bands are Status Indians in the same way that Treaty Indians are Status.

If that makes sense.

Prior to 1985 and Bill C-31, when Native men with Status married non-Status women, Native or non-Native, the women and any children gained Status. However, when Native women with Status married non-Status men, Native or non-Native, they and any children lost Status. In this regard, the Indian Act was clearly discriminatory and blatantly sexist.

When Bill C-31 was passed, Native women who had lost Status because of marriage were able to apply to have Status reinstated. The bill also closed the loophole of non-Native women gaining Status through marriage by legislating that no one could gain or lose Status through marriage, though this is slightly disingenuous.

While you can't gain or lose Status through marriage, whom you marry can affect your children.

So long as Status Indians marry Status Indians and their children marry Status Indians, then no one loses Status. But if Status Indians begin marrying non-Status Indians or non-Indians, then Status for any offspring is at risk.

And once you lose Status, you can never get it back.

So, let's say that you have a brother, an identical twin. Both of you are Status, full-blood Indians. You marry a full-blood Native woman who is Status, but your brother marries a full-blood Native woman who is non-Status. You have a daughter. Your brother has a daughter. Both of the girls are Status.

The two girls grow up, fall in love, and marry. Your daughter marries a full-blood Status Native man. Your brother's daughter marries a full-blood non-Status Native man. Your daughter and your brother's daughter have boys.

Watch closely. Nothing up my sleeve.

Your daughter's son, who is a full-blood Native, has Status. Your brother's daughter's son, who is a full-blood Native, does not.

One child is Status. One child is not. Even though each child has the same Status grandparents, even though everyone involved married full-bloods. What you just watched happen is referred to as the "two-generation cut-off clause." Marry out of Status for two generations, and the children of the second union are non-Status.

Was this draconian measure something that Native people requested? Or was it an initiative that the government came up with to eliminate Status Indians?

Let's think about that for a minute.

Because Indians marry both Status and non-Status individuals, so long as the "two generation cut-off clause" remains in place, more of our children will lose Status. If this continues, at some point, perhaps in the lifetime of my grandchildren, there could be no Status Indians left in Canada. There will still be treaty land, held in trust for Status Indians. There will still be Indians, full-bloods and mixed-bloods who have maintained their tribal affiliations and their cultures and perhaps even their languages. But the reserves at Hobbema and Standoff, at Curve Lake and Brantford, at Penticton and Bella Bella, at Cross Lake and Nelson House will all be ghost towns. Or museums.

It is a brilliant plan. No need to allocate money to improve living conditions on reserves. No reason to build the new health center that's been promised for the past thirty years. No reason to fix the water and sewer systems or to update the science equipment at the schools. Without Status Indians, the land can be recycled by the government and turned into something useful, such as estate lots and golf courses, and Ottawa, at long last, can walk away from the Indian business.

They were never much good at it anyway.

Bill C-31 will probably wind up before the courts, but what I don't understand is why the loss of Status and the potential loss of our land base hasn't been a hot issue for Native organizations in Canada. Perhaps it has and I haven't been paying attention. What Native leaders and government officials *have* talked about is amending the Indian Act to allow for more local autonomy, and about eliminating the Act altogether. So far, none of the talking has gone anywhere. Treaties are the sine qua non of the Act. Technically, I think treaties could function without the legislation. They might even function better.

But without the treaties, the Indian Act is a parasite without a host. The disheartening reality is that, even if the combined efforts of national and grassroots organizations were successful in getting rid of this particular assault on Status, it simply means we'd be back to 1985. No further ahead. All of the problems we face as Native people would still be there waiting for us. And such a campaign, in spite of its success, would do little to help the more than 200,000 non-Status Natives in the country, who have little vested interest in either the Indian Act or in band land.

The alternative is to do nothing—which I'll admit is far more comfortable and appealing—and leave the next seven generations, if there are that many left, to fend for themselves.

While Bill C-31 gives us a quick glimpse into the metaphysics of federal Indian-hating, the *Report of the Royal Commission on Aboriginal Peoples*, its reception, and its implementation provide us with a panoramic view.

The Royal Commission on Aboriginal Peoples was formed in 1991, with a blue-ribbon panel of four Aboriginal members and three non-Native members. The report was originally budgeted at $8 million for three years, but the research ran to five years at a cost of some $58 million. The commission visited 96 communities, held 178 days of hearings around the country on reserves, in community centers, and in jails where Aboriginal people—who are 4 percent of the Canadian population—make up over 18 percent of the federal prison population.

The final report ran to over four thousand pages contained in five volumes (six books), and was the most comprehensive and complete study of Aboriginal people, Aboriginal history, and Aboriginal policy that has ever been done in North America.

The last volume of the report contained 440 recommendations, which included recognizing that "Aboriginal people are nations vested with the right of self-determination," that Aboriginal people in Canada enjoy "a unique form of dual citizenship," that the government abolish the Department of Indian Affairs and Northern Development and replace it with "two new departments: a Department of Aboriginal Relations and a Department of Indian and Inuit Services," that the government of Canada meet with First Nations governments and people to "meet the need of First Nations people for adequate housing within ten years," and that "Representatives of Aboriginal peoples be included in all planning and preparations for any future constitutional conference convened by the government of Canada."

The report went on to make recommendations in areas such as governance, health, housing, education, Native women's rights, Métis rights, and economic development. The expectation was that the government would see the report as an opportunity to renew, amend, and restructure its relationship with Canada's First Nations.

But that's not what happened. Almost as soon as the report was released, it was placed on the shelf with all the rest of the reports from Royal Commissions—the Royal Commission on the Status of Women, the Royal Commission on Radio Broadcasting, the Royal Commission on Bilingualism and Biculturalism, the Royal Commission on Capital Punishment, the Royal Commission on the Electoral System—though, to be fair, some of the recommendations from these other Royal Commissions have actually been acted upon.

Probably the most embarrassing aspect of the Royal Commission on Aboriginal Peoples affair was the speed with which the report was buried. Alive. Perhaps it fell prey to the vagaries of politics.

The Mulroney Conservatives had commissioned the study, but the Chrétien Liberals were the party in power when the report was tabled. Or perhaps the reason is not to be found in the intrigue of partisan politics. Perhaps, as Helen explained to me, Royal Commission reports have become the Canadian alternative to action.

Since we're looking at 1985 and beyond, we shouldn't ignore the Meech Lake Accord, which was a set of amendments to the Canadian Constitution designed to encourage Quebec to join Canada's "constitutional family." Even though the Accord straddles both sides of our date, the critical meeting took place at Meech Lake, Quebec, in April of 1987, with the final text of the Accord being approved in June of the same year.

The Accord officially recognized Quebec as a "distinct society," and it gave the province new and wide-ranging powers in the areas of immigration, Senate and Supreme Court appointments, and changes to national institutions. It also granted Quebec (and the other provinces) the ability to opt out of any program that the province did not feel was in its best interests.

But while the Meech Lake Accord dealt with many of Quebec's concerns, it completely ignored Aboriginal people. The Accord called for a First Ministers' conference to be held at least once a year to consider matters of national concern. Native leaders wanted a place at that table. They wanted official recognition of Indian societies as "distinct societies," a term that Quebec had used successfully. They wanted acknowledgment of Native rights and aspirations. And they wanted guarantees that the veto and opting-out powers that the Accord granted the provinces would not adversely affect Canada's First Nations.

Instead, Native people weren't even mentioned in the document.

Canada was the confluence of three founding peoples, Aboriginal, English, and French, but the Accord acknowledged only the English and French streams.

The Meech Lake Accord had a three-year timeline that expired on June 23, 1990. All ten provinces had to ratify the agreement within that period or the Accord would die. By early June of 1990, eight of the provinces had voted to accept the Accord. Only two had not: Manitoba and Newfoundland.

In the Manitoba provincial elections of 1990, Gary Filmon's Progressive Conservatives won control of the government, with thirty of the fifty-seven seats. The New Democrats captured twenty seats, and the Liberals limped in with seven. Support for the Meech Lake Accord was not unanimous, but the leaders of all three parties agreed to bring it to the floor for a vote.

Before there could be a vote, however, the Accord required public hearings. Public hearings at this late date would have pushed the debate beyond the deadline for ratification. So Filmon introduced a motion to bypass such debate and bring the Accord to the floor for a vote. The vote to dispense with public hearings had to be unanimous, and here the Meech Lake Accord ran into Elijah Harper.

Harper was Cree, a member of the Red Sucker Lake First Nation in northern Manitoba, and the first Treaty Indian to be elected in Manitoba. When the vote to forgo public hearings on the Accord was called, he stood up and said no.

No. No. No.

And with that, the Meech Lake Accord died.

Two years later, another package of proposed amendments to the Canadian Constitution, the Charlottetown Accord, was brought forward. This time, unlike with the Meech Lake Accord, representatives of the Assembly of First Nations, the Native Council of Canada, the Inuit Tapirisat of Canada, and the Métis National Council participated in the public consultations.

The text of the Accord stipulated the rights of Aboriginal peoples to "promote their language, cultures and traditions and to ensure the integrity of their societies," and acknowledged that Aboriginal governments "constitute one of the three orders of government in Canada." And it also assured Native people that nothing in the Accord "abrogates or derogates from the aboriginal and treaty rights of the aboriginal peoples of Canada," and that the people have "the inherent right to self-government." The Accord even suggested the possibility of guaranteed seats for Aboriginals in a reorganized Canadian Senate.

Mind you, the "possibilities" that appear in government documents are generally euphemisms for "no way in hell." And the "inherent right to self-government" is clarified later on by the provision that "No aboriginal law or any other exercise of the inherent right of self-government . . . may be inconsistent with federal or provincial laws that are essential to the preservation of peace, order and good government in Canada."

Which makes perfect sense. Otherwise, Aboriginal Nations would be . . . sovereign.

Unlike the Meech Lake Accord, which was voted on at the provincial level, the Charlottetown Accord was decided by public referendum. And was soundly defeated. Even though this Accord had guarantees in it for Native people that Meech Lake did not, and even though Native leadership supported the agreement and spoke out in favor of the Accord, Aboriginal people, on the whole, voted against it.

I don't know why, exactly. Perhaps, at this point in our relationship with non-Natives, we were not convinced that the government was here to help.

But it wasn't the Aboriginal vote that killed Charlottetown.
In 1992, voters in Alberta, British Columbia, Manitoba, Nova
Scotia, Saskatchewan, and Quebec voted against it. Voters in
New Brunswick, Newfoundland, Ontario, and Prince Edward
Island voted for it. The Northwest Territories said yes. The
Yukon said no. Still, it was a close vote: 49.6 percent in favor;
50.4 percent against.

The Accord did give Native people assurances that Meech had
not, and this "generosity" might have played a small part in its
defeat. I certainly heard people complain about "more money
being wasted on Indians," even though the Accord didn't throw
any dollars our way. However, most of the rancor that the
Charlottetown Accord produced was centered on Quebec.

And after the dust of two failed Accords had settled, Native
people in Canada were right back to 1985.

Almost forgot. Remember that land-claim dispute at Caledonia,
Ontario, in 2006 that I mentioned earlier? Where Mohawks took
over a housing development to protest the building of new homes
on what the Mohawk considered to be their territory? That ended
happily. In 2011, the Ontario government agreed to a $20 million
settlement.

But not for the Mohawk.

No, the money went to homeowners and businesses adversely
affected by the six-week blockade. That the settlement came just
months before the provincial election when the sitting Liberal government was behind in the polls had, according to government

sources, nothing to do with the timing of the cash award. The concerns of the Mohawk and the land claim itself were shoved into a closet, yet another testament to North America's willingness to ignore commitments and its capacity for self-deception.

In the United States, the post-1985 period was redeemed by the 1990 Native American Graves Protection and Repatriation Act, which required federal agencies and institutions to return Aboriginal cultural materials and human remains to the appropriate tribes. It was also marked by the settlement of a number of land claims—the Massachusetts Land Claims Settlement with the Wampanoag in 1987, the Washington Indian Land Claims Settlement with the Puyallup in 1989, the Seneca Nation Land Claims Settlement in 1990, the Mohegan Nation Land Claims Settlement in 1994, the Crow Boundary Settlement in 1994, the Cherokee, Choctaw, and Chickasaw Nation Claims Settlement in 2002, and the Pueblo De San Ildefonso Claims Settlement in 2006, just to mention a few. However, more than anything else, the period was dominated by the rise of Native gaming, and depending on your point of view, gaming could be seen as economic enterprise or economic war.

It began simply enough in 1972, with a property tax bill that Itasca County sent to Russell and Helen Bryan, a Chippewa couple living on the Greater Leech Lake Indian Reservation in northern Minnesota. The Bryans refused to pay the bill, arguing that the mobile home they owned was on tribal land. The court ruled in favor of Itasca County, and the case was appealed to the Minnesota Supreme Court, where the lower court ruling was upheld.

In due course, the case wound up in the lap of the U.S. Supreme Court, where Justice William Brennan Jr. wrote the unanimous decision. The simple version is that states did not have the right to tax Indians who lived on federal reservations. As well, the court held that states lacked the authority to regulate Indian activities that took place on Indian reservations. The Bryan case was not about whether Indian tribes could run gambling casinos, but the Brennan decision did open the door to this possibility, and when this basic concept of Indian self-determination was tested in two other major cases, *Seminole v. Butterworth* in 1981 and *California v. Cabazon Band of Mission Indians* in 1987, the matter was settled. Tribes now had the right to develop gambling on tribal land.

Of course, not everyone was happy. State governments were furious, in part because of the loss of control over land that they felt was their domain, and in part because of the lost tax revenues. National gambling interests had a massive stake in places such as Atlantic City and Las Vegas and saw the advent of Native gambling as direct competition to their fiefdoms. Donald Trump, looking after his own profits, was particularly vocal in his opposition to Native gaming.

The idea that Native people had something resembling agency and independence was just too much to bear, and almost immediately state governments, along with citizen groups opposed to gambling of any sort, the gambling cabal itself, the Bureau of Indian Affairs, and Congress all climbed into bed together to figure out a way to get around the Brennan decision.

After all, the notion of Indians in charge of themselves and their businesses was antithetical to the American ideals of democracy, fair play, and free enterprise.

What happens next is complicated, illegal, and sleazy. But, given the history of Indian affairs, not unexpected. The states, along with the federal government and private interests, made it quite clear that while tribes might have the legal right to run gaming enterprises on their reservations, that right could be tied up in the courts until hell froze over. What we need, tribes were told by the powers that be, is a compromise.

Compromise is a fine word. So much more generous than blackmail.

In 1988, Congress formally recognized the right of Native Americans to conduct gaming operations with the passage of the Indian Gaming Regulatory Act (IGRA). The states supported the Act because it required the tribes to negotiate with the states concerning the games that were to be played. And while the Act allowed that tribal governments were the sole owners and primary beneficiaries of gaming, the reality was that the tribes were forced to sign compacts guaranteeing the states a generous portion of the money Indians made from the slots and the tables.

A deal you can't refuse.

In the United States, under the Indian Gaming Regulatory Act of 1988, there were three classes of gambling possible on Native reservations: Class I, Class II, and Class III.

Class I gaming was defined as traditional gaming or social gaming with minimal prizes. Authority for this form of gaming was vested with the tribe itself and was not subject to the regulations of the Indian Gaming Regulatory Act.

Class II gaming was generally understood to cover bingo and other games similar to bingo. Class II gaming was regulated by tribal governments, with oversight of the National Indian Gaming Commission.

Class III gaming dealt with all other types of gaming not

covered by Class I and Class II, and was generally concerned with casino-style gaming. It differed little from the kind of gambling that went on in places such as Atlantic City and Las Vegas, and it was here that the matter of Indian gaming got . . . entertaining. If a tribe wished to engage in Class III gaming, Class III gaming had to be allowed in that state. The tribe also had to negotiate a compact with the state, to be approved by the Secretary of the Interior. Finally, the tribe had to put together a gaming ordinance, to be approved by the National Indian Gaming Commission.

I'm not particularly happy about gambling as a fiscal base for Native people. That kind of money generally brings out the worst in folks, Native as well as non-Native. But after several centuries of economic oppression, and given the lack of alternatives, professional gaming, for many tribes, holds the most potential for the least effort. Still, apart from raw cash and jobs, industrial-strength gambling contributes little of value to the world.

But then, the same thing could be said about land mines and reality television.

To date, there are about 15 Native-run casinos in Canada and over 350 casinos and bingo halls in 30 states, which bring in over $25 billion a year. And these numbers keep growing. In Manitoba, a consortium of Native bands in the province and the Red Lake Chippewa from northern Minnesota have joined forces to build the Spirit Sands Casino near Spruce Woods Provincial Park. The casino will be one of the first Native-to-Native gaming enterprises and may be a model for further development.

The new buffalo. That's what someone called Indian Gaming. *The new buffalo.*

In the fall of 2010, my brother and I went on a car trip that took us through Oklahoma. As we travelled Highway 40 to Oklahoma City and Highway 44 to Tulsa, we ran into a series of small, road-side casinos that the Cherokee have built. They were clean and slick. Bigger than a fast-food restaurant, smaller than the MGM Grand in Vegas. Chris called them "drive-by casinos."

I'm not a gambling enthusiast, but in the spirit of curiosity and tribal solidarity, Chris and I stopped and fed the buffalo. Fifteen dollars each. All things considered, I would have rather put the money into a hospital or a clean-water system on a reserve.

Over one-third of the federally recognized tribes in North America have moved into some form of gaming, with more tribes coming on board all the time. Even the Navajo, who had twice voted against allowing gambling on the reservation, finally succumbed to the promise of easy money and jobs. The tribe's first venture into Class III gaming, the Fire Rock Casino a little east of Gallup, is expected to generate close to $32 million a year.

It's hard to argue with money like that and the jobs that such an industry creates.

No one knows what long-term effects on-reserve gaming will have on Native people. I would hope that we're smart enough to make use of gaming as an enabling industry, hope that, as we create and improve tribal infrastructures, we will also direct some of the profits to more diversified and sustainable businesses.

But make no mistake. When states and provinces and munici-palities look at Native gaming, all they see is a deep-dish pie. Since 2003, Arizona tribes have given about $430 million to that state. Connecticut, with the large Native casinos at Foxwoods and Mohegan Sun, gets about $200 million annually. In 2003, California

Governor Gray Davis "called on" tribes to donate $1.5 billion, about one-third of their gaming profits, to help a mismanaged state out of its deficit.

Ironically, California is the same state that in the mid-nineteenth century actively encouraged the slaughter of Native people, offering bounties for Indian bodies and scalps with no regard for gender or age. Twenty-five dollars for adults. Five bucks for a child. It is the same state that sold over four thousand Native children into slavery at prices ranging from sixty dollars for a boy to two hundred for a girl.

Thank goodness that the past is the past, and today is today. We'd much rather be appreciated than hunted, though we do need to understand that each time our new political friends drop by, they will want another and larger piece of our pie, and that they will keep coming back until there is little left but crumbs on a plate.

After all, it's Indian pie and we don't need that much.

But the post-1985 period isn't just about legislation and government and politicians with their hands in the Indian till. The present, like the past, also has its fair share of bad behavior, racism, and murder.

There are people who are genuinely disturbed by what they erroneously perceive to be preferential treatment for Native people. Many of these voices have banded into small groups and local organizations such as Protect Americans' Rights and Resources or Stop Treaty Abuse, which were formed in 1987 and 1988 respectively to protest Ojibway spear-fishing treaty rights in Wisconsin. Other organizations, such as the Citizens Equal Rights Alliance (CERA), with chapters in over a dozen states, are larger and better funded, with access to state and federal lawmakers. CERA's mission statement is succinct and straightforward. "Federal Indian Policy is unaccountable, destructive, racist and unconstitutional. It is therefore CERA's mission to ensure the equal protection of the law as guaranteed to all citizens by the Constitution of the United States of America."

You might have mistakenly thought that CERA is talking about the harm that federal Indian policy is doing to Native people. Not so. The "injured" group that CERA is sworn to protect is Whites.

Bigotry and misinformation feed many of these organizations. Other groups don't even try to pretend. In 1999, a flyer was distributed in South Dakota and Nebraska. It was worked up to look like an official notice from the South Dakota State Fish and Game Department announcing a special season on local Lakota reserves during which White hunters could hunt Native people, or as the flyer called them, "Worthless Red Bastards, Gut Eaters, Prairie Niggers." The hunt, according to the notice, was intended to "thin out the fucking Indians."

The flyer set a limit on the number of Indians you could kill—ten Indians a day—and restricted hunting parties to no more than 150 persons and thirty-five "bloodthirsty, rabid hunting dogs." Other rules forbade shooting at an Indian in a public tavern as the "bullet might ricochet and hit civilized white people." You could not set traps within fifteen feet of a liquor store, you couldn't shoot an Indian sleeping on the sidewalk, and you couldn't shoot length-wise in a welfare line.

Damn. These people are witty.

Benjamin Nighthorse Campbell, a U.S. senator from Colorado, the third Native American to be elected to Congress and the first to chair the Senate Committee on Indian Affairs, took the matter of the flyer up with the Department of Justice, but by then, with the dim light of judicial interest flickering in their general direction, the framers of the document scurried back to their hidey-holes and disappeared.

I'd like to be able to say, as a matter of Canadian pride if nothing else, that such behavior is an exclusively American pastime, but I'd be lying.

In 1988, Helen and I were living in Lethbridge, Alberta. We had one of those newer, suburban, split-level tract homes, with stucco walls and a faux-tile roof. The yard consisted of grass and a Russian Olive tree, which was about the only kind of tree able to survive on the high prairies. Its thin, grey leaves made it look as though it were on the verge of dying, thereby fooling the elements and the bad weather into thinking that they didn't have to bother with something so spindly and bent, something so obviously on its last legs.

One Saturday, I was roaming around, going to open houses. I wasn't looking to buy. I was just curious. And, in Lethbridge, in 1988, dropping in at open houses was pretty much the most excitement one could find on a Saturday afternoon.

So, I was looking, and I happened to stumble across a small bungalow on Seventh Avenue, just a short walk from the Woodward's Mall, the Lethbridge Lodge, and the coulees overlooking the river bottom. It was a lovely bungalow on a corner, surrounded by a tall hedge. Inside, it had three bedrooms, one bath, a kitchen, a dining room, and a living room on the main floor. The basement was undeveloped, but you could see where you could put in a full bath, two bedrooms, and a family room without much difficulty.

I hurried home, told Helen about the place. She looked at it, and before the month was out, we had sold our house and bought the bungalow.

Lethbridge sits on the edge of the Blackfoot reserve, and it contains, as Walt Whitman might have said, all of the accommodations and prejudices that one might expect from such a social geography: "I am large, I contain multitudes." Not that these multitudes always got along, but at that time, there was an uneasy peace between the cowboys and Indians. Racism was audible but muted, visible but filtered.

We had been living in our new bungalow for a few months when I arrived home one evening to find a flyer in the mailbox. It was from one of the city's prominent realtors. I won't mention his name because I have no wish to open old wounds and because, at this point, there is nothing to be gained or lost.

The flyer was a single sheet of paper, yellow in color, and it alerted folks to the fact that a Treaty Seven family had moved into the neighborhood. I'm reasonably sure we weren't the family in question. Treaty Seven didn't deal with the Cherokee. It was the treaty struck with the Blackfoot in September of 1877. In the case of the flyer, however, "Treaty Seven" was simply code for "Indians," so perhaps the realtor was thinking of me as well.

You don't need Alan Turing to break this code. Indians have moved in. Your property values are about to fall. To save your investment and yourself, call me and I'll sell your home and help you move to a safer—economically and socially speaking—part of town.

At first, I was amused. Then I was angry, as were a number of people in Lethbridge and on the reserve. And why not? This fool had broken the first rule of racism. Think it, but do not speak it out loud.

So the flyer hit the fan. As it were. The agent took one step backward (it was a fair-sized fan) and then leaned into the wind, explaining, as he lumbered forward, that it was all a misunderstanding. His flyer wasn't racist, it was an opportunity. If one Treaty Seven family had liked this particular neighborhood well enough to move there, then other Treaty Seven families might also want to buy in the area. House prices might well go up. Supply and demand. It wasn't racism that we had heard, he argued, it was the engine of capitalism as it chugged down Main Street.

The engine of capitalism. That must have been what I'd heard years before in Salt Lake City when I tried to buy a house there. After I had spent several weeks looking at dozens of homes and frustrating the real estate agent with my indecision, he finally turned to me and asked, "What do you want to do? Spend the rest of your life in a tipi?"

Somebody once told me that racism hurts everyone. Perhaps in the broader sense of community, this is true. All I know is that it seems to hurt some much more than others.

A number of us complained about the Treaty Seven flyer. I don't know what I expected, but I was surprised when I was told by a city official that "you people should calm down." Live and let live, he told me. No harm, no foul. Everybody makes mistakes. Go with the flow. Let he who is without sin cast the first stone. Judge not lest ye be judged.

That's the problem with the Bible, isn't it? While the Old Testament is filled with angry gods and bad business, and the New Testament is awash in gospels and epistles, there just aren't many good quotations that deal with confronting hate. "Vengeance is mine, I will repay" (Romans 12:20) might seem to suggest a possible course of action, but the verse is really an admonishment *not* to indulge in revenge. It is a reminder that the settling of injustices is the realm of God himself, and no one else. We (humankind) are supposed to forgive our tormentors, turn the other cheek and all that, though the Good Book does not explain the nobility in being despised. Or the profit in being hit.

Oh, sure, the Beatitudes make all sorts of promises for passivity and faith: the poor in spirit and the persecuted will inherit heaven, the merciful will receive mercy, the pure in heart will see God, mourners will be comforted, and the meek will inherit the earth. If you take Matthew at his word, you have most of your bases covered. And Romans 12:20–21 allows that if you feed your enemy, you heap coals of fire on his head, but, like the Beatitudes, this is just a general metaphor with no real contractual obligations.

I had expected that the real estate agent would be censured by the real estate board, but he wasn't even admonished. I don't think anyone believed his explanation, but then again, his flyer wasn't a lynching in Mississippi or a massacre at Sand Creek. It was just another of those sharp shards of bigotry you find when you run your fingers across the Canadian mosaic.

And then there was the sad sign that a young woman working at a Tim Hortons in Lethbridge, Alberta, taped to the drive-through window in 2007. It read, "No Drunk Natives." Accusations of racism erupted, Tim Hortons assured everyone that its coffee shops were not centers for bigotry, but what was most interesting was the public response. For as many people who called in to radio shows or wrote letters to the *Lethbridge Herald* to voice their outrage over the sign, there were almost as many who expressed their support for the sentiment. The young woman who posted the sign said it had just been a joke.

Now, I'll be the first to say that drunks are a problem. But I lived in Lethbridge for ten years, and I can tell you with as much neutrality as I can muster that there were many more White drunks stumbling out of the bars on Friday and Saturday nights than there were Native drunks. It's just that in North America, White drunks tend to be invisible, whereas people of color who drink to excess are not.

Actually, White drunks are not just invisible, they can also be amusing. Remember how much fun it was to watch Dean Martin, Red Skelton, W. C. Fields, John Wayne, John Barrymore, Ernie Kovacs, James Stewart, and Marilyn Monroe play drunks on the screen and sometimes in real life? Or Jodie Marsh, Paris Hilton, Cheryl Tweedy, Britney Spears, and the late Anna Nicole Smith, just to mention a few from my daughter's generation. And let's not forget some of our politicians and persons of power who control the fates of nations: Winston Churchill, John A. Macdonald, Boris Yeltsin, George Bush, Daniel Patrick Moynihan. Hard drinkers, every one.

The somewhat uncomfortable point I'm making is that we don't seem to mind our White drunks. They're no big deal so long as they're not driving. But if they *are* driving drunk, as have Canada's coffee king Tim Horton, the ex-premier of Alberta Ralph Klein, actors Kiefer Sutherland and Mel Gibson, Super Bowl star Lawyer Milloy, or the Toronto Maple Leafs' Mark Bell, we just hope that they don't hurt themselves. Or others.

More to the point, they get to make their mistakes as individuals and not as representatives of an entire race.

Racism is endemic in North America. And it's also systemic. While it affects the general population at large, it's also buried in the institutions that are supposed to protect us from such abuses.

On a November evening in 1971, in The Pas, Manitoba, a nineteen-year-old Cree woman, Helen Betty Osborne, was walking home. She was approached by four White men, who threw her into their car and took her to a cabin near Clearwater Lake where she was beaten, raped, and stabbed over fifty times. To call Osborne's death a murder is to ignore the mindless savagery of the crime. It was more a slaughter.

The initial investigation focused on Osborne's Aboriginal friends, but in May of 1972, police received a letter naming three White men, Lee Colgan, James Houghton, and Norman Manger, as Osborne's killers. Later, a fourth name was added to this list, Dwayne Johnston.

Police seized Colgan's car and found trace evidence to indicate that this was the vehicle that had been used to kidnap Osborne.

Osborne was killed before my 1985 cutoff date, so you might feel that I'm cheating, but I've included this crime because the real investigation didn't start *until* 1985 when the Royal Canadian Mounted Police (RCMP), who had sat on their hands for fourteen years, finally got serious about the murder.

In 1983, Constable Robert Urbanoski of the Thompson detachment opened up the cold case and began a new review of the murder. Two years later, in June of 1985, the RCMP placed an article in the local newspaper asking the people of The Pas for their assistance. Amazingly, after all this time, several individuals came forward. Colgan and Johnston had talked openly about the murder and shared details with friends, and in October of 1986, the police, armed with the old and new evidence, charged Colgan and Johnston with murder. Colgan immediately asked for immunity and got it in exchange for his testimony against Johnston and Houghton. In 1987, Johnston was convicted of murder, Houghton was acquitted, and Colgan walked away without a scratch. Norman Manger was never charged.

Perhaps I was unfair when I said that the police "sat on their hands." The official reason for the years of delay was that the police, while they knew who killed Osborne, didn't feel they had enough evidence to take the case to trial. Perhaps they hadn't thought of asking for the public's help in 1971. Or perhaps back then, they hadn't been all that concerned with solving the murder of an Aboriginal woman. Perhaps it was partly Osborne's fault. Perhaps she should have been White.

In 1999, the Manitoba Aboriginal Justice Inquiry concluded that the murder of Betty Osborne was motivated by racism. "It is clear," the report said, "that Betty Osborne would not have been killed if she had not been Aboriginal." However, the inquiry did not take the RCMP to task for their lack of interest all those years, choosing instead to focus on the special effort that Constable Robert Urbanoski made in bringing Osborne's killer to justice.

Fair enough. In March of 2012, the Aboriginal Commission on Human Rights and Justice and the Institute for the Advancement of Aboriginal Women presented Urbanoski with their Social Justice Award for his efforts in the Osborne case. Well deserved.

But sixteen years? With everything in plain view? With the murderers talking freely about their crime? Even the most generous observer would have to wonder about the police force and its attitude toward Aboriginal people.

Or maybe not.

On another November evening, this time in 1990, a seventeen-year-old Cree man, Neil Stonechild, disappeared just blocks from his mother's home. The next day, he was found frozen to death in a field on the northern outskirts of Saskatoon. A friend, Jason Roy, had seen Stonechild the night before, handcuffed in the back of a police cruiser driven by Saskatoon police officers Larry Hartwig and Brad Senger. The police department did a cursory and sloppy investigation, concluded that Stonechild had died of exposure, and closed the case.

For the next ten years, the Stonechild case stayed closed. Then, in January of 2000, another Native man, Darrell Night, was picked up by Saskatoon police officers Dan Hatchen and Ken Munson, driven out of town, and dropped off by the side of the road. He almost froze to death, but was able to walk to a power plant where a shift worker, Mark Evoy, let Night in out of the cold.

Night was lucky. He lived. The next day the body of Rodney Naistus, a twenty-five-year-old man from the Onion Lake reserve, was found frozen to death about a kilometer south of where Night had been dropped off. Then days later, in early February, Lawrence Wegner from Saulteaux First Nation was discovered frozen to death in the same area.

The three deaths—Wegner, Naistus, and Stonechild ten years earlier—were remarkably similar. All three were young Native men who had been found frozen to death in the same area just outside Saskatoon. Besides being Native, the other common element that three of the four men shared was that they had last been seen in the back of a Saskatoon police cruiser.

With three similar, suspicious fatalities and one near-fatality, the Saskatoon public might have suspected that the deaths were racially motivated. And they would have been correct. The police even knew where to look to find the perpetrators. As far back as 1976, Saskatoon police officers had been driving young Native men to the outskirts of town and dropping them off. Within the urban mythology of Saskatoon, these rides were known as Starlight Tours. You could argue that this activity was no more than simple harassment, the kind of harassment that police forces around North America have engaged in for centuries, the kind that usually results in inconvenience and bad feelings rather than death.

But on the prairies, in the dead of winter, these Starlight Tours were executions.

This is what happened to Neil Stonechild, Rodney Naistus, and Lawrence Wegner. Darrell Night would have died as well, had he not found shelter in time.

The police.

There was a public inquiry. A number of high-ranking and retired police officials had their feelings hurt and their reputations impugned. The two officers responsible for Darrell Night's ordeal were convicted and sentenced to eight months in jail, then released early. The two officers who had been seen with Lawrence Wegner in their squad car were fired.

No one was ever formally accused or convicted of any of the deaths.

1985.

In terms of attitudes, in terms of dispossession and intolerance, nothing much has changed; 2012 feels remarkably similar to 1961. That was the year I graduated from high school, and the year that four hundred delegates from sixty-seven tribes met in Chicago to draw up a Declaration of Indian Purpose, which emphasized the preservation of culture and freedom for Native people to choose their own way. And 2012 also feels similar to 1911, when the Lakota writer Charles Eastman published *The Soul of the Indian* and when Ishi walked out of the Butte County wilderness in northern California and into the modern world. Or 1864, when Kit Carson and the U.S. Army rounded up the Navajo and marched them at gunpoint for eighteen days to Bosque Redondo. Or 1812, when the British cut and ran and left Tecumseh to face the Americans alone at the Battle of the Thames. Or 1763, when Pontiac led a loose confederation of Great Lake tribes against the British in an effort to drive them out of the area.

One story from this period has the British army contemplating using blankets infected with smallpox in an attempt to break the back of Indian resistance, but whether or not that plan was ever carried out, or carried out successfully, has never been proven, so I'm not going to repeat it.

1985.

You see my problem. The history I offered to forget, the past I offered to burn, turns out to be our present. It may well be our future.

8

WHAT INDIANS WANT

What we need is a cultural leave-us-alone agreement, in spirit
and in fact.

—Vine Deloria Jr., *Custer Died for Your Sins*

A future.

What a good idea. But there's a problem. If Native people are
to have a future that is of our own making, such a future will be
predicated, in large part, on sovereignty.

Sovereignty is one of those topics about which everyone has an
opinion, and each time the subject is brought up at a gathering or
at a conference, a hockey game breaks out. To be honest, I'm
reluctant to mention it. But if you're going to talk about Indians
in contemporary North America, you're going to have to discuss
sovereignty. No way around it.

Sovereignty, by definition, is supreme and unrestricted

authority. However, sovereignty in practice, as a functional form of governance, is never an absolute condition. Rather, it is a collection of practical powers that include, among others, the authority to levy taxes, set the criteria for citizenship, control trade, and negotiate agreements and treaties.

Aboriginal sovereignty, by the way, is a given. It is recognized in treaties, in the Canadian and American constitutions, and in the Indian Act. It has been confirmed any number of times by Supreme Court decisions in both countries. Just in case you didn't know.

In 2007, the United Nations passed its Declaration on the Rights of Indigenous Peoples, in which it recognized that indigenous people had the right "to self-determination" and that they could "freely determine their political status and freely pursue their economic, social and cultural development." The declaration doesn't use the word "sovereignty" but the forty-six articles that set out the rights and freedoms and responsibilities of indigenous people are close enough to sovereignty. At least, close enough for government work.

The Canadian columnist Jeffrey Simpson, in a *Globe and Mail* article in August of 2009, offered a more pragmatic approach to the subject of Native sovereignty. "We have been living a myth in aboriginal policy," said Simpson, "that 'nations,' in the sociological sense of the word, can be effective 'sovereign' entities, in the sense of doing what sovereign governments are expected to do. When the population of a 'nation' is a few hundred people, or even a few thousand, we are kidding ourselves, aboriginal or non-aboriginal, if we think that sovereignty can be anything more than partial."

The Cherokee–Creek scholar Craig Womack is less dismissive and more practical. "Sovereignty, for all its problems and contradictions," says Womack, "is a reality in Indian country, embedded in the U.S. Constitution and two centuries of federal Indian law. In short, it is what Native people have to work with, the hand that has been dealt us. This, of course, does not mean Native people should not dream of more, or even advocate for more, but present realities must also be acknowledged."

One of the realities that Simpson may have missed is that the Navajo in the Southwest, the Blackfoot in Alberta, and the Mohawk on both sides of the border have been looking after their own affairs for some time now. All three tribes have taken control of on-reserve services for health, education, and housing. Meanwhile, the Iroquois have been practicing sovereignty by issuing and using their own Haudenosaunee Confederacy passports.

In 2009, the National Congress of American Indians (NCAI) finished work on the Embassy of Tribal Nations in Washington, D.C. At the opening ceremony, President Jefferson Keel said he expected that the embassy would allow Native people to "more effectively assert their sovereign status and facilitate a much stronger nation-to-nation relationship with the federal government."

Even American President Barack Obama has spoken publicly about the "nation-to-nation relationship" that North America has with Indian tribes.

It all *sounds* good. Of course, government has been only too happy to download services onto reservations and reserves. Ottawa and Washington still control the budgets and set the regulations, while avoiding most of the liabilities. The issuing of passports is a legitimate exercise of sovereignty, but in 2010, when the Iroquois Nationals lacrosse team tried to travel to Manchester for the International Lacrosse Championships on those documents, they were refused entry into England. They had been able to cross from Canada to the United States on their passports, but that was only because Secretary of State Hillary Clinton had interceded in the matter and arranged for a one-time waiver. In the end, however, instead of playing in the tournament, the team wound up watching television at a Comfort Inn in New York.

The Embassy of Tribal Nations is a fine idea, and to hear President Obama speak the word "sovereignty" in the same breath as the word "Indian" is certainly encouraging, even though we all know that political rhetoric has little to do with political action. But more telling, to my way of thinking, is the 2010 radio show during which New York City mayor Michael Bloomberg called on New York governor David Paterson to take a more proactive approach to the state's dispute with the Seneca tribe over the collection of sales tax on cigarettes. "I've said this to David Paterson," said Bloomberg. "Get yourself a cowboy hat and a shot-gun. If there's ever a great video, it's you standing in the middle of the New York State Thruway saying, 'Read my lips—the law of the land is this, and we're going to enforce the law.'"

That Mayor Bloomberg. Such a funny guy. Reminds me a lot of John Wayne in *The Searchers*.

The American historian David Wilkins is direct and to the point. "The relationship," says Wilkins, "between American Indian tribes and the U.S. federal government is an ongoing contest over sovereignty." And while there are no clear winners at this moment, the reality is that, no matter what the historical and legal precedents, neither Canada nor the United States has much enthusiasm for recognizing any varietals of Native sovereignty. Both governments are concerned with cutting the cost of Native Affairs. They are certainly concerned with reducing the Indian estate. But they have shown little interest in prolonging the authority of treaties, and none whatsoever in encouraging stand-alone sovereign or semi-sovereign nations within the borders of either country.

Ask Quebec about that one, if you don't believe me. Or take a refresher course on the American Civil War.

Indeed, one of the contentions currently in vogue is that Native people in North America need to be rescued from reserves and reservations, the Indian Act, the Department of Indian Affairs, and the Bureau of Indian Affairs. Aboriginal people have suffered unduly from government interference and bureaucratic oppression, so the thinking goes, and the only solution is to abrogate treaties, eliminate federal guarantees, divide First Nations land into fee-simple blocks, and allow Native people to participate freely in the economic markets that western capitalism has created.

Tribes are obsolete forms of governance. Treaties are an obstacle to Native–non-Native *rapprochement*.

Rapprochement. There's nothing like a French word thrown in every now and then to give an argument *puissance*.

This is the twenty-first century, after all. We no longer tolerate child labor (family-owned convenience stores don't count). We have done away with public executions. Capital punishment is conducted humanely in state-approved facilities. Women have gained control of their reproductive rights. For the time being, at least. And having made these strides, why should individual enterprise be limited or western civilization's advance be hindered by ancient agreements and promises?

Slade Gorton, the Washington State politician, made a political career out of pursuing a termination vendetta against the tribes in his state and around the nation. In 1998, Gorton sponsored a Senate bill, which he disingenuously called "The American Indian Equal Justice Act." The legislation was a direct attack on tribal sovereignty. Item 8 under "Findings" argued that the idea of Native sovereignty "frustrates and provokes social tensions and turmoil inimical to social peace," while item 9 called on Congress to do away with Indian sovereignty because "no government should be above the law."

The New York Times was not amused. "Senator Slade Gorton," the article said, "has once again declared war on the Indians. Having failed last year to undermine the concept of Indian sovereignty with a sneaky amendment to an appropriations bill, the Washington State Republican has now offered a freestanding bill, erroneously labeled the 'American Indian Equal Justice Act,' that is a reprise of last year's rider."

To his credit, Gorton did not stand with the angry mobs who gathered in Wisconsin in 1989 to throw rocks at Indians and shout racial epithets, including old favorites such as "timber niggers" and newer creations such as "welfare warriors," nor did he hold up one of the signs that said "Save a Fish, Spear a Squaw, Save Two Fish, Spear a Pregnant Squaw."

Still, he probably agreed with Washington State Senator Jack Metcalf's 1983 Senate Joint Memorial that urged Congress to "abrogate all existing treaties," and the resolution that John Fleming introduced at the 2000 Washington State Republican convention that called for the termination of all tribal governments in the state. Fleming bragged that if the tribes resisted such an effort, "then the U.S. Army and the Air Force and the Marines and the National Guard are going to have to battle back." You might want to write Fleming off as a clown and his resolution as a piece of political rhetoric, but the resolution passed on a vote of 248 in favor and 2 against and became part of that state's Republican Party platform.

One of neo-termination's strongest supporters is Thomas Flanagan, a University of Calgary political science professor and author of *First Nations? Second Thoughts* and *Beyond the Indian Act.* Flanagan has little patience with treaties and Native Status, and has argued vigorously, in his role as educator and as an advisor to Prime Minister Stephen Harper, for the dissolution of Indian reserves and federal Status. "Call it assimilation, call it integration, call it adaptation," says Flanagan, "call it whatever you want: it has to happen."

Adherents to Flanagan's particular vision for Indians in the twenty-first century are adamant that Aboriginals should not be entitled to self-determination to any degree, in any form, nor should they receive federal funding or qualify for special tax exemptions. Closing down the Department of Indian Affairs and the Bureau of Indian Affairs, they contend, would save billions of dollars a year. But most of all, these latter-day terminators want tribal lands taken out from under the protections of treaties, turned into fee-simple parcels, and turned loose on the prairies.

Where the properties can be picked off by real estate agents or shot at from moving trains.

All else considered, the main attraction of this line of reasoning is that it is simplistic and requires no negotiation or compromise. Let's get rid of Indians as a legal entity, and let's do it now.

But why would we want to repeat the mistakes of the past? Why drag a failed policy such as termination out of its grave, when history has already shown us that this particular strategy was an utter disaster? For Indians *and* for Whites. Why argue for closing the Department of Indian Affairs or the Bureau of Indian Affairs, or for dismantling the Indian Act, when the problem is not simply the legislation but how it has been interpreted and employed?

Speaking specifically of the Indian Act, Harold Cardinal, in his 1969 best-seller *The Unjust Society*, said, "We do not want the Indian Act retained because it is a good piece of legislation. It isn't. It is discriminatory from start to finish. But it is a lever in our hands and an embarrassment to the government, as it should be. No just society and no society with even pretensions to being just can long tolerate such a piece of legislation, but we would rather continue to live in bondage under the inequitable Indian Act than surrender our sacred rights. Any time the government wants to honor its obligations to us we are more than ready to help devise new Indian legislation."

In 2010, Assembly of First Nations National Chief Shawn Atleo echoed Cardinal's earlier concerns about the Indian Act and began a running discussion on how the Act might be abolished and what would replace it. Atleo points out, quite rightly, that the treaties and the body of Aboriginal rights that have been formally recognized under international law and under section 35 of Canada's 1982 Constitution Act could form a usable structure for a working relationship between First Nations and the federal government. While I haven't heard him say so, this is the same framework that was used in the early days, before the Indian Act and assimilation came along.

It's a great idea, but I don't think it's going to happen. Treaties and Native rights have one fatal flaw: they are predicated on

Aboriginal sovereignty, and while Ottawa and Washington can imagine a world in which federal responsibility for Indians has been eliminated, neither will countenance any deal that revisits the question of Native sovereignty. It took both countries long enough to bury the concept. They're not about to buy a shovel and dig it up.

None of this debate around Native rights, self-determination, and sovereignty is particularly new. Even Ely S. Parker (Seneca), the first Native American to be Commissioner of Indian Affairs, had concerns about Native sovereignty. In his 1869 report, Parker offered that "the Indian tribes of the United States are not sovereign nations, capable of making treaties, as none of them have an organized government of such inherent strength as would secure a faithful obedience of its people in the observance of compacts of this character."

The year before Parker wrote his report, the U.S. government had signed the Treaty of Fort Laramie with the Lakota, which guaranteed them the exclusive use of the Black Hills. Nine years later, after gold had been discovered, Parker watched as non-Natives flooded into the Black Hills, watched as the government stood by unable to "secure a faithful obedience of its people in the observance of compacts of this character." In 1877, Parker was on hand when Washington unilaterally confiscated the Black Hills and turned the land over to the White miners and settlers.

Parker died in 1895. By then, the United States had become quite efficient at breaking the agreements and the promises it had made with Native people. Perhaps by then Parker realized the irony of his earlier observation. Perhaps he understood that sovereignty had little to do with the ability of a nation to control its people.

The wonderful irony of Aboriginal sovereignty is that if we collected the Indian Act, the treaties, the Canadian and U.S. constitutions, the Canadian Charter of Rights and Freedoms, the U.S. Bill of Rights, all the Supreme Court decisions, along with the cases that the Canadian Human Rights Commission has generated, we would have a composite and contradictory manuscript much like the Bible. A manuscript in which both saints and scoundrels can find satisfaction and validation for contrary principles and beliefs in the same passage, where they can find a precedent for every comfort and every larceny.

But perhaps discussing sovereignty as an absolute concept is a waste of time. Perhaps we should concern ourselves instead with practical sovereignty and ask the question, what part of sovereignty is critical to Aboriginal Nations in North America? Each Nation will, of course, have to answer that for itself. However, seeing as my advice is free and as I'm more than happy to give it, I suggest that we concentrate on the issues of tribal membership and resource development. I'd even go further and propose that these two topics may well be two of the more important issues of the twenty-first century for Aboriginal people in North America.

Membership in an Aboriginal Nation is a somewhat bewildering combination of federal legislation, federal treaties and agreements, blood quantum, and nineteenth-century enumeration lists, along with tribal regulations and customs. In Canada, the Indian Act, along with the treaties, sets some of the terms of reference for band membership, while in the United States, membership, in part, is based on federal recognition of a tribe and the lists that the government created to keep track of Aboriginal people.

In Canada, as we saw earlier, Native people are divided, more or less, into three categories: Status Indians, Treaty Indians, and non-Status Indians. In most instances, Status Indians and Treaty Indians are the same. Legal Indians. Non-Status Indians are simply not Indians, or, more accurately, not Legal Indians.

In the United States, Legal Indians are members of a tribe that is recognized by the federal government, while the rest of Native people in that country are, like their counterparts in Canada, not Indians. In fact, with the passage of the Indian Arts and Crafts Act in 1990, Native artists who produce and sell their work cannot call themselves by their tribal affiliation unless they are official members of the tribe. To do so is to risk fines of up to $250,000.

The Arts and Crafts Act was designed to stop the trade in counterfeit "Native art" that unscrupulous dealers were bringing in from places such as Japan, Taiwan, Korea, and India, and in this regard, the act was a welcome law. But the unfortunate side effect of the act was to "terminate" a great many Native artists who were Indians by blood but who, for a variety of reasons, were not official members of a tribe. Many of them had home communities. Many of them had blood relatives living in those communities. Yet under the terms of the act, they could be prosecuted for claiming they were who they were because, legally, they weren't.

Jimmie Durham is one such artist. He's Cherokee, but because he can't legally say he's Cherokee, he's not. I probably shouldn't have mentioned this since it may be illegal for me to . . . you know, say this. Durham himself is somewhat circumspect about the issue of identity. "I'm a full-blood contemporary artist," says Durham, "of the sub-group (or clan) called sculptors . . . I am not a 'Native American,' nor do I feel that 'America' has any right to either name me or un-name me. I have previously stated that I should be considered a mixed-blood: that is, I claim to be a male but in fact only one of my parents was male."

Today, almost all Aboriginal Nations control their memberships. While the rules and regulations differ from tribe to tribe, band to band, the general requirement is that a blood relationship exist between a registered Indian or an ancestor on the tribal rolls and an individual seeking membership. Sometimes there is a blood-quantum requirement as well. The Blackfoot in Alberta and the Comanche in Oklahoma, for example, currently require that, in addition to a blood tie, their members be at least one-quarter blood. But they could, if they wished, lower that blood-quantum requirement or dispense with it altogether. This is what the Ottawa, Seminole, Wyandot, Creek, Choctaw, and Chickasaw have done. For these tribes and others, any descendant of a tribal member is also entitled to be a member of the tribe, regardless of blood quantum.

But there can be other factors as well. The Cherokee, for example, have fifteen tribal rolls that were created between 1817 and 1914. A great many Cherokee can trace their family back to a name on one of these rolls, but unless your ancestor appears on the 1924 Baker rolls that cover the Eastern Cherokee or the 1898–1914 Dawes–Gaion–Miller rolls that cover the Western Cherokee, you cannot qualify for membership in one of the three federally recognized Cherokee tribes: the Eastern Cherokee, the Western Cherokee, and the United Keetoowah Band. Neither the Baker nor the Dawes–Gaion–Miller rolls are a comprehensive or complete compilation of Cherokee families,

but these rolls are the only sources that the tribe uses for deter-
mining who can be a citizen of the nation.

The Keetoowah, to complicate things further, require that a
member be one-quarter blood and have an ancestor on either the
Dawes rolls or the United Keetoowah Band Base Roll, which was
created in 1949. Up until about 1994, the Keetoowah also gave
associate memberships to Cherokees who could not demonstrate via
the rolls that they were Cherokee, and they gave associate memberships to folks who were famous or influential, such as Bill Clinton.
Some of the associate members were given an enrollment card
with a number, but these associate members could not appear
on the official Keetoowah tribal rolls, nor could they receive any
federal benefits.

Just in case you thought membership in a Native Nation was a
straightforward thing.

Currently, the trend among bands and tribes in North America
is to try to limit membership. The land base and the resources that
Native people control are finite. But Aboriginal populations continue to grow, and the thinking is that tribal assets should only be
used for the benefit of those who are "authentic," a term that is
fraught with dangerous assumptions and consequences. Among the
Cherokee, you have Cherokees who are Cherokee by blood and who
have an ancestor on the required rolls, and you have Cherokees who
are Cherokee by blood but whose ancestors were not listed on the
required rolls. The one group is "authentic." The other group is not.

To my way of thinking, such a distinction is self-serving and
self-defeating at the same time.

In Canada, where First Nations people are defined by the Indian
Act, there is currently no possibility for creating new Status

Indians, apart from birth. Bands may grant membership to non-Status Indians and even to non-Indians, and it's possible that these individuals could be given the right to vote in band elections and allowed to live on Indian land (though the jury is still out on the question of residency), but they could not share in any benefits that came to the tribe by way of the Indian Act or a treaty.

Sovereignty allows that Aboriginal Nations can either erect barriers to membership or lower those barriers and create new opportunities for citizenship. There are arguments to be made for both of these approaches. Barriers can create security. Numbers can create strength. In the twenty-first-century conversation around tribal membership, I hope that Aboriginal Nations use this sovereign power with intelligence and generosity.

After membership, the second question that Native people have to consider with regards to sovereignty is how we go about creating an economic base for reserves and reservations. If the statistics are correct, there are almost as many Native people on reserves as off reserves, and while off-reservation Native-run businesses are important to the overall health of Native as well as non-Native communities, the development and expansion of on-reservation enterprise is critical if we expect to maintain our communities and our land base.

Up to this point, while reserves and reservations with a large land base have had more economic choices than those with a small land base, the range of the choices itself has been limited. And some of the choices have been downright disquieting.

Garbage dumps, for example.

In the late 1980s and 1990s, North America decided that Native land would be a perfect place to dump its garbage. Waste management companies that handle everything from nonhazardous materials to nuclear waste began riding into Indian country armed with beads and promises, hell-bent on convincing tribal leaders that turning part of the reservation into a landfill was good economics. This scenario made for excellent theater of the absurd, with the waste management companies suddenly championing Native rights and tribal sovereignty. Not that these com panies gave a damn about Native sovereignty. But they *were* excited by the prospect that the legal status of Indian land might protect them from the tyranny of environmental regulations.

I don't want to suggest that Native communities were simply victims in this or that they were completely opposed to the enterprise of garbage disposal. Many reservations were so poor that any business was good business. From small tribes such as the Campo Band of Mission Indians just outside San Diego to larger groups such as the Chickasaw and Sauk and Fox in Oklahoma, the Yakama in Washington, and the Mescalero Apache in New Mexico, First Nations began approaching companies on their own to talk about joint ventures that would create commercial landfills on trust land and generate much-needed money for the community.

The garbage issue was, as might be expected, controversial, and the debate split many of the tribes. What was mildly amusing was watching environmentalists and concerned non-Natives lecture Indians on traditional beliefs and ethical standards. While Native people have, for a long time now, been adversely affected by White development near reservations and reserves— the mercury poisonings at Grassy Narrows in northern Ontario, the General Motors landfill near Akwesasne, the draining of

Pyramid Lake in Nevada, the Kinzua Dam in Pennsylvania—the level of concern seems far greater, the reaction more intense, when White communities are faced with the consequences of Native development.

John Dossett, the general counsel for the National Congress of American Indians, sees the land-use battles as a reflection of race and privilege. "It is more than a little unfair," says Dossett, "that tribes, who have been among the last to receive the benefits of economic development, would be expected to keep their lands pristine while everyone has developed all around them."

For a tribe such as the Navajo, the benefits of economic development and the need to protect the land are parts of a long-running deliberation. So far, economic development has carried the day. The Navajo have, since the 1940s, been involved in resource mining. While most of Navajo country is desert, it is also home to major deposits of uranium and even larger deposits of coal. In 1948, the U.S. Atomic Energy Commission set off a mining boom in New Mexico, Colorado, Utah, and Arizona when it announced that it would purchase all uranium ore at a guaranteed price.

Uranium meant jobs for the Navajo. No one talked about the hazards of uranium, though the science in and around radon gas, particularly by the 1950s, was reasonably well established. Nor did anyone discuss with the tribe the bottom-line costs to the environment and to the lives of the people who worked in the mines.

Then in March 1979, a few months after the partial meltdown of the nuclear reactor at Three Mile Island in Pennsylvania, a dam at the United Nuclear Corporation's Church Rock facility in New Mexico, on the edge of the Navajo reservation, collapsed, and over 1,100 tons of radioactive waste and 93 million gallons of mine effluent poured into the Puerco River, permanently contaminating the river and the water supply.

Three Mile Island got all the press, but Church Rock was a much larger ecological disaster, and when the Navajo finally banned uranium and uranium processing on the reservation in 2005, all they were left with for their efforts at creating a working economy was a deadly legacy of contaminated tailings, polluted water supplies, abandoned mines, and chronic illness.

In addition to uranium deposits, the Navajo Nation has one of the largest coal-mining operations in the world. The royalties that the Navajo receive from Peabody Energy account for most of the tribe's annual budget. As well, coal mining, along with the attendant industries, provides jobs for thousands of Navajo.

But as with uranium, the downside of this industry is huge. If anything, coal is even more polluting than uranium. The Four Corners power plant, which came on line in 1963, operates outside normal regulations, without any significant limits on its emissions. By any measure, Four Corners is an environmental nightmare, emitting over 15 million tons of sulfur dioxide, nitrogen oxides, and carbon dioxides each year, as well as some 600 pounds of mercury. No other power plant in the United States puts more pollutants into the air and the water than Four Corners. It's in a category all by itself. The Navajo and Hopi reservations used to have some of the cleanest air in the country. Now, because of Four Corners and the other coal-burning power plants in the Southwest, air pollution on the reservations is at least ten times worse than in a city such as Los Angeles.

I have great concerns about resource mining on Native lands, and I don't much like the idea of reserves and reservations being

used as landfills. It all feels too much like *Colonialism: Part Two*.
I understand that these projects generate much-needed revenues
for many Aboriginal communities who are living at poverty
levels. But I also know that once the resource is gone and the
dumps are filled, all that Native people will have to pass on to
their children will be a blasted and poisoned landscape.

There has been a great deal of talk about the prospects of solar,
wind, and tidal-surge energy on Indian reserves and reservations.
The Laguna Pueblo in New Mexico, the Cowessess First Nation
in Saskatchewan, the Assiniboine and the Sioux in Fort Peck,
Montana, the Blackfeet in Browning, Montana, the T'Sou-ke
Nation near Sooke, British Columbia, the Spirit Lake Sioux at
Fort Totten, North Dakota, and the M'Chigeeng First Nation
and the Wikwemikong First Nation on Manitoulin Island are all
engaged in renewable-energy projects that may make the transition from demonstration projects to full-blown industries.

Which brings us back to the previous chapter and the growth
of Aboriginal gaming. Compared to commercial landfills,
resource mining, aluminum processing, nuclear-waste storage,
and waste incineration, Indian ventures in gaming and tourism
are relatively pristine activities with a limited impact on the
physical environment.

But I'm not going to suggest that the economic development
of Aboriginal resorts and casinos is an improvement. The potential downside of gaming—alcohol, drugs, prostitution, gambling
addiction, organized crime—may be just as damaging as a toxic
holding pond. But casinos and the large amounts of money that
they generate have allowed certain tribes to do something I never
thought I'd ever see.

I knew that Indian gaming was big business. I knew that many casinos were making a healthy profit from slot machines, bingos, blackjack, and the like. What I didn't know was what tribes were doing with the profits. I assumed that band councils were giving part of the profits to the members of the tribe as per capita payments or spending it on much-needed infrastructure or buying stocks and bonds as long-term investments.

And they were. But they were also buying land.

In upstate New York, the Oneida Nation has used some of the money made from its Turning Stone Resort and Casino to purchase over 17,000 acres of land. In Minnesota, the Shakopee Sioux have taken money from their Mystic Lake Casino Hotel, have bought 750 acres, and are looking at another 1,000 acres. The Cherokee in Oklahoma have purchased acreage along the major highways in that state, while the Sycuan Band of the Kumeyaay Nation in southern California is buying up land in downtown San Diego and the surrounding area.

But instead of pursuing the American dream of accumulating land as personal wealth, the tribes have taken their purchases to the Secretary of the Interior and requested that the land they acquired be added to their respective reservations and given trust status. This is not merely a return to a communal past. It is a shrewd move to preserve and expand an indigenous land base for the benefit of future generations.

This type of purchase and conversion is now being emulated by tribes across the United States. In 2003, the Tohono O'odham Nation purchased a 130-acre parcel of land in Glendale, Arizona. The land was converted from fee simple to trust land, and the tribe is making plans to build a $600 million casino on the site.

This acquisition has caused no small amount of consternation for politicians in Glendale, who watched as a perfectly good block of fee-simple land was taken out of local and state control and removed from the tax base.

Raising the Western specter of wild and uncontrolled Indians, Craig Tindall, the city attorney, warned, "As soon as people step off that land into our jurisdiction, we have to deal with them. Whatever condition they are in, when they come off that land, it's up to us."

I had assumed that the "people" Tindall was talking about were Indians, and that his comments were just an intemperate outburst. But now that I think about it, I wonder if he was expressing concern about White Glendalians returning to the city after an evening of fun and frolic at the Tohono O'odham Nation casino.

The fact that the casino will create a great many permanent jobs and stimulate the local economy has not been lost on city planners, but the thought of a reservation on the edge of Glendale has been too much for local bureaucrats. In 2010, the city sued the federal government, charging that the 1986 federal law that allowed the Tohono O'odham as well as other tribes to acquire new reservation property was unconstitutional. But I shouldn't pick on Glendale. All around America, local reaction to tribes buying up property and having the land converted to trust status has been predominantly negative.

Almost 150 years ago, then Secretary of the Interior Carl Schurz said: "Many treaty reservations have turned out to be of greater value in agricultural and mineral resources than they were originally thought to be, and are now eagerly coveted by the white population. . . . It is argued that the Indians cannot and will not develop these resources; that the country cannot afford to maintain large and valuable districts in a state of waste. . . . This demand becomes more pressing every year, and although in many cases urged entirely without regard to abstract justice, it is a fact . . . which must be taken into account in shaping an Indian policy."

This nineteenth-century complaint that Native people weren't using their land base and developing their resources in an acceptable fashion and the veiled warning that Indian land was "eagerly coveted by the white population" remain potent factors in contemporary Indian–White politics. Glendale's anger is not simply over the new reservation and casino at the edge of town. It is over the fact that the land in question is owned by Indians and no longer available to the city.

So far, reserves in Canada have not tried to follow the American example. Any expansion of First Nation lands would have to come via land-claim settlements or parliamentary decrees. But it would be interesting to see what might happen if, for example, the Ojibway at Rama bought up some of the land on the outskirts of Orillia, Ontario, and attempted to expand their reserve.

This new twist on land has just begun to play its way through the courts in the United States and may not be settled in my lifetime. However the matter turns out, I can't help but enjoy the irony. North Americans, all along, have believed that private ownership of land would turn Indians into Whites, while Native people have learned that the control of land can allow us to remain ourselves.

What remains distressing is that much of what passes for public and political discourse on the future of Native people is a discourse of anger, anger that Native people are still here and still a "problem" for White North America, anger that we have something non-Natives don't have, anger that after all the years of training, after all the years of having assimilation beaten into us, we still prefer to remain Cree and Comanche, Seminole and Salish, Haida and Hopi, Blackfoot and Bellacoola.

All of which brings us to the perennial North American question. Just what is it that Indians want? Sovereignty? Self-determination? A future? Good jobs? A late-model pickup truck? I get asked that question all the time. What do Indians want? The good news is that you could choose from any of the above and be right.

And you'd be wrong.

9

AS LONG AS THE GRASS
IS GREEN

Buy land. They ain't making any more of the stuff.

—Will Rogers

What do Indians want?

Great question. The problem is, it's the wrong question to ask. While there are certainly Indians in North America, the Indians of this particular question don't exist. The Indians of this question are "the Indian" that Canada and the United States have created for themselves. And as long as the question is asked in that way, there will never be the possibility of an answer. Better to ask what the Lubicon Cree of Alberta want or the Brantford Mohawk of Ontario or the Zuni of New Mexico or the Hupa of northern California or the Tlingit of Alaska.

But I'd just as soon forget the question entirely. There's a better question to ask. One that will help us to understand the nature of contemporary North American Indian history. A question that we can ask of both the past and the present.

What do Whites want?

No, it's not a trick question. And I'm not being sarcastic. Native history in North America as writ has never really been about Native people. It's been about Whites and their needs and desires. What Native peoples wanted has never been a vital concern, has never been a political or social priority.

The Lakota didn't want Europeans in the Black Hills, but Whites wanted the gold that was there. The Cherokee didn't want to move from Georgia to Indian Territory (Oklahoma), but Whites wanted the land. The Cree of Quebec weren't at all keen on vacating their homes to make way for the Great Whale project, but there's excellent money in hydroelectric power. The California Indians did not ask to be enslaved by the Franciscans and forced to build that order's missions.

What do Whites want?

The answer is quite simple, and it's been in plain sight all along. Land.

Whites want land.

Sure, Whites want Indians to disappear, and they want Indians to assimilate, and they want Indians to understand that everything that Whites have done was for their own good because Native people, left to their own devices, couldn't make good decisions for themselves.

All that's true. From a White point of view at least. But it's a lower order of true. It's a spur-of-the-moment true, and these ideas have changed over time. Assimilation was good in the 1950s but bad in the 1970s. Residential schools were the answer to

Indian education in the 1920s, but by the twenty-first century governments were apologizing for the abuse that Native children had suffered at the hands of Christian doctrinaires, pedophiles, and sadists. In the 1880s, the prevailing wisdom was to destroy Native cultures and languages so that Indians could find civilization. Today, the non-Native lament is that Aboriginal cultures and languages may well be on the verge of extinction. These are all important matters, but if you pay more attention to them than they deserve, you will miss the larger issue.

The issue that came ashore with the French and the English and the Spanish, the issue that was the *raison d'être* for each of the colonies, the issue that has made its way from coast to coast to coast and is with us today, the issue that has never changed, never varied, never faltered in its resolve is the issue of land. The issue has always been land. It will always be land, until there isn't a square foot of land left in North America that is controlled by Native people.

At the Lake Mohonk conference in October of 1886, one of the participants, Charles Cornelius Coffin Painter, who served as a lobbyist for the Indian Rights Association, pointed out the obvious, that the treaties made with Native people had been little more than expediencies. In his talk, Painter quoted General William Tecumseh Sherman, who had said that treaties "were never made to be kept, but to serve a present purpose, to settle a present difficulty in the easiest manner possible, to acquire a desired good with the least possible compensation, and then to be disregarded as soon as this purpose was tainted and we were strong enough to enforce a new and more profitable arrangement."

This is the same General Sherman who philosophized that "The more Indians we kill this year, the fewer we will need to kill the next."

Painter didn't necessarily agree with Sherman, but he understood that the overall goal of removals, allotments, treaties, reservations and reserves, terminations, and relocations was not simply to limit and control the movement of Native peoples, but more important to relieve them of their land base.

Land. If you understand nothing else about the history of Indians in North America, you need to understand that the question that really matters is the question of land.

Land has always been a defining element of Aboriginal culture. Land contains the languages, the stories, and the histories of a people. It provides water, air, shelter, and food. Land participates in the ceremonies and the songs. And land is home. Not in an abstract way. The Blackfoot in Alberta live in the shadow of Ninastiko or Chief Mountain. The mountain is a special place for the Blackfoot, and friends on the reserve at Standoff have told me more than once that, as long as they can see the mountain, they know they are home.

For non-Natives, land is primarily a commodity, something that has value for what you can take from it or what you can get for it.

Helen thinks that this is a gross generalization. She believes that there are all sorts of people in Canada who have a deep attachment to land that extends beyond the family cottage on the lake, and that there are Native people who have little connection to a particular geography. I don't disagree. Individuals can fool you, and they can surprise you. What I'm talking about here is North America's societal attitude toward land.

The Alberta Tar Sands is an excellent example of a non-Native understanding of land. It is, without question, the dirtiest, most environmentally insane energy-extraction project in North America, probably in the world, but the companies that are destroying landscapes and watersheds in Alberta continue merrily along, tearing up the earth because there are billions to be made out of such corporate devastation. The public has been noticeably quiet about the matter, and neither the politicians in Alberta nor the folks in Ottawa have been willing to step in and say "Enough," because, in North American society, when it comes to money, there is no such thing as enough.

We all know the facts and figures. Carbon emissions from the production of one barrel of tar sands oil are eight times higher than the emissions from a conventional barrel. The production of each barrel of tar sands oil requires at least three barrels of fresh water, 90 percent of which never makes it back into the watershed. The waste water winds up in a series of enormous tailing ponds that cover some fifty square kilometers and is so poisonous that it kills on contact. It is only a matter of time before one or more of the earthen dams that hold these ponds in place collapse and the toxic sludge is dumped into the Athabasca River.

Just as disturbing are the surreal structures that have begun to appear on the Alberta landscape. Sulfur, a by-product of the bitumen-to-oil process, is being turned into large blocks and stacked in high-rise piles on the prairies because no one knows what else to do with it. Predictably, these blocks are slowly decomposing, allowing the sulfur to leech out and spoil the ground water.

Yet, in spite of all the scientific evidence, oil corporations, with the aid and abetment of government, are expanding their operations, breaking new ground, as it were, and building thousands of miles of pipeline—the Keystone Pipeline, the Northern Gateway Pipeline, the Transmountain Pipeline—that will take Alberta crude from Fort McMurray to refineries and markets in the United States (Illinois, Oklahoma, and Texas) and in Canada (Kitimat and Vancouver).

I know, I know, there are organizations that have been fighting this kind of ecocide for years, but unfortunately, they constitute only a small portion of the overall population. To be sure, they have had the occasional success, but there is little chance that North America will develop a functional land ethic until it finds a way to overcome its irrational addiction to profit. Unfortunately, there are no signs that that's going to happen any time soon.

In 1868 the Lakota and the U.S. government signed a peace treaty at Fort Laramie, which guaranteed that the Black Hills would remain with the Lakota Nation and that the Powder River Country in northeastern Wyoming would be closed to White settlement. However, just six years later, in 1874, an army expedition led by, of all people, George Armstrong Custer discovered gold in the Black Hills at French Creek, and before you could say "Fort Laramie Treaty," White miners swarmed into the Black Hills and began digging mines, sluicing rivers, blasting away the sides of mountains with hydraulic cannons, and clear-cutting the forests in the Hills for the timber. The army was supposed to keep Whites out of the Hills. But they didn't. A great many histories will tell you that the military was powerless to stop the flood of Whites who came to the Hills for the gold, but the truth of the matter is that the army didn't really try.

By the spring of 1875, the situation had become untenable, and the Lakota went to Washington to try to persuade President Grant to honor the treaty that the two nations had signed. The Lakota wanted Whites out of the Black Hills. They wanted the destruction of their forests and rivers stopped. They wanted the Hills left alone. Instead, the administration told the Lakota that a new treaty was needed, one in which the Lakota would have to give up all claim to the Black Hills for the princely sum of $25,000, and that the tribe would have to move to Indian Territory.

The Lakota refused to sign a new treaty. You can keep your money, they told Grant. And of the move to Indian Territory, Spotted Tail said that "If it [Indian Territory] is such a good country, you ought to send the white men now in our country there and let us alone."

The Fort Laramie Treaty still stands as a valid agreement, and the Lakota have never given up their claim to the Hills, nor have they stopped fighting for the land's return. So I can only imagine how they felt as they watched Six Grandfathers being turned into a national tourist attraction.

Six Grandfathers is the mountain in the Hills that became Mount Rushmore after it was renamed for a New York lawyer in 1885. From 1927 to 1941, the American sculptor Gutzon Borglum chiselled and hacked and blasted the rock face, until the granite looked remarkably like the faces of George Washington, Thomas Jefferson, Theodore Roosevelt, and Abraham Lincoln.

The Lakota, for whom the mountain is sacred, must have been particularly pleased with the dandy new artwork.

Then in 1980, in *United States v. Sioux Nation of Indians*, the Supreme Court ruled that the Black Hills had been illegally taken. The solution, however, wasn't to return the Hills to the Lakota. Instead the court instructed that the original purchase price of $25,000 plus interest be paid to the tribe. After the long addition was over, the total came to over $106 million.

$106 million.

And as they had done in 1875, the Lakota refused the settlement. Money was never the issue. They wanted the Hills back. As for the money, it stays in an interest-bearing account to this day.

Alberta Tar Sands. Black Hills. So much for Helen's spurious objection.

Oh, sure, two examples do not a treatise make, and I'm confident someone can find instances where tribes have engaged in what could be seen as dubious enterprises in the area of land husbandry. In fact, let me help you. The Navajo and the Crow have leases with companies to strip-mine coal on their respective reservations. The Cree in Quebec signed agreements that led to the damming of the Great Whale River for hydroelectric power. Tribes in the Northwest and British Columbia have parlayed their timber holdings and fishing rights into nascent economies.

I would like to make the point that there is a difference between depredation and development, but I'm forced to admit that I probably couldn't draw a line between the two clear enough for all parties to agree.

So, Helen may be right. As for me, I still find it impossible to imagine the Alberta Tar Sands ever coming out of an Aboriginal ethos.

One of the problems in any discussion about Indian land is that you also have to talk about treaties. In North American Indian history, land and treaties are so tightly intertwined that it is hardly possible to separate them. It is no coincidence then that, while the relationship that Native people have with Canada and the United States contains both historical and social aspects, the primary relationship is legal.

Remember our earlier chat about Legal Indians?

From a Native perspective, Indian land is Indian land. From a contemporary, somewhat legal North American perspective, Native land is land that belongs to the federal government and is on indefinite loan to a certain category of Native people. To say that these two views are in conflict is to state the obvious.

Indian land as Indian land was certainly the idea behind early treaties and agreements. But by the middle of the nineteenth century, new attitudes had taken over, and a treaty such as the one struck with the Yanktonai band of the Dakota at Fort Sully in 1865 stipulated, "Any amendment or modification of this treaty by the Senate of the United States shall be considered final and binding upon the said band, represented in council, as a part of this treaty, in the same manner as if it had been subsequently presented and agreed to by the chiefs and head-men of said band."

One of the great phrases to come out of the treaty process is "as long as the grass is green and the waters run." The general idea behind the phrase is not new. Charlemagne supposedly used such language in the eighth century, when he declared that "all Frisians would be fully free, the born and the unborn, so long as the wind blows from heaven and the child cries, grass grows green and flowers bloom, as far as the sun rises and the world stands."

Great Britain, the United States, and Canada, depending on how you want to count, signed well over 400 treaties with Native tribes in North America. I haven't read them all, but none of the ones I have read contains the phrase. So, I've always wondered if "as long as the grass is green and the waters run" was ever actually used in a treaty.

I know that Andrew Jackson promised the Choctaw and Cherokee that, if they left their lands east of the Mississippi and moved west of the river, "There beyond the limits of any state, in possession of land of their own, which they shall possess as long as grass grows or water runs, I am and will protect them and be their friend and father." And I know that over a century later, in 1978, David Sohappy Sr., a Yakama fisherman, said that he had been told by elders that the 1855 treaty with the Yakama had come with the promise that the treaty would last so long as Mount Adams was standing and so long "as the sun rose in the east and long as the grass grows green in the spring and rivers flow."

I'm betting that poetic constructions such as "as long as the grass is green and the waters run," "Great White Father," and "Red Children" were part of the performances, the speeches, and the oral promises that attended treaty negotiations and did not necessarily find their way into the official transcript. While a phrase such as "the hatchet shall be forever buried" does appear in Article 13 of the treaty the Cherokee signed in 1785, I suspect that, in general, lawyers and politicians were not comfortable with metaphors. As a rule, easily understood language is not welcome in legal documents.

Treaties, after all, were not vehicles for protecting land or even sharing land. They were vehicles for acquiring land. Almost without fail, throughout the history of North America, every time Indians signed a treaty with Whites, Indians lost land. I can't think of a single treaty whereby Native people came away with more land than when they started. Such an idea, from a non-Native point of view, would have been dangerously absurd.

In fact, treaties have been so successful in separating Indians from their land that I'm surprised there isn't a national holiday to honor their good work. But we could fix that. We could, if we were so inclined, turn Columbus Day and Victoria Day into Treaty Day. After all, Columbus didn't discover America, and Queen Victoria never set foot in Canada. Folks in the United States would get a day off in October, just as the leaves were turning color in New England, and folks in Canada—perhaps even in Quebec—would get a day off in May, just as most of the snow had melted. We could encourage schoolchildren in both countries to memorize the top ten treaties in terms of land acquisition, and turn that knowledge into a contest. Maybe get the Blackfoot to donate ten acres of reserve land along the Old Man River as first prize.

Of course, no one in Canada or the United States is going to support a holiday that isn't a celebration of national power and generosity, so we'd have to disguise it, much the way we do Thanksgiving.

There it is. Treaty Day. I'd do my part. Read Robert Frost's poem "The Gift Outright." Sing a few verses of Woody Guthrie's "This Land Is Your Land" as part of the festivities.

Now I don't want to give anyone the impression that I think treaties are a bad idea. Treaties aren't the problem. Keeping the promises made in the treaties, on the other hand, is a different matter.

One of the complaints that Whites have had about Aboriginal people is that they didn't know what to do with land, or that they weren't using the land to its full potential. And North America has been quick to rally around the old aphorism "use it or lose it." Ironically, Canada currently finds itself in a pseudo-Native position with regard to the far north. Knowing that the Arctic is a treasure trove of oil and gas, minerals and precious metals, and fish, the United States has been pushing jurisdictional boundaries, insisting that the Northwest Passage is an international waterway rather than a part of Canada. In 1969, the United States sent the S. S. *Manhattan* to sail into the Passage without first getting Canadian permission. In 1985, the U.S. icebreaker *Polar Sea* did the same thing. Nasty words flew back and forth. One solution to this problem that is being bandied about is to strike a treaty, wherein the United States recognizes the Passage as Canadian waters and Canada gives the United States the right to travel the waterway unimpeded.

A treaty with the United States. That should work out well.

Lost in all of this gunship diplomacy was the 1953 saga of eighty-seven Inuit who were moved from Port Harrison to Grise Fiord. The official reason Canadian bureaucrats gave for the move was that it would allow the Inuit to continue to live off the land and maintain their traditional ways. The unofficial reason was that Canada wanted to use the Inuit as placeholders in the continuing debate over who had territorial rights to the High Arctic and its resources. The government has always maintained that the families who relocated did so voluntarily, while the Inuit maintain that the moves were forced.

Wherever the truth lies, it is amusing to watch politicians validating Canada's land claims in the far north on the backs of Aboriginal people. It's ours, Ottawa tells the world. Our people are there.

When it comes to the matter of land, one of the key questions is: "What is the proper use of land?" This is both a historical and a contemporary consideration in Native rights. In the early days, hunting and gathering were seen as inferior uses of the land compared to farming. Where Indians did farm, their farming practices were considered inferior to those of Whites. And these days, heaven help the tribe or band that wishes to keep a section of land in its natural state when a golf course or a ski resort or a strip mine comes looking for a home.

Sometimes a close reading of history is helpful in understanding the question of land, and sometimes representative stories will do just as well. Personally, I prefer stories. And I happen to have several that you might consider.

One.

In 1942, during World War II, the Government of Canada went looking around for a place to set up a military-training base. Surprise of surprises, they found such a site on the Stoney Point Ojibway reserve in Ontario.

Ipperwash.

The government offered the band fifteen dollars an acre for the land. The band refused, and the government confiscated the land with the explicit promise to return it after the war.

I should mention that wars have provided excellent opportunities for the theft of Indian land. The Stoney Point Ojibway were not the only people to have land confiscated in the interests of a war effort. In 1917, in the dead of winter, the U.S. Army moved the Nisqually out of their homes in Washington State and "condemned" more than two-thirds of the reservation. Then the land was transferred to the U.S. Department of War, which used the gift of 3,300 acres to expand Fort Lewis and construct an artillery range.

Further west on the prairies following World War I, amendments to the Indian Act in 1918 gave Canada's Department of Indian Affairs the power to lease band land and give it to non-Natives for proper cultivation. "We would be only too glad to have the Indian use this land, if he would," lamented Arthur Meighen, the Minister of the Interior and Superintendent of Indian Affairs. "But he will not cultivate this land, and we want to cultivate it; that is all."

But back to Ipperwash. The war came and went as wars will do, yet the land was not returned. Over the years, at various times, the Stoney Point Ojibway protested the original confiscation, and, in 1996, that protest took on a new life.

In September of that year, about thirty-five Natives took over the park to call attention to the long-standing land claim. At first, things were reasonably peaceful. And then harsh words were exchanged. An Ontario Provincial Police cruiser had its window smashed. A band councillor had a rock thrown at his car. One story about a woman in a car being attacked with a baseball bat proved to be a fabrication by the police, supposedly for public relations reasons. The pushing and shoving escalated, and the confrontation came to a head with police firing on a car and a school bus, wounding two of the Native protesters and killing Dudley George.

I must admit, I know little about Ipperwash. I've never been to the park. What I know of the confrontation that led to Dudley George's death, I know from newspaper and television reports, and I have always had a problem trusting those accounts. But I did have an interesting conversation with a government official a year or so after the tragedy.

I had gone to Ottawa to give a lecture, and, on the flight back to Toronto, I sat next to a fellow who was actually involved with the Stoney Point Ojibway land claim at Ipperwash. He had heard me speak and wanted to get my opinion on the matter. Now, it's not every day that I get asked by the government for my opinion. Helen hardly ever asks me for my opinion. So, I was flattered.

Ask away, I said.

Ipperwash, he agreed, had been part of the Stoney Point Ojibway reserve, and it had been taken as part of the war effort, and with the war long gone and the military-training base dismantled, the perception, on the part of the Ojibway certainly, was that the land should be returned. However, the official told me, besides the problem of public perception—the government returning land to Indians, no matter what the circumstances, was not a vote-getter—there was the problem of live ordinance. Because the land had been used as a military range, there were unexploded shells and nasty whatnots in the ground, which made some areas dangerous.

What are we supposed to do about that? the official wanted to know. How could the government, in good faith, return land that was unsafe to the Ojibway?

I suggested that the government clean up the land and then return it. The government didn't make the mess, the man told me, the Army did.

Now, in my house, if you make a mess, you clean it up. Most of the time.

Okay, I said, have the Army clean it up.

They don't have enough money in their budget to do that.

Then put the money in their budget.

If we do, they'll just spend it on things that are higher priorities.

It was a pleasant conversation, and, the more we talked, the more I felt as though I were talking to a bowl of Jello. By the time we landed, I realized that I wasn't being asked *how* the land could be given back so much as I was being given a briefing on *why* that wasn't going to happen.

The real problem, the official told me as we sat next to each other on the plane, is the "cultural recalcitrance" of the Ojibway. The hostile feelings, the takeover of the park, the killing of Dudley George could all have been avoided if the Ojibway had simply sold the land to the government in the first place.

Well, that's certainly one way to look at it.

Since that conversation, the government of Ontario, in 2007, did announce that it plans to return the fifty-six-hectare park to the Chippewa of Kettle and Stony Point First Nation, though not right away. In May of 2009, a transfer-process agreement was signed stipulating a full transfer of the land within a year. In 2010, legislation was passed to deregulate the park lands, a legal move that was supposed to be the next step in actually returning the land. By May of 2012, nothing more had happened. Though the cleanup of the old military base had begun, the bottom line remains the same. The land still hasn't been returned.

Two.

Kinzua Dam, in the Allegheny National Forest in Pennsylvania, is one of the largest dams east of the Mississippi River. Work on the dam began in 1960 and was finished in 1965. The dam cost more than $120 million and is over 1,900 feet long and 179 feet high.

The main purpose of the dam is to control the Allegheny River while, at the same time, providing hydroelectric power for homes and industry, and places for folks with leisure time on their hands to park their boats. The reservoir that the dam created is twenty-seven miles long and has about ninety miles of shoreline.

The dam created the deepest lake in Pennsylvania, around

130 feet deep, and at the bottom of that lake is the Seneca Indian reservation.

The reservation wasn't supposed to be at the bottom of the reservoir. The Seneca had signed a peace treaty with the United States that guaranteed this particular piece of land for the Seneca. Article Three of the 1794 treaty allowed that "the United States acknowledge all the land within the aforementioned boundaries, to be the property of the Sencka nation; and the United States will never claim the same, nor disturb the Seneka nation."

That was 1794. So in 1956, the Seneca were probably surprised to learn that Congress had appropriated funds to build a dam on their land. The government had held hearings. The Army Corps of Engineers had briefed all of the interested parties. Except the Seneca. No one invited the Seneca to the hearings. They weren't even advised that hearings were being held. They found out about the dam project after the fact.

The tribe immediately filed a number of injunctions to stop the project, and, at the same time, in a rather savvy move, hired two well-known engineers, Arthur Morgan, who had been chair of the Tennessee Valley Authority, and Barton Jones, who had been responsible for the building of the Norris Dam within the TVA complex. Morgan and Jones were to look at the proposed dam to see if there was an alternative site that would serve the project without breaking the treaty and forcing the Seneca to move. Morgan found such a site, but the Army Corps of Engineers was not keen on changing its plans, and instead of looking at the new site in any detail, they forged ahead, pushing the dam project through Congress and condemning the Seneca reservation by right of eminent domain.

In 1961, the Seneca went as far as to write President John F. Kennedy, requesting that he terminate the project. I'm guessing that the Seneca supposed that Kennedy might be a sympathetic ear. After all, he had made all sorts of encouraging noises about civil rights and had lectured the Russians and other countries on the need to honor treaties.

Just not Indian treaties.

Alvin Josephy, in his book *Now That the Buffalo's Gone*, argues that the Seneca had a large number of supporters in Congress who tried to get the dam site moved so the Seneca could stay where they were, but that the forces massed against the Seneca, led by the Army Corp of Engineers, were simply too great to overcome.

I don't doubt that Josephy is correct. But I also know enough about money and politics to say that much of the public support for the Seneca and a good deal of the hand-wringing on the part of politicians was probably just for show. Treaty or no, I can't imagine that many folks in Washington really gave a damn whether or not Seneca land wound up on the bottom of a lake.

I know that's a rather cynical attitude, but, if you look at the history of dam building in North America, you might be surprised to discover how many excellent dam sites just happen to have been found on Indian land.

Then again, maybe you wouldn't.

Three.

The year is 1717. Voltaire is sent to the Bastille because his rather edgy writing makes powerful people uncomfortable, a massive earthquake strikes Antigua, Guatemala, and France gives a portion of land along the Ottawa River to the Sulpician

Missionary Society. France doesn't own the land, but for the French Crown, such matters are neither here nor there.

The gift did not sit well with the Mohawk, since the land in the French grant was their land, and for the next 151 years, this piece of real estate would be a thorn in the side of Mohawk and Sulpician relations.

In 1868, a year after Confederation had overtaken Canada, Joseph Onasakenrat, a chief of the Mohawk, wrote a letter to the Sulpicians demanding the return of the land within eight days. The Sulpicians ignored the warning, and Onasakenrat led a march on the Sulpician seminary, weapons in hand. After a short and rather unpleasant confrontation, local authorities arrived and forced the Mohawk to retreat. Then, in 1936, the Sulpicians sold the property and left the area. The Mohawk protested the sale, and again, the protest fell on deaf ears.

Twenty-three years later, in 1959, a nine-hole golf course, Club de golf d'Oka, was built on the land, right next to the band's cemetery. This time the Mohawk launched a legal protest, hoping that the courts would provide them with some relief from White encroachment. The authorities and the courts dillied back and dallied forth, and in the meantime, the developers went ahead with the construction of the course, and happy golfers began roaming up and down the fairways in their little carts.

Finally, in 1977, the Mohawk filed an official land claim with the federal Office of Native Claims in an attempt to recapture the land. Nine years later, the claim was rejected because it failed to meet certain legal criteria. Which was a fancy way of saying that the Mohawk couldn't prove that they owned the land, at least not in the way that Whites recognized ownership.

For the next eleven years, relations between the town of Oka and the Mohawk were spotty. Then, in 1989, the mayor of Oka, Jean Ouellette, announced the exciting news that the old golf course was going to be expanded into an eighteen-hole course, and that sixty luxury condominiums would also be built. In order to manage this expansion, the town prepared to move on the Mohawk, taking more of their land, levelling a forest known among the Mohawk as "the Pines," and building new fairways and condominiums on top of the band cemetery.

That did it. After 270-odd years of dealing with European arrogance and indifference, after trying every legal avenue available, the Mohawk had had enough. On March 10, 1990, Natives began occupying the Pines, protecting their trees and their graveyard. Their land.

Five months later, in the heat of July, the confrontation became a shooting war. Neither the provincial government nor the federal government wanted to deal with the situation. Jean Ouellette had no intention of talking with the Mohawk and said so on television. Instead, he insisted that the province send in the Sûreté du Quebec, and in they came, storming the barricades that the Mohawk had erected with tear gas and flash-bang grenades. Shots were fired. No one knows who fired first. Not that it would have made much difference. And when the smoke cleared, Corporal Marcel Lemay had been mortally wounded and a Mohawk elder, Joe Armstrong, had suffered what would be a fatal heart attack trying to escape an angry mob.

So began the Oka Crisis.

Very quickly the Sûreté was reinforced by members of the Royal Canadian Mounted Police, and the RCMP was joined by around 2,500 members of the Canadian military. Jets arrived, along with tanks and armored personnel carriers. The Mohawk were joined by other Natives, and for seventy-eight days the two sides remained locked in a standoff.

To say that Oka could have been avoided is an understatement. John Ciaccia, Quebec's Minister of Indian Affairs at the time, had realized the potential for disaster months before matters got out of hand. Ciaccia had urged the federal government to buy the disputed land from Oka and give it to the Kanesatake Mohawk. Of course, the Kanesatake Mohawk already had Aboriginal title to the land, had had title to the land long before France gave it to the Sulpicians, but Ciaccia's idea was, given the circumstances, a reasonable compromise.

But rather than do something creative or at least intelligent, local, provincial, and federal politicians stood around and pointed fingers at each other. And did nothing.

The confrontation at Oka cost well over $200 million. In 1997, some seven years after the fact, the Department of Indian Affairs and Northern Development quietly purchased the disputed land for $5.2 million and "gave" it to the Mohawk for their use. At the discretion of the federal government, of course.

Anyone with a calculator can figure out that it would have been $195 million cheaper to have bought the land earlier, as the confrontation began to take shape. Of course, if the Mohawk land claim had been settled in 1977, the costs would have been minimal. Hardly more than a good dinner and a movie. But from Ottawa's point of view, Oka was never about the money. Or justice, for that matter.

Of the confrontation at Oka, Georges Erasmus, National Chief of the Assembly of First Nations at the time, said, "This is not going to be the last battle. This is not the last stand. This could be the first stand."

Four.

The Northwest coast is one of my favorite places in the world. I've spent a good deal of time along the northern California coast, the Oregon and Washington coasts, and, in particular, the coast of British Columbia. I like the fog and the gloomy, cool weather, and I have a long-lived love affair with the ocean that makes me prone to multisyllable adjectives. But if I were required to find a single noun to describe this part of the planet, it would be "fish."

Salmon. In fact, many of the tribes in the Northwest refer to themselves as the "Salmon People."

The salmon have been coming up the rivers along the Northwest coast for millennia. They are one of the staple foods and figure heavily in the language and the cultural life of the Native people along these waterways.

By 1854 Europeans had settled in numbers in the Puget Sound area of Washington Territory. In that year, the territorial governor, Isaac Stevens, was able to impose a treaty—the Treaty of Medicine Creek—on the Nisqually, the Puyallup, the Steilacoom, the Squawshik, the Squaxin Island, and other western tribes, a treaty that forced the tribes to give up most of their good farming land in exchange for $32,500 and the promise that they could continue to fish. One of the Nisqually chiefs, a man named Leschi, objected to the treaty and the loss of land. Skirmishes broke out between Indians and Whites, and the conflict turned into what history likes to call the Puget Sound War.

Puget Sound War sounds more dramatic that it was. Few people died on either side, but Stevens, outraged that the Nisqually would resist his land grab and angered over the deaths of two of his militiamen, sent troops to capture Leschi. No one knew for sure if Leschi had anything to do with the deaths of the two men, but it didn't matter. Leschi's real crime was his resistance to White desires, and, on February 19, 1858, he was hanged.

Whites were quick to take over the land that the Treaty of Medicine Creek had given them and slow to honor their promises, particularly the promise about fishing rights, and for the next hundred years, the matter of fishing rights would be a continuing irritant to Indian–White relations.

Any question about fishing rights should have been settled by the Medicine Creek treaty, and, if not by that treaty, then by two U.S. Supreme Court cases, *United States v. Winans* (1905) and *Suefert Brothers Co. v. United States* (1919). In both these cases, the central question was whether Indians had access to the rivers of the Northwest and whether they could fish as they had been accustomed to fishing. And in each of the cases, the court ruled that Native people indeed had those rights.

Yet in 1945, a fourteen-year-old Nisqually named Billy Frank Jr. was arrested for fishing on the Nisqually River. Frank had the right to fish, guaranteed by treaty. That right had been upheld in at least two Supreme Court cases, but for the next twenty-nine years that right would be ignored by Washington State officials.

Maybe they were fans of Andrew Jackson.

Just in case anyone has forgotten, Georgia, in the late 1820s and early 1830s, was hell-bent on removing the Cherokee from the state. Then, in 1832, the U.S. Supreme Court under John Marshall, in *Worcester v. Georgia*, ruled that states had no power or authority to pass laws that affected "domestic, dependent" Indian Nations.

That decision should have put Georgia's plans on hold, but Andrew Jackson, who was president at the time and sympathetic to Georgia, pushed ahead with the forced removal of the Cherokee anyway. "Marshall has made his decision," Jackson is credited with saying, "now let him enforce it."

But perhaps Washington State officials weren't thinking of Jackson. Perhaps they just decided, like Jackson, that when it came to a matter of land and natural resources, a bunch of Indians, treaty or no, Supreme Court decisions or no, weren't going to set the rules of engagement.

In 1954, a Puyallup named Bob Satiacum was arrested for illegally fishing along the Puyallup River. He was convicted, but, in 1957, on appeal, the Washington State Supreme Court overturned the conviction. However, the matter of who could fish and who controlled the fishing was far from settled, and in no time at all, the rivers of the Northwest became the site of "fish-ins," as tribes pushed to have their fishing rights recognized and reaffirmed.

During these "fish-ins," Indians went fishing with a vengeance. Game wardens arrested them, destroyed their equipment, and confiscated their boats. While the Indians were fishing and the wardens were arresting, courts of various jurisdictions were busy turning out a flurry of rulings. In 1960, the Pierce County Superior Court ruled that the Puyallup tribe didn't exist. Another ruling denied the existence of the Puyallup reservation. In 1963, in *Washington v. McCoy*, the court upheld the right of the state to subject Indians to reasonable and necessary regulations.

The fishing wars escalated quickly. Hollywood celebrities such as Marlon Brando, Buffy Sainte-Marie, and Dick Gregory came to the Northwest to help call attention to Indian fishing rights.

The National Indian Youth Council showed up. Many of the fishing protests were led by the Survival of American Indians Association (SAIA), an organization formed out of the dispute itself.

Neither side was willing to back down. Native people wanted their fishing rights as guaranteed by treaty. But neither the Department of Fish and Game nor the state's sports fishery associations were willing to allow the power to regulate any part of the fishery slip through their fingers. One of the fears voiced in newspaper articles and on radio talk shows was that Native fishers would ruin the fishery by overfishing. Little was said about the destruction to the fishery by foreign offshore trawlers with their factory ships, or the army of sports fishers who waited in ambush at the mouth of the river each year for the salmon to return.

The idea was that Indians had no business competing with the commercial and sports fishery. This was never said out loud. It was just in the air. Certainly, this was the attitude of the Department of Fish and Game. And as Indians pushed to secure their treaty rights to the salmon, a strange dance began. Indians would push off in their boats and set their nets in the river, all of which, under the terms of the Medicine Creek treaty, was legal. Game wardens would arrest, fine, and jail the fishers and confiscate their boats and nets. The Indians would go to court, and the court would throw the government's case out. The Indians would claim their boats and nets and go back on the river.

But the arrests and fines and court costs took their toll. Boats and nets were never returned in a timely manner, and, many times, they would somehow sustain damage during their impoundment. As soon as the Indians got back on the river, the game wardens would arrest them once more, and the great legal mandala would begin to turn again.

One of my historian friends, who wishes to remain anonymous, told me the story of his time on the rivers of the Northwest assisting some of the tribes with their fishing protests. He said that, after a while, the people would go out on the river with their worst boats and their worst nets. As soon as the wardens confiscated the equipment and were busy dragging the derelict boats and nets back to town, the Natives would bring out their good boats and their good nets and continue fishing.

The situation on the rivers became increasingly violent. Boats rammed each other. There were beatings. Folks began shooting at each other. On September 9, 1970, state law-enforcement officials raided a large fishing camp on the banks of Puyallup River. Sixty people were arrested, and the fishing village was bulldozed. No one was killed, but that was the only good news.

And, as one might expect, the question of treaty rights went back to court, this time to the District Court for the Western District of Washington. *United States v. State of Washington*. If you're surprised that the U.S. government sued the State of Washington on behalf of Native people, don't be. One of the legal issues in the fishing wars was federal jurisdiction versus state jurisdiction. Treaty land, let's not forget, was federal land.

The arguments in *United States v. State of Washington* were the same as they had been for the past hundred years. On the one hand, it was argued, the Treaty of Medicine Creek gave Indian people the right to fish. On the other hand, it was argued, the State of Washington had the right to regulate its fishery, regardless of any treaty. And when all the motions had been made and all the points had been argued, the district court, under Justice George Boldt, ruled not only that Indians had a guaranteed right to fish but that they had the right to 50 percent of the harvestable fish.

The sound you just heard was the State of Washington passing out.

In the end, no one won much. The salmon fishery had already been in decline. And that decline has continued. Offshore trawlers continue to take the lion's share of the salmon. The state, the sports fishery, and the Natives have come to some tentative agreements to try to conserve the salmon, but with the new threat from fish-farm diseases and the lack of regulation or responsibility in that particular industry, a once-vibrant fishery may be on its way to extinction.

Five.

You like golf? I do.

The Shaughnessy Golf and Country Club is one of the premier clubs in Vancouver. It's a private club, so unless you're a member or know a member, you can't play. The club had its beginnings in 1911 as the Shaughnessy Heights Golf Course, with a nine-hole course that was expanded to eighteen holes the following year. The club didn't own the land. The sixty-seven acres that encompassed the course had been leased from the Canadian Pacific Railroad.

In 1956, the CPR began making noises that it wanted its land back, and the club went looking for another site. And in 1958, they found it. A lovely 162-acre site overlooking the Fraser River and the Strait of Georgia. Views, views, views. The only problem was that the land belonged to the Musqueam Nation.

Actually, that wasn't really a problem. Since all Indian land and all Indian business was handled by Ottawa, the club leadership simply got together with the resident Indian agent, and in a series of mostly private meetings, negotiated a long-term lease for the site.

The Musqueam had had little or no input regarding the lease. They weren't given a copy of the agreement, and they had no idea what the exact terms were until 1970, when Graham Allen, a Department of Indian Affairs employee, showed the lease to Chief Delbert Guerin.

Guerin and the Musqueam suspected that the golf club had got a bargain, so they weren't all that surprised to discover the deal had actually been a steal. While the land on which the golf course sat had originally been appraised at a rental price of $53,450 per year, the government gave the club a seventy-five-year lease for $29,000 a year and locked that amount in for the first ten years with no possibility of an increase. For the second fifteen years, any increase on the lease could not exceed 15 percent.

There's nothing like a government that's here to help. Nor was the government finished helping the Musqueam. In 1965, Ottawa, on behalf of the band, signed a development deal with a private developer for about forty prime acres of Musqueam land. The parcel was turned into a subdivision of seventy-four executive building lots, which were rented to non-Natives for ninety-nine years. Leases were set at about $400 per year for each of the 10,000-plus square-foot lots, and the lease prices frozen for the first thirty years with no incremental increases.

Four hundred dollars a year for a one-hundred by one-hundred-foot building lot in the exclusive Point Grey area of Vancouver. Twelve thousand dollars for the first thirty years.

For thirty years, the Musqueam watched as the land around the leases skyrocketed in value, and for thirty years the Musqueam were unable to realize a fair share of that market increase. So, when the leases came up for renewal in 1995, the Musqueam tried to raise the rent to market value.

Human nature is a rather predictable thing. The non-Natives who had been paying next to nothing for their leases were angry that the rent was going to be raised and furious that the increase was going to be to market value. One of the arguments against this hike was that the houses increased the property value, a somewhat spurious argument since the real value was in the land and its location and not what was on it.

Just so we keep things straight, any other landlord or corporation would have raised the rates to market value with no questions asked. That's Real Estate 101. But the leases were on Indian land, and, following the lead of Ottawa, the homeowners decided that Indian land was different from non-Indian land. Indian land, they argued, could not be valued in the same way as non-Indian land. It was unfair for their rates to be raised, they also argued, since they had no say on the Musqueam Council and could not vote in Musqueam elections, a creative variation on "no taxation without representation."

A Canadian friend of mine owns a condo in Costa Rica. He pays taxes on his property. He pays condo fees. He doesn't get to vote in Costa Rican elections. Another Canadian friend owns a small house in Fort Myers, Florida. He pays property taxes. He doesn't get to vote in that state, either.

Chief Ernest Campbell, in a *Vancouver Sun* interview, reminded everyone that "For the first thirty years, the tenants paid rents at very low fixed amounts. In 1995, tenants would have paid more to rent a parking stall downtown than for their home's lease. Annual rents were in the range of $375 to $400, or $31.25 to $33.33 per month."

Low rents or no, the homeowners stopped paying rent altogether, hired a lawyer, and went to court.

There was a series of court decisions, one in 1997 and one in 1998, but the one that counted was the 2000 review by the Supreme Court of Canada, which concluded that Musqueam land, for the purposes of lease agreements, was worth about 50 percent of adjacent non-Indian land. At the same time, the court also suggested that if the band were to sell the land, it could be appraised at full market value.

So, in essence, what the court said was that land held by First Nations was worth half the value of the same land held by non-Natives.

Still, good things come to them that waits. The lease on the Shaughnessy Golf and Country Club ends in 2033, while the leases on the estate lots will be up in 2064. I won't be around when that two hundred acres of prime Vancouver real estate is returned to the Musqueam, so I don't know what they will decide to do with the land, but I'm sure Ottawa will help the Musqueam come up with something.

Six.

And while we're waiting, why don't we go for a hike?

How about New Mexico? The population density is sixteen people per square mile, so you won't be bumping into neighbors. The state has the third-highest percentage of Indians after Oklahoma and Alaska. Among other things, the state is known for sandhill cranes, Native art, Carlsbad Caverns, balloon festivals. And atomic bombs.

It's also home to the Carson National Forest, a park in the northern part of the state that covers over 1.5 million acres and contains Wheeler Peak, the highest mountain in New Mexico. The park was created by Theodore Roosevelt in 1906, and, to do so, his administration confiscated about 50,000 acres of Taos Pueblo Indian land.

No treaty. No payment. No nothing.

For Roosevelt, the land he took was simply land. Rocks, trees, lakes, rivers. For the Taos Pueblo, it was far more than that. When Roosevelt appropriated Taos land for the national forest, he took Ba Whyea, or Blue Lake, a remote mountain lake that was and is sacred to the Taos people. Oral tradition has it that the Taos tribe was created out of the waters of the lake, and the area around the lake has always been part of the tribe's ceremonial life.

Nevertheless, the park was created, and in 1916, the Forest Service ran a trail up to the lake and stocked the lake with trout for the pleasure of backpackers and tourists. Ten years later, the service built a cabin near the lake for the use of the park's forest rangers.

The Taos protested the taking of the land and the lake. They protested opening the area to public recreation. Without much success.

In the 1920s, the Pueblo Lands Board, which had been established by the Pueblo Lands Act of 1924, awarded the Taos Pueblo $297,684.67, which was the 1906 valuation of the land that had been taken. The Pueblo countered, offering to waive any cash compensation in exchange for a clear and exclusive title to Blue Lake and the land around it.

The Forest Service objected to the proposal, and that was the end of that.

In 1933, with the help of the Commissioner of the Bureau of Indian Affairs, John Collier, who was the driving force behind the 1934 Indian Reorganization Act, the Taos were able to get a statute passed for a fifty-year permit that was supposed to allow them year-round exclusive use of the lake and the area around the lake. The Forest Service was none too pleased with this arrangement, and, like many bureaucracies, was able to stall and delay and postpone. Finally, about seven years after the fact, the service reluctantly issued a permit that allowed the Taos Pueblo exclusive use of the lake for three days in August.

This wasn't a solution so much as it was an insult.

In 1951, the Indian Claims Commission, which had been set up to hear and adjudicate Native claims, affirmed that Blue Lake had been taken illegally. But predictably, while the commission had the power to hear cases and to recommend monetary compensation, it did not have the power to return land to any tribe. In fact, it was expressly forbidden even to consider the return of land.

But the Taos hadn't changed their minds. They weren't interested in money. They wanted the lake and the land back. Taos elder Juan de Jesus Romero summed it up nicely. "If our land is not returned to us, if it is turned over to the government for its use, then it is the end of Indian life. Our people will scatter as the people of other nations have scattered. It is our religion that holds us together." He might have gone on to say that Taos religion was in the land and the land in the religion, but for him, that would have been stating the obvious.

The Taos continued pushing for the return of the land. Pushing, pushing, pushing. Sixty-four years of pushing.

And then, in 1970, after more pushing, President Richard Nixon signed House of Representatives Bill 471 into law, which gave back to the Taos people trust title to 48,000 acres of their land including Blue Lake, and 1,640 acres surrounding the lake.

Sixty-four years.

These six instances do no more than frame the issue of Native land. I have not mentioned the Quinault or the Menominee or the Lumbee or the Siletz and Grand Ronde tribes or the Klamath or the Passamoquoddy or the Blackfoot or the Pit River or the Havasupai or the Yakama at Warm Springs or the Lubicon Lake Cree, nor have I listed any of the hundreds of land claim cases that are currently outstanding in Canada and the United States.

Earlier in this book, I hinted that I didn't think that legal action was going to provide a solution to the problems that centuries of North American Indian policy and action had created. I suggested that the legal gauntlet created by legislation and the courts better served the powerful and the privileged than it did Native people.

I still believe this.

But I do have to admit that, in spite of such impediments, Native people in the late twentieth and early twenty-first centuries have begun to find moments of success within the legal systems of North America. Perhaps, after all this time, the laws of the land will finally ride to the rescue and we will all live happily ever after.

10

HAPPY EVER AFTER

Out of a past, I make truth for a future.

—Beth Brant, *Mohawk Trail*

Since *The Inconvenient Indian* is set in North America, and since North Americans love happy-ever-after endings, I thought I'd try to close the book on an optimistic note. So, I asked Native friends who keep abreast of current affairs if they'd noticed any encouraging signs that Native–White relations were moving in positive directions. I wasn't expecting that we'd be talking about outright victories or triumphs for, in the tumble of Native history, in the ongoing pursuit of Native sovereignty and self-determination, such things don't yet exist.

That being said, two contemporary topics came up in our running conversations with some regularity: the Alaska Native Claims Settlement Act and the Nunavut Land Claims Agreement.

But before I tackle the two largest land-claim settlements in North American history, I want to take a moment and begin with another affair that was widely publicized at the time, though now mostly forgotten. Unlike the Alaska Native Claims Settlement Act or the Nunavut Land Claims Agreement, the creation of the Gwaii Haanas National Park and Haida Heritage Site was not a land-claim settlement. It was one of those rare occasions when Aboriginal concerns, environmental ethics, political will, and good sense came together in common cause.

In the 1980s some of the large wood-product companies began pressing the British Columbia government for access to timber stands largely untouched by logging activities. In 1983, MacMillan Bloedel received permits to cut old-growth cedar on Meares Island in Clayoquot Sound on the west coast of Vancouver Island. The reaction was immediate. By the time logging crews arrived on the island in November of 1984, they were met by a blockade of Natives and non-Natives. "This land is our garden," Tla-o-qui-aht Chief Moses Martin told the loggers. "If you put down your chainsaws, you are welcome ashore, but not one tree will be cut here."

MacMillan Bloedel and the Tla-o-qui-aht took the matter to court, and, in what must have been a surprise to the corporation, the judiciary sided with Native people, issuing an injunction that suspended logging activities on Meares Island until such time as Native land claims in the area were settled.

The following year, 1985, across the water on Haida Gwaii, logging interests turned their attention to Lyell Island. This was Haida territory, and the Haida immediately threw up a blockade to stop any cutting. The Haida were tired of having their territory destroyed, and they were joined by environmentalists who shared the tribe's concern about preserving old-growth forests, animal habitats, and watersheds. People who worked in the timber industry were furious at what they saw as an assault on their livelihood, and, predictably, tempers flared. In November of that year, the police moved in and began arresting protesters, many of whom were Haida elders who had insisted on being on the front lines.

Generally protests of this sort can be tense, sometimes even lethal events. But the confrontations over Lyell Island were — from time to time—unexpectedly civil and periodically humorous. The Haida shared their food with the police and the loggers. Guujaaw, one of the Haida leaders, told a reporter that the police ate with the Haida because the Haida had the better food. The RCMP, in the spirit of community, arranged for satellite service so that everyone could watch the B.C. Lions beat the Hamilton Tiger Cats 37–24 in the Grey Cup. At one point, a truce was struck in which loggers agreed not to cut any trees while the Haida left Lyell Island to attend a funeral.

For the next twenty-one months, the Haida, the loggers, the environmentalists, and the police moved back and forth among each other, arguing jobs, culture, land claims, environmentalism, and the law, sometimes heatedly, sometimes calmly and with respect. And then, in July of 1987, Ottawa, British Columbia, and the Haida signed a memorandum of agreement that created Gwaii Haanas National Park Reserve and Haida Heritage Site.

In May of 1996, my family and I, along with Greg Staats (Mohawk), a fine-art photographer from Toronto, began a month-long tour of remote Native villages along the west coast of British Columbia, where Greg and I offered workshops in photography and writing. At the end of our time on the coast, I packed Helen and two of our three children, Benjamin and Elizabeth, into a very small seaplane and flew down to Rose Harbour in the middle of Gwaii Haanas. We took a Zodiac from there across the water to Sgaan Gwaii to see the Haida village of Ninstints and the stand of old totem poles on the island.

I think that many non-Natives find it hard to understand why Native people are willing to fight so hard to protect their land. In the case of Gwaii Haanas, all you have to do is stand at the ocean's edge with the cedars at your back and the sky on your shoulders, and you will know.

The place is magic. No doubt about it. Now, I know that not everyone is going to understand the affinity that the Haida have for their land. Which is why the creation of the Gwaii Haanas National Park Reserve and Haida Heritage Site was such an important event. The agreement protects an astonishing landscape and allows North America the time to mature and to come to an appreciation of what the oft-abused term "sacred" truly means.

Okay, the moment's over. Let's get back to work.

The Alaska Native Claims Settlement Act (ANCSA)

When Alaska became a state in 1959, one of the contentious issues that followed it into statehood was the matter of Native land claims. The Alaska Statehood Act, which had passed the year before, allowed the territory to help itself to over 100 million acres of "vacant, unappropriated, and unreserved" public land. At the same time, the Act forbade Alaska from selecting lands that were held by Native tribes. As a result, for most of the next decade Native groups and the state spent a great deal of time, effort, and money arguing over who owned what.

Then, in 1966, Alaska Natives came together, formed the Alaska Federation of Natives (AFN), and began an organized and concerted effort for a comprehensive, state-wide, land-claim settlement. In that same year, Stuart Udall, the Secretary of the Interior, announced that he would refuse to approve any of the land selections that Alaska had made until the state first settled Native claims. Three years later, in 1969, Udall made his earlier order permanent, with Public Land Order 4582. Predictably, this did not go over all that well with Alaska's Governor Walter J. Hickel or the state's petroleum lobby. Not only did the order stop Alaska's land selection, it also halted the sale of oil leases and blocked the construction of a much-anticipated 800-mile oil pipeline that was to bring Arctic crude from the Beaufort Sea down to Prince William Sound.

The federal moratorium was a strong incentive to settle the claims, but what put the train on the track was the 1968 discovery of oil at Prudhoe Bay on Alaska's North Slope. Now, with the scent of money in its nose, and with the oil industry pushing it from behind, the state began the process in earnest.

The land-claim issue in Alaska was massive. Natives claimed most of the state. Alaska claimed most of the state. This should have been a recipe for political disaster. Instead, in three short years, a time frame unheard of in such negotiations, the Alaska Native Claims Settlement Act (ANCSA) was passed by Congress, approved by the Alaska Federation of Natives, and signed by President Richard Nixon.

ANCSA, in many ways, resembled early treaties, with Aboriginal people giving up claim to large chunks of territory in exchange for smaller portions of guaranteed land. Under the settlement act,

Natives in Alaska received about 44 million acres of land and some $963 million in cash. To put that settlement into perspective, 44 million acres is more land than is currently held in trust for *all* other Indian tribes in the United States. The cash compensation is nearly four times the combined amount that Native people had won from the U.S. Indian Claims Commission over the twenty-five years the commission was in business. On paper, the settlement looked to be a reasonable compromise. A win-win situation. Alaska was able to abrogate all Native claims with one slash of the pen, and Alaska Natives came away with the largest land-and-cash settlement that Aboriginal people had ever negotiated.

Prior to ANCSA, Native land in Alaska was trust land, subject to the control and protection of the U.S. government. But from the start of the negotiations, it was clear that neither Alaska nor Washington was interested in continuing this arrangement. Instead, federal and state authorities insisted that any land that was transferred to Alaska Natives be transferred as fee simple.

This should have set off alarm bells. The conversion of trust land to fee-simple land had been the centerpiece of earlier legislation: the 1887 Allotment Act and termination in 1953. Both policies had been a disaster for Native people. But for whatever reason, when the Alaska Federation of Natives met in December of 1971 to consider the Alaska Native Claims Settlement Act as passed by Congress, the delegates voted 511 to 56 to support the legislation and to take the land designated in the settlement as fee simple.

Native people have complained for years about the paternalism of the Bureau of Indian Affairs and the extent to which this agency has tried to micromanage Aboriginal affairs, so I can only suppose that AFN believed that a fee-simple land arrangement would allow for more control than was possible under a federal trust agreement. Certainly, the lived experience of the tribes in North America would seem to support this conclusion.

But while ANCSA may have contained some elements of allotment and termination, it was neither. Both allotment and termination were blunt weapons that had been used to relieve tribes of their land. Under those two policies, tribal lands were broken into fee-simple pieces, and Native people who had been part of a communal whole suddenly found themselves set adrift as private landowners. Within one generation, much of the land was lost and the people scattered.

One of the major differences between ANCSA and allotment or termination was that the fee-simple land Alaska Natives received in the settlement was protected in a number of ways. Neither the land nor the cash was given to individuals. Both were placed under the control of twelve Native regional corporations (a thirteenth corporation was added later) and over two hundred Native village corporations. Not a trust relationship exactly, but close enough for government work.

In addition to cash and land, Alaska Natives also retained surface and sub-surface rights to the land, all of which promised a much-needed economic base. As a rough and loose rule, sub-surface rights, such as oil, were vested with the regional for-profit corporations, while surface rights, such as timber, were vested with the village corporations, which could be either profit or non-profit in nature.

In quick order, tribal and village councils were whisked through the corporate looking glass, emerging on the other side as boards of directors, while individual Alaska Natives, who had been members of the Tlingit, Haida, Tsimshian, Aleut, Yupik Nations, et al., were suddenly, presto change-o, shareholders in the Sealaska Corporation or Doyon Limited or the Arctic Slope Regional Corporation or the Bering Straits Native Corporation or Cook Inlet Region Inc. or one of the seven other ANCSA-created corporations.

When I was in Juneau in 2011, a Tlingit friend of mine told me that, since the advent of ANCSA and the changes the act has had on traditional Native culture, there is a generation of Tlingit who "no longer know their clan or their house, but they sure know the name of their corporation."

Corporations. The new reservations.

From a distance, ANCSA looked good. But the devil, as usual, was in the details. What quickly became clear was that Alaska Natives were simply not prepared to move from the heart of the country to the boardroom in one generation. Nor were they ready to take on the financial and legal complexities that attend corporations. ANCSA contained provisions to protect the land from loss and seizure for the first twenty years, but by the late 1980s, it was clear that if the protections were lifted in 1991 as scheduled, all Native land in Alaska would be exposed and vulnerable.

By the by, this twenty-year protection provision was remarkably similar to the twenty-five-year provision that was supposed to have protected Native land under the policy of allotment. And everyone knows how well that turned out.

To their credit, Native leaders went to work, and, in 1991, Congress passed House Resolution 278 (HR 278), which amended the original 1971 settlement act. While the new amendments dealt with wide-ranging concerns, the two most critical changes were in the area of corporate stock and protection of the land base. Under the 1971 agreement, stock in the regional corporations was given only to Alaska Natives who were born before 1971 and who met ANCSA criteria for enrollment. Alaska Natives born after 1971 received no stock, though they could inherit it. Under HR 278, corporations were given the flexibility to issue different categories of stock as they saw fit, and to set the rules as to how the stock might be voted and conveyed. Still, the amendments did not solve the problem completely, and Native corporations in Alaska are currently looking at the somewhat absurd spectacle of generations of Alaska Natives who may have no stock and no vested interest in the very corporations that were formed for their benefit.

Equally important, HR 278 extended protection for ANCSA land, granting it immunity from bankruptcy, civil judgments, liens, taxation, and the like, so long, in some cases, as the land remained undeveloped.

These amendments were welcomed by Alaska Natives, but I suspect such amendments are temporary at best. The lessons of history tell us that, at some point, both the State of Alaska and the federal government will move to eliminate any and all shelters, and force Native corporations into the marketplace. Corporations raise money in a variety of ways. They can issue and sell stock, they can adjust the price of their goods and services, and they can borrow against assets. Because ANCSA corporations are closed corporations—more or less—they can't really sell stock on the open market, since such a move would allow Native corporations to be taken over by non-Native interests. The prices of goods and services are, in large part, dependent on the economy and market fluctuations, over which Native corporations have little control. The easiest way to raise capital is to borrow against corporate assets using the land as collateral. It is also the most dangerous.

The eminent Canadian jurist Thomas Berger warned of such a scenario. In his book *Village Journey: The Report of the Alaska Native Review Commission*, Berger urged that the land held by village corporations be returned to tribal ownership. "My objective," said Berger, "is to ensure that Native people do not lose their land. The only way to do that, the only way to ensure that Native land remains in Native ownership, is to re-tribalize the land. I do not see any alternative. As long as the land is a corporate asset, it will be vulnerable."

The Alaska settlement is substantial. The economic potential of the land and resources, along with the profit-sharing agreements that have been negotiated among the Native regional corporations, should be able to provide a strong financial base for generations to come. Yet Berger isn't the only one disturbed by this fee-simple business model. It makes me uneasy as well, makes me suspect that corporations are just the latest fashion in assimilation.

Still, apart from my alarmist apprehensions, there is no reason to believe that Native people in Alaska won't prosper. All that is needed is a little traditional imagination, a modicum of generosity, and some political goodwill.

Along with a skid of lawyers and a truckload of accountants.

The Nunavut Land Claims Agreement

Canada, until 1993, consisted of ten provinces and two northern territories, the Yukon Territory and the Northwest Territories. In that year, Parliament passed the Nunavut Land Claims

Agreement (NLCA) and the Nunavut Act. Six years later, on April 1, 1999, the new territory of Nunavut came into being.

The initial step in this process was, of course, the abrogation of all Aboriginal rights. "In consideration of the rights and benefits provided to Inuit . . ." the agreement read, "Inuit hereby: cede, release and surrender to her Majesty The Queen in Right of Canada, all their aboriginal claims, rights, title and interests, if any, in and to lands and waters anywhere within Canada and adjacent offshore areas within the sovereignty or jurisdiction of Canada; and agree, on their behalf, and on behalf of their heirs, descendants and successors not to assert any cause of action, action for a declaration, claim or demand of whatever kind or nature which they ever had, now have or may hereafter have against her Majesty The Queen in Right of Canada or any province, the government of any territory or any person based on any aboriginal claims, rights, title or interests in and to lands and waters . . ."

Human beings were not involved in the formulation of the preceding sentence, but the views expressed do reflect the attitudes of management.

Jean Chrétien, the prime minister du jour, used the occasion to take a bow. "Canada," he said, "is showing the world, once again, how we embrace many peoples and many cultures."

Nunavut, which means "Our Land" in Inuktitut, was the end game of a land claim that the Inuit began in 1976. The Inuit could have argued for a homeland within the existing Northwest Territories, but they correctly concluded that, if that happened, they would find themselves at a substantial disadvantage as a minority within a much larger non-Native, non-Inuit population. They could have insisted on the establishment of an exclusively

Inuit enclave, but instead they lobbied for a new territory that would include Inuit and non-Inuit citizens and that would have the same standing within Canada as the other two territories.

Nunavut is a 2-million-square-kilometer chunk of Canadian arctic carved out of the eastern portion of the Northwest Territories, and whenever I look at a map of the area with its raggedy, puzzle-piece geography, I'm reminded, more than anything else, of a Rorschach test. Under the terms of the Nunavut Land Claims Agreement, the Inuit received over 350,000 square kilometers of land within the new territory, along with over a billion dollars in cash to be paid over a fourteen-year period.

I'm tempted to compare the Nunavut Land Claims Agreement with the Alaska Native Claims Settlement Act to see who got the better deal. Under ANCSA, Alaska Natives received about half the land that the Inuit negotiated, while both groups came away with the same amount of cash. The difference that stands out between the two agreements is the status of the land. Inuit land is divided into two types. Of the 350,000 square kilometers that the Inuit received, 315,000 square kilometers is Crown land held in trust for the Inuit by the Canadian government, while 35,000 square kilometers, about 10 percent of the total, is fee-simple land managed by the Inuit under the corporate aegis of Nunavut Tunngavik Incorporated. In Alaska, all the land that Alaska Natives received under their agreement is fee simple.

But such comparisons are of little value. The situation of Alaska Natives is considerably different from that of the Inuit in Nunavut. In Alaska, Native people make up approximately 14 percent of the state's population. In Nunavut, the Inuit make up 85 percent of that territory's inhabitants. In Alaska, Native people have access to state government primarily through the ballot box. In Nunavut, at least for the time being, the Inuit *are* the government.

Since the Inuit are Nunavut's primary constituency and since Inuktitut is the main language, you might expect to find Inuktitut-speaking Inuit professionals in the majority of government positions in the territory. You might expect that Inuktitut would be taught in the schools with English and/or French offered as a secondary language to help ensure bilingualism. In fact, this was the general sentiment of the Bathurst Mandate that the Government of Nunavut released in 2000. The Mandate set forth a series of ambitious objectives that the territory hoped to meet by 2020. One of the objectives was that Nunavut be "a fully functional bilingual society, in Inuktitut and English, respectful and committed to the needs and rights of French speakers," while a second objective committed the territory to "a representative workforce in all sectors."

Yet, in spite of the population advantage, the strength and range of Inuktitut, and the commitment the territorial government has to education and training, there seems little hope that either of these objectives will be reached. The high school graduation rate for Inuit students hovers at around 25 percent, and few graduates go on to colleges and universities. Article 23 of the Nunavut Land Claims Agreement calls for Inuit participation in the territory's public-service sector "to match the proportions of Inuit in the population," but that hasn't happened. Most estimates of Inuit in government positions are around 45 percent, with the majority of those jobs at the lower levels of administrative support. While Inuktitut is taught in the schools, it is only taught until grade three/four. Instruction beyond that is in English.

In his 2008 discussion paper, "*Aajiiqatigiingniq*," York University professor Ian Martin looks at the "long-term threat to Inuit language from English" and warns that abruptly dropping Inuktitut in favor of English in elementary school risks the consequence that Inuit students will develop neither language to its full potential.

Equally worrisome is the role of the federal government. Financial support for teaching French in Nunavut is around $4 million a year, while support for teaching Inuktitut comes in at the $1 million mark. Ottawa may be philosophically inclined to multiculturalism, but it has yet to provide the Inuit with the necessary funds and assistance to establish and maintain an Inuktitut bilingual language program that starts at kindergarten and runs through to grade twelve.

Interestingly enough, the concerns that currently face the Inuit are the same concerns that the 1960 Royal Commission on Bilingualism and Biculturalism considered when it recommended that French be encouraged and supported, that French-speaking Canadians have adequate educational opportunities, and that they have access to their fair share of jobs in the country's public service. These recommendations were echoed in the Official Languages Act of 1969 and embedded as constitutional guarantees in the 1982 Canadian Charter of Rights and Freedoms.

I was going to say that it's too bad the Inuit aren't French, but using that logic, they would be even better off if they were English.

The Nunavut Legislative Assembly currently consists of nineteen members, including a Premier and a Speaker of the Assembly, the majority of whom are Inuit, and I'm confident of the government's commitment to Native language, bilingualism, education, and jobs. Unfortunately, the problem isn't commitment. The problem is time. And resources. Each year that these matters go unresolved intensifies the situation and invites consequences over which the Inuit may have little control.

If an object lesson is needed, Nunavut might want to consider the history of Manitoba. When that province came into Confederation in 1870, the population was overwhelmingly French-speaking Métis. The Manitoba Act set out French and English as the two official languages, guaranteed public funding for Catholic schools, and established a Métis land base. But within a dozen years, intense settlement had changed the demographics of the province dramatically, and the Métis found themselves a minority. Predictably, subsequent provincial legislatures began clawing back or ignoring the guarantees contained in the Manitoba Act, and the Métis spent the next hundred years in court trying to get those promises honored.

I'm not suggesting that Nunavut should be a territory where Inuit culture and philosophy frame governmental and social interaction, where residents are expected to be bilingual with Inuktitut as the primary language and English or French as the second, but neither do I see any reason why it shouldn't.

Nunavut. The Quebec of the North.

Both the Alaska Native Claims Settlement Act and the Nunavut Land Claims Agreement are flawed accords. Some of the flaws were apparent even before the agreements were signed. Others have appeared after the fact. Now that the "honeymoon" is over, perhaps it's time for Alaska Natives and the Inuit to ask the question: how are the needs of our people served by these documents? There is nothing to stop Alaska Natives from returning to the

Alaska Native Claims Settlement Act, and there is no reason that the Inuit in Nunavut can't revisit the Nunavut Land Claims Agreement. After all, both Ottawa and Washington have been rewriting treaties and amending agreements to suit themselves for the past two centuries.

In the meantime, old attitudes continue to bluster about with each new storm. Certainly, as I've travelled around the continent, and around the world for that matter, there's always been someone willing to sit me down and set me straight on the matter of Native history. You people, I'll be told, really have to stop complaining. What happened can't be undone. None of us is responsible for the sins of our ancestors. Times have changed. Attitudes have changed. Get over it.

You can't judge the past by the present.

It's a splendid slogan. It permits us to set aside the missteps of history and offers a covenant with the future, allowing us to be held blameless for the decisions we make today. Ignorance. That's our defense. Our grandparents didn't know any better. We didn't know any better. If we knew then what we know now, we wouldn't have done what we did.

You can't judge the past by the present. One of history's grand maxims. It's convenient, and it's specious.

This needs to be said. In the history of Indian—White relations, it is clear that politicians, reformers, the clergy, the military, in fact the whole lot, knew the potential for destruction that their policies and actions could have on Native communities. They were betting that something good would come out of the devastation. And they were able to make these decisions with easy confidence, because they weren't betting with *their* money. They weren't betting with *their* communities. They weren't betting with *their* children.

Ignorance has never been the problem. The problem was and continues to be unexamined confidence in western civilization and the unwarranted certainty of Christianity. And arrogance. Perhaps it is unfair to judge the past by the present, but it is also necessary.

If nothing else, an examination of the past—and of the present, for that matter—can be instructive. It shows us that there is little shelter and little gain for Native peoples in doing nothing. So long as we possess one element of sovereignty, so long as we possess one parcel of land, North America will come for us, and the question we have to face is how badly we wish to continue to pursue the concepts of sovereignty and self-determination. How important is it for us to maintain protected communal homelands? Are our traditions and languages worth the cost of carrying on the fight? Certainly the easier and more expedient option is simply to step away from who we are and who we wish to be, sell what we have for cash, and sink into the stewpot of North America.

With the rest of the bones.

No matter how you frame Native history, the one inescapable constant is that Native people in North America have lost much. We've given away a great deal, we've had a great deal taken from us, and, if we are not careful, we will continue to lose parts of ourselves—as Indians, as Cree, as Blackfoot, as Navajo, as Inuit— with each generation. But this need not happen. Native cultures aren't static. They're dynamic, adaptive, and flexible, and for many of us, the modern variations of older tribal traditions continue to provide order, satisfaction, identity, and value in our lives.

More than that, in the five hundred years of European occupation, Native cultures have already proven themselves to be remarkably tenacious and resilient.

Okay.

That was heroic and uncomfortably inspirational, wasn't it? Poignant, even. You can almost hear the trumpets and the violins. And that kind of romance is not what we need. It serves no one, and the cost to maintain it is too high.

So, let's agree that Indians are not special. We're not . . . mystical. I'm fine with that. Yes, a great many Native people have a long-standing relationship with the natural world. But that relationship is equally available to non-Natives, should they choose to embrace it. The fact of Native existence is that we live modern lives informed by traditional values and contemporary realities and that we wish to live those lives on our terms.

I'm sorry that I won't be around when the next millennium rolls into town. Just to see how we managed. Just to hear the stories. If the past five hundred years are any indication, what the Native people of North America do with the future should be very curious indeed.

Acknowledgments

The Inconvenient Indian has been a work-in-progress for most of my adult life. Its origin dates back to at least the early 1970s, when I worked at the University of Utah's American West Center where Floyd O'Neil rode herd on a motley crew of graduate reprobates that included myself as well as Greg Thompson, Laura Bayer, John Alley, Geno Defa, David Lewis, and Kathryn MacKay. Native history was the topic of research and conversation at the Center, and we spent our time reading oral histories and treaties, drawing maps, working with tribes in the Southwest, and engaging in running pranks that involved potatoes. Floyd introduced me to the discipline of history. More than that, he was a mentor and a friend who, along with Edward Lueders and William Mulder, professors in the English Department, helped to drag me through the rigors of a Ph.D. Floyd also introduced me to many of the historians and scholars whose work is a part of this book: Richard White, Alvin Josephy, Francis Paul Prucha, Patricia Limerick, David Edmunds (Cherokee), Brigham Madsen, Gerald Vizenor (Anishinaabe), S. Lyman Tyler,

Terry Wilson (Potawatomie), Richard Hart, Louis Owens (Choctaw–Cherokee), Robert Berkhofer, and Arrell Morgan Gibson.

As important were the conversations that I had with fellow graduate students in the English department—Steve Tatum, Robert Haynie, Bob King, and Barry Sarchett—who were engaged in the disciplines of western literature and western history. We all played on the English department's intermural softball team, the Hot Tamales, which contributed nothing to this book but was fun nevertheless.

When I was working and studying in Salt Lake City, I met Leroy Littlebear (Blood) who was finishing a law degree at the university. We became friends, and when he returned to the University of Lethbridge in Lethbridge, Alberta, to head up the Native Studies Department, he offered me a job teaching Native literature and Native history. I spent the next ten years on the high Alberta prairies, braving the wind and the cold winters, working with Native and non-Native students, and hanging out with folks on the reserve. I even played (badly) in an Indian basketball league with Narcisse Blood (Blood), Martin Heavyhead (Blood), and Morris Manyfingers (Blood), in which tribal history was always a topic of conversation. My time in Lethbridge with colleagues such as Christine Miller (Blackfeet), Marie Small Face-Marule (Blood), Don Frantz, Meno Boldt, Alfred Youngman (Cree), Tony Long, and Amethyst First Rider (Blood) was an intensive course in contemporary reserve politics, oral history, small-town sociology, and very bad puns.

I should mention that I also met my partner, Dr. Helen Hoy, at the University of Lethbridge. Which just goes to show that treasures can be found in unlikely places.

Helen and I went on to the University of Minnesota in 1990, where I taught Native literature, got an interesting though not always pleasant crash course in urban Indian politics, and had the pleasure of working with other scholars on that campus—Carol Miller (Cherokee), Alan Kilpatrick (Cherokee), Ron Libertus (White Earth Ojibway), Terry Collins, Jean O'Brien (White Earth Ojibway), George Lipsitz, John Wright, Brenda Child (Red Lake Ojibway), Elaine and Lary May, and Carter Meland (White Earth Ojibway)—whose thoughts and ideas are a part of this book.

I landed at the University of Guelph in Guelph, Ontario, in the summer of 1995 and began the actual work of writing *The Inconvenient Indian* sometime in 2006. In that enterprise I had the help of a great many people, Native and non-Native, throughout North America, many whose work I've read and others who took the time to talk with me—in many cases, pointing out the errors in my research and in my thinking: Jace Weaver (Cherokee), Linda Vandenberg, Daniel Fischlin, Ajay Heble, Jeannette Armstrong (Okanagan), Christine Bold, Basil Johnston (Anishinaabe), Ric Knowles, Drew Hayden Taylor (Ojibway), Harry Lane, Douglas Sanderson (Opaskwayak Cree), Philip Deloria (Standing Rock Sioux), Buzz and Judy Webb, Craig Womack (Creek–Cherokee), Evan Connell, Paul Chaat Smith (Comanche), Robert Warrior (Osage), N. Scott Momaday (Kiowa–Cherokee), Robert Conley (Cherokee), Donald Smith, Pamela Palmater (Mi'kmaq), John Ralston Saul, and others whom I have forgotten at the moment. I will be embarrassed by my memory lapse when I am reminded of their contribution. I should also recognize the University of Guelph, especially the English Department, for the support and encouragement of my research and writing.

In particular, I want to acknowledge Carol Miller (Cherokee), Brian Dippie, Daniel Justice (Cherokee), and Margery Fee, all of whom took time from their hectic schedules to read early drafts and provided me with critical comments and sage advice. My thanks also to Benjamin Hoy, who helped with the research at a crucial stage of the book.

Yet for all this, *The Inconvenient Indian* wouldn't have happened had it not been for the presence in my life of my partner, Helen Hoy, who is always prepared to wrestle me to the ground on points of Native literature and history. It was her intelligence, kindnesses, and perseverance that helped keep me and the book on track when all I wanted to do was to run away to Tofino and hide out in a fog bank. This book is as much hers as it is mine. No one knows that more than I do. Now you know it, too.

Index

Thomas King is one of Canada's premier Native public intellectuals. He was the first Aboriginal person to deliver the prestigious Massey Lectures, and he is the best-selling, award-winning author of six novels, two collections of short stories, and two nonfiction books. *The Inconvenient Indian* won the BC National Award for Canadian Non-Fiction and the RBC Taylor Prize. He is a recipient of the Order of Canada and lives in Guelph, Ontario.